Homeownership and the Labour Market in Europe

Homeownership and the Labour Market in Europe

Edited by

Casper van Ewijk and Michiel van Leuvensteijn

OXFORD
UNIVERSITY PRESS

OXFORD
UNIVERSITY PRESS

Great Clarendon Street, Oxford OX2 6DP

Oxford University Press is a department of the University of Oxford.
It furthers the University's objective of excellence in research, scholarship,
and education by publishing worldwide in

Oxford New York

Auckland Cape Town Dar es Salaam Hong Kong Karachi
Kuala Lumpur Madrid Melbourne Mexico City Nairobi
New Delhi Shanghai Taipei Toronto

With offices in

Argentina Austria Brazil Chile Czech Republic France Greece
Guatemala Hungary Italy Japan Poland Portugal Singapore
South Korea Switzerland Thailand Turkey Ukraine Vietnam

Oxford is a registered trade mark of Oxford University Press
in the UK and in certain other countries

Published in the United States
by Oxford University Press Inc., New York

© Oxford University Press 2009

The moral rights of the authors have been asserted
Database right Oxford University Press (maker)

First published 2009

British Library Cataloguing in Publication Data
Data available

Library of Congress Cataloging in Publication Data
Data available

Typeset by SPI Publisher Services, Pondicherry, India
Printed in Great Britain
on acid-free paper by
the MPG Books Group

ISBN 978–0–19–954394–6 (Hbk.)

1 3 5 7 9 10 8 6 4 2

Preface

Some ten years ago, Andrew Oswald first put forward the intriguing hypothesis that homeownership may be a hindrance to smooth working of the labour markets. As homeowners face higher transaction costs of moving than renters, they are less inclined to accept a job outside their own region. Homeownership may then be a crucial factor in the explanation of unemployment.

This book takes up the challenge put forward by Oswald, and brings together leading economists from across Europe to analyse the relationship between housing markets and labour markets. The research covers both macroeconomic, cross-country analysis and microeconomic-oriented country studies focusing on the impact of housing status on job mobility and unemployment duration. Tackling these issues from the perspective of different European countries is especially fruitful, as it provides insight into how specific national institutions affect the performance of housing markets and labour markets.

This book serves two goals. First, it contributes to research at the very frontier of current knowledge of housing markets and labour markets. Second, it has immediate relevance for economic policy. In EU countries, homeownership rates have been on the rise, often as a result of government policies, which makes the barrier that homeownership puts up for labour mobility increasingly important. This book shows that higher transaction costs related to homeownership hamper job-to-job changes and may increase unemployment on the country level. This insight provides a clear policy message to European policymakers: reforms in the housing market, aiming at lower transaction costs and less generous subsidies on homeownership, could be an effective instrument for reducing unemployment and improving labour market flexibility. But the problem is not confined to the homeowner sector alone. Also in social renting, rigid institutions causing rationing and imperfect portability of entitlements may hamper mobility of workers, and thus affect the labour market negatively.

The book consists of three parts. Part I introduces the general problem from a European perspective, and provides a theoretical framework. It also includes Oswald's original paper, which has been unpublished hitherto. Part II focuses on how housing status affects unemployment, and presents country studies for Denmark, France, and the Netherlands. Finally, Part III analyses the impact of the housing market on job-to-job mobility and family migration in the United Kingdom, Denmark, and the Netherlands. Of the ten chapters, five have previously been published in high-quality economic journals (Chapters 1, 4, 7, 8, 9).

The research reported in this book originally emerged from the project on 'Homeownership, Commuting, and Labour Mobility' sponsored by the European Science Foundation and national scientific councils in Denmark, the Netherlands, Spain, and the United Kingdom. This financial support is gratefully acknowledged. We would like to thank Geraldine Hilgersom-Van der Meer and Maartje Kreuzen, of the Netherlands Organization for Scientific Research (NWO) and Caroline Eckert of the European Science Foundation, for their patient and flexible support of the project. The book has benefited from discussions by the participants during the workshop on homeownership held at the Tinbergen Institute in Amsterdam, September 2006, of whom we would like to mention Anthony Murphy, Peter Nijkamp, Andrew Oswald, Jan Rouwendal, Coen Teulings, and Jos van Ommeren. Finally, we thank Jeannette Verbruggen (CPB Netherlands Bureau for Economic Policy Analysis) for her perfect assistance during the different stages of the project, and Sarah Caro, Chris Champion, and Jennifer Wilkinson of Oxford University Press for their excellent advice and guidance.

Casper van Ewijk
Michiel van Leuvensteijn

Contents

Contents

List of Contributors

Harminder Battu is Senior Lecturer in Economics at the University of Aberdeen.

Carole Brunet is a Researcher at the University of Lyon.

Thomas de Graaff is Assistant Professor at VU University, Amsterdam.

Thomas J. Dohmen is Director of the Research Centre for Education and the Labour Market at Maastricht University.

Pierre Koning is Program Leader at the CPB Netherlands Bureau for Economic Policy Analysis in The Hague.

Jean-Yves Lesueur is Professor of Economics at the University of Lyon.

Ada Ma is a Research Fellow at the University of Aberdeen.

Jakob Roland Munch is Professor of Economics (MSO) at the University of Copenhagen.

Andrew Oswald is Professor of Economics at the University of Warwick.

Euan Phimister is Professor of Economics at the University of Aberdeen.

Michael Rosholm is Professor of Economics, Aarhus School of Business, at the University of Aarhus.

Michael Svarer is Professor (MSO) at the University of Aarhus.

Casper van Ewijk is Deputy Director of the CPB Netherlands Bureau for Economic Policy in The Hague.

Michiel van Leuvensteijn is Senior Economist at the CPB Netherlands Bureau for Economic Policy in The Hague.

Aico van Vuuren is Assistant Professor at VU University, Amsterdam.

Introduction and Policy Implications

Casper van Ewijk and Michiel van Leuvensteijn

Introduction

Labour market mobility in Europe is at the forefront of academic and policy debates in Europe. Facing growing competition due to globalization, the EU countries have agreed to increase flexibility in the labour market. Labour market mobility has been accepted as one of the official goals of the Lisbon Agenda. The reasons for rigidities in Europe have traditionally been sought in labour market institutions such as employment protection and unemployment insurance. It has recently become clear, however, that the housing market may also play a crucial role in rigidities in the labour market. Due to the spatial nature of these markets, mobility in the housing market and mobility in the labour market are natural complements. If people are less mobile in the housing market, then their opportunities to find jobs in the labour market will be limited as well.

In this respect, an intriguing hypothesis (see Oswald 1999, reprinted as Chapter 2 of this book) is that homeownership is an important barrier to flexibility in the labour market, and will lead to higher unemployment in the aggregate. The underlying reason is that homeowners will find it more difficult to move residence than renters will, as they face higher transaction costs of selling and buying their homes. Figure I.1, a simple plot of aggregate homeownership and the effect of housing market institutions on the probability of becoming unemployed for EU-15 (minus Sweden), illustrates the relationship between homeownership and unemployment. Countries with low homeownership, such as Germany, the Netherlands, and Portugal, feature lower probabilities of individuals becoming unemployed than countries with higher homeownership rates, such as Greece and Spain.

Homeownership is not the only source of inflexibility in the labour market. Other sources of rigidities in the housing market may also prevent the labour market from working smoothly. A clear example is social housing, which—dependent on the exact design—may also present a barrier to mobility,

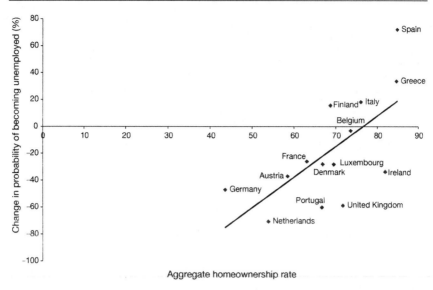

Figure I.1. The relationship effect of homeownership institutions on the probability of becoming unemployed. *Source*: De Graaff and Van Leuvensteijn (2007)

particularly when the entitlements to social housing that have been acquired in one municipality cannot be transferred to other municipalities. This aspect of the housing market will also be considered in this book, although it is admittedly more difficult to draw strong conclusions from the material provided.

This book focuses on the way in which the housing market affects mobility in the labour market. Other aspects of the relationship between the housing market and the labour market, such as the issue of commuting (which is the obvious third cornerstone of the spatial triangle 'home–job–commuting'), are beyond the scope of this book. In the course of this introduction, we explain the book's main findings, and put them in a broader perspective. To that end, we first revisit Oswald's hypothesis on homeownership and its possible explanations. This is followed by a look at the empirical evidence. We then continue by exploring what we can learn from a policy perspective, and finally we investigate which questions are still open for further research.

The Oswald puzzle

The research on homeownership and unemployment was initiated by two seminal—although unpublished—papers by Oswald (1996, 1999). The latter paper is included in its original form as Chapter 2 of this book. Looking at aggregate data for twenty-two industrialized countries and for US states, Oswald finds a clear positive association between the fraction of homeownership and aggregate unemployment.

Oswald's hypothesis on the relationship between homeownership and unemployment is not undisputed, however. A remarkable divide seems to exist between empirical macroeconomic studies and microeconomic studies. While the evidence at the macroeconomic level seems convincingly to confirm Oswald's hypothesis, a similar positive association between homeownership and unemployment is not found at the microeconomic level. On the contrary, the body of evidence suggests that homeowners tend to be less likely to be unemployed than renters are.

The contradictory results at the macro and micro levels, which we may designate as the 'Oswald puzzle', together form one of the leading themes in this book. In order to appreciate the various results, and to establish whether the results are really irreconcilable, we must dig deeper into the underlying relationships between the housing market and the labour market, and explore the mechanisms that may explain the association between unemployment and homeownership by studying data on different countries.

General framework

The key mechanism underlying Oswald's hypothesis on homeownership and unemployment concerns the transaction costs of moving. Figure I.2 illustrates how moving costs (as a percentage of property value) affect residential mobility

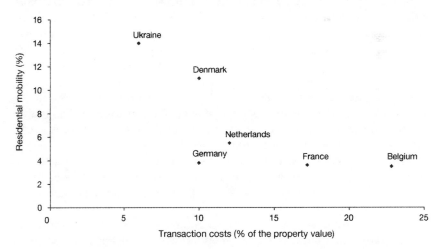

Figure I.2. Residential mobility and transaction costs. *Source*: Van Ommeren and Van Leuvensteijn (2005)

for a number of EU countries. On the basis of these data, Van Ommeren and Van Leuvensteijn (2005) find that residential mobility decreases by 8 per cent for each 1 percentage point increase in transaction costs.

Other explanations may be found for why homeownership may lead to unemployment. Green and Hendershott (2001) point out that housing becomes an illiquid asset in bad states of the economy, thereby aggravating the immobility of homeowners in times when they need most to be mobile. From a more general point of view, Oswald argues that when rigidity in the housing market reduces aggregate efficiency in the economy, this may also lead to higher unemployment.

To this we can add that the tax system may also cause a positive association between homeownership and labour market distortions. In many European countries tax regimes tend to favour homeownership. This can, for instance, be implemented by some kind of tax relief for mortgage interest payments, or low tax rates on imputed rents, or exemptions for capital gains on houses. To the extent that these—implicit—subsidies are financed by raising taxes on labour, this will directly affect the labour market and raise unemployment. Here, it is not so much homeownership that causes unemployment directly, but rather the tax system, which increases homeownership and unemployment concurrently (see also Van Ewijk *et al.* 2007).

From a microeconomic perspective, the housing status of an individual agent can interfere at different stages of labour market dynamics. Transaction costs associated with distant moves will probably hamper job mobility. The way in which transaction costs influence unemployment is more complex, however. Unemployment in the steady state depends on the inflow into, and outflow out of, unemployment. Transaction costs may affect both inflow and outflow rates. At first sight, one might expect that transaction costs increase the inflow into unemployment while reducing the outflow—in which case unemployment rises unambiguously in the steady state. This is too simple, however, as more factors play a role. First, homeowners tend to be more committed to their work than renters are, which mitigates the inflow into unemployment (discussed in Chapter 8 of this book). Second, the penalty of becoming unemployed may be larger for homeowners than it is for renters. This may be due to, for example, means testing in the tax system, so that homeowners are keener to avoid unemployment. For this same reason homeowners will also leave unemployment sooner in the unfortunate case that they lose their jobs. In order to disentangle these different effects, one must pay attention to each of the different transitions in the labour market separately.

Chapter 1 describes how Dohmen (Chapter 1 below) develops a theoretical framework to analyse the above-mentioned mechanisms in a consistent manner. Using a two-region model, he analyses the labour market behaviour of homeowners and renters, where homeowners typically face higher costs of moving than renters do. This model explains why higher transaction costs of moving lead to higher unemployment in the aggregate, while maintaining the result, at the individual level, that homeowners tend to be less unemployed than are renters. This latter result is driven by the fact that homeowners are assumed to be higher skilled on average than renters, so that the drop in income when becoming unemployed is larger.

In Chapter 3, De Graaff, Van Leuvensteijn, and Van Ewijk broaden the scope of the analysis by analysing the impact of both homeownership and social housing on labour market flows. Using European data for fourteen countries in 1994–2001, they find that homeownership tends to reduce labour market flexibility (as measured by job-to-job mobility), as predicted by theory. With regard to social renting, the results are mixed, with significant differences between individual countries. This may point to differences in how social renting is organized in various countries. With regard to the inflow into unemployment, social renters are found to have a higher risk of becoming unemployed, while homeowners feature a lower risk than average.

Country studies on homeownership and unemployment

The way in which homeownership affects unemployment at the level of individual agents is central in three country studies—for Denmark, the Netherlands, and France. Chapter 4 describes how each of these studies uses a similar framework extending the standard search model of the labour market by adding a spatial dimension and including housing status. Here, Munch, Rosholm, and Svarer analyse unemployment duration using micro data covering 1 per cent of the Danish population for the years 1993–2001. Although homeownership is found to hamper geographical mobility, the impact of homeownership on unemployment duration is unambiguously negative. Unemployed homeowners thus tend to leave unemployment earlier than would renters with the same individual characteristics. This contrasts with the Oswald hypothesis, which predicts that homeowners will have a harder time finding a job than renters will, due to their geographical immobility.

In Chapter 5, Van Vuuren, using the same framework, investigates the impact of homeownership on unemployment duration in the Netherlands. Using a dataset for taxpayers in the period 1989–2001, he confirms the results that were found for Denmark. Also in the Netherlands, homeowners are more likely to find a job in the local market than are renters, and on balance tend to leave unemployment earlier. Again, this contrasts with the Oswald hypothesis. The overall impact of the likelihood of finding a job outside the local market increases during the first months of unemployment. This suggests that unemployed homeowners start looking for a job primarily in the local labour market during the first months of unemployment. Thereafter, the focus on the non-local labour market increases gradually. In Chapter 6, Brunet and Lesueur, in a microeconomic study for France of a cohort of unemployed persons in 1995, find that homeowners indeed tend to have longer spells of unemployment, which coincides with the Oswald hypothesis. This result, contrary to the results of our book, described in Chapters 4 and 5, can be partly explained by the fact that the authors also correct explicitly for search intensity. Search intensity is correlated with homeownership.

Each of these studies is partial, focusing on one aspect of the relationship between housing status and unemployment: namely, the impact on the outflow out of unemployment. For a more comprehensive assessment of the impact on unemployment, one should also consider the inflow into unemployment in relation to the other transitions in the labour market.

Country studies on homeownership and job-to-job mobility

In Chapter 7 Battu, Ma, and Phimister consider the impact of housing tenure on both job-to-job transitions and unemployment duration in the UK. In line with theory, homeownership proves to be an obstacle to job-to-job mobility with a distant move—for skilled manual workers more so than for the professional managerial socio-economic class. However, as in the studies for Denmark and the Netherlands discussed above, they find no support for the Oswald hypothesis that private homeownership increases unemployment duration. In contrast, these transaction costs of moving appear to be relevant for social renters, who are less likely to accept a distant job than private renters are. These results on social renting for the UK coincide with the findings of De Graaff *et al.* discussed in Chapter 3.

One of the explanations for why homeowners tend to be less unemployed at the individual level is that they are more committed to their jobs than are renters. As it is more difficult to move, homeowners will be more attached to their jobs, will invest more in human capital, and will put more effort in their careers. However, the causation may also be the reverse: agents with stronger commitment to their jobs will be more likely to become homeowners. In Chapter 8, Van Leuvensteijn and Koning, testing this for the Netherlands, indeed find such a reverse causation. Taking account of this endogeneity, the authors find no support for the negative effect of homeownership on job-to-job mobility. They do find, however, that homeowners are less likely to become unemployed. The fact that no negative effect is found for job-to-job mobility might be due to the small geographical scale of the Netherlands, where people often change jobs without moving residence.

In Chapter 9 Munch, Rosholm, and Svarer do find a negative effect of homeownership on job-to-job mobility in Denmark. Interestingly, this applies to both local jobs and distant jobs. This suggests that homeowners are more committed to their jobs than are renters. Consistent with this finding, the authors show that homeownership also has an upward effect on wages. Due to their reduced mobility, firms may be more willing to invest in homeowners, and homeowners may be more willing to invest in their jobs. Homeownership thus serves as a commitment mechanism that can help to solve the hold-up problem of investment in human capital.

In Chapter 10 Battu, Ma, and Phimister discuss another extension of the model, in their study of family migration in the UK. They find that females in dual career households are more likely to be the trailing spouse; they move at the behest of their partners, and in doing so experience a labour market loss. Although married females may encounter a penalty for moving, in terms of employment, this penalty may be largely transient.

Policy implications: the forgotten chapter in the Lisbon Agenda

What can the evidence in this book teach us from a policy perspective? In general terms, it is clear that the housing market can no longer be neglected if flexibility and efficiency in labour markets are at the top of the agenda. This also pertains to the Lisbon Agenda, in which mobility in the housing market appears to be a forgotten chapter. The European Commission may want to reconsider this matter and devise a programme to encourage national authorities to reduce transaction costs in the housing markets for both homeowners and renters as part of the Lisbon Agenda.

In many European countries, promoting homeownership is an official objective of government policy, usually supported by favourable tax regimes. Although there is a general tendency to reduce the (implicit) subsidization of homeownership, it is still considerable in many countries (Hendershott and White 2000), and in some countries has even been recently introduced (France, for instance). Furthermore, governments also often intervene in the renting sector through social housing schemes featuring rents below market-clearing levels and some directive allocation schemes. The research covered in this book may shed new light on these housing market policies. Both types of interventions tend to increase the transaction costs of residential mobility and—as a side effect—harm labour market flexibility.

A traditional argument for promoting homeownership is that homeownership creates positive externalities (i.e. homeowners care better for their homes and neighbourhood). Although these externalities are found to exist, their size is probably too small to warrant policy interventions (Glaeser and Shapiro 2002). Although for social housing other—social—arguments come into play, even these arguments have to be balanced against the welfare losses caused by the interventions.

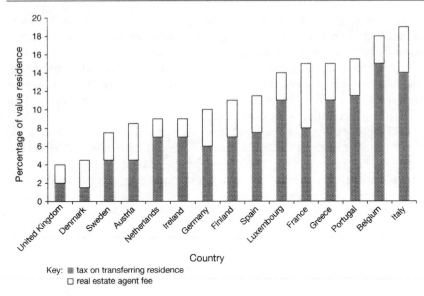

Figure I.3. Taxation for moving residence and real estate agent fee for several European countries. *Source*: Belot and Ederveen (2005)

As can be seen in Figure I.3, transaction costs of moving residence are quite substantial for homeowners in most countries. Remarkably, the government in all countries imposes an additional burden in the form of transfer taxes, on top of the already high transaction costs due to notary costs and commissions. These taxes range from 0.6 per cent in Denmark to 10 per cent in Greece and Portugal, and even 12.5 per cent in Belgium. Rather than promoting mobility, as one would expect, the government thus directly adds to rigidity in the housing market. This may cause substantial welfare losses. In fact, it is difficult to think of any rational reason for levying taxes on transactions of private housing property. Table I.1 provides a rough estimate for the welfare gains of abolishing transfer taxes by calculating the deadweight loss associated with the transfer tax. In general, the deadweight loss (DWL) can be expressed in terms of the revenue of this tax according to the formula $DWL = 1/2\,\varepsilon t$, where t stands for the tax rate and ε reflects the elasticity of the tax base for the tax rate. Using the elasticity of 8 reported by Van Ommeren and Van Leuvensteijn (2005), the table reports the welfare effects that follow from the tax rate and the size of the tax base as a percentage of GDP. A range is given to indicate uncertainty as to whether the notary costs and commissions, which vary widely between countries, should be interpreted as a real social cost or as an indirect tax due to regulation. Abolition of transfer taxes on residential property would result in an overall gain of somewhere between 0.15 per cent and 0.40 per cent of GDP in the sixteen European countries presented in Table I.1. Welfare gains

Table I.1. Welfare gains of the abolition of transfer taxes on residential property in 2006

Countries	Transfer tax (%)	Welfare effect in billions of euros (2006)	Welfare effect as percentage of GDP
Austria	3.5	0.08–0.30	0.03–0.11
Belgium	12.5	1.27–2.40	0.40–0.76
Denmark	0.6	0.00–0.03	0.00–0.02
Finland	4	0.02–0.11	0.01–0.06
France	4.89	1.44–7.41	0.08–0.41
Germany	3.5	0.40–1.88	0.02–0.08
Greece	10	1.60–3.19	0.75–1.49
Ireland	6	0.60–1.21	0.35–0.69
Italy	8	3.75–14.04	0.25–0.95
Luxembourg	6	0.03–0.11	0.09–0.33
Netherlands	6	0.71–1.42	0.13–0.27
Portugal	10	1.20–2.52	0.77–1.62
Spain	6	3.24–9.17	0.33–0.94
Sweden	1.5	0.02–0.16	0.01–0.05
Switzerland	3	0.07–0.32	0.02–0.10
United Kingdom	1	0.09–0.62	0.00–0.03
Total		14.52–41.70	0.13–0.38

Source: Belot and Ederveen (2005), own calculations.

would be especially large in absolute terms in Belgium, France, Italy, and Spain. In most of these countries, transfer taxes are relatively high compared to the average. Although Italy is an exception, here the maximum welfare loss is relatively high, because the overall transaction costs on the housing market in Italy are large, at 19 per cent.

These welfare effects concern taxes on buying and selling homes only. Additional welfare gains can be achieved by reforming other policies that hamper mobility in the residential market. First, one may have to reconsider current policies that aim at encouraging homeownership, since these policies indirectly may lead to lower mobility in the labour market. The size of these externalities for the labour market is hard to quantify. Moreover, there may be positive externalities of lower mobility in the form of better commitment to jobs as well. It is obvious, however, that policies that hamper mobility in the housing market are hard to justify, given the general emphasis in economic policy on improving flexibility in labour markets, as is prominently stipulated in the Lisbon Agenda of EU members.

A similar rethink may also be needed for social housing policies—to the extent that these produce obstacles for spatial mobility. This is the case if social housing is associated with rigid allocation mechanisms, waiting lists, entry barriers for newcomers, and lock-in effects of rent control for those who benefit from rents below market rents.

Further analysis necessary: research agenda

The complex relationship between the housing market and the labour market is a rich and fruitful area for economic research. This book focuses on the effects of an individual's housing status on labour market performance. By using a consistent framework applied to different countries, this study has gained important insights. There is scope, however, for a wide range of future research. A number of issues stand out.

First, this book focuses on homeownership as a possible obstacle for mobility in the labour market. Some chapters also touch upon social housing as another potential cause of labour market rigidities. Provisional evidence indicates that this is an important area for future research. EU countries feature widely different institutions in social housing. By studying each other's successes and failures, European countries can learn from one another and draw lessons to improve their housing policies.

A second area for research concerns the endogeneity of housing tenure. Most of the chapters in this study take housing tenure to be given exogenously. A comprehensive approach would require simultaneous modelling of housing choice and labour market behaviour.

Third, as mentioned already, this book neglects the third corner of the home–job–commuting triangle. It is obvious that lowering commuting costs is an alternative to lowering transaction costs in the housing market in order to promote mobility. A full analysis should take account of commuting as well. From a policy point of view, it is evident that if commuting costs are on the rise because of congestion and environmental externalities, then reforming the housing market will become all the more pressing.

Finally, also in the area of homeownership and labour market flexibility, which is the focus of this book, many issues and puzzles remain. The definitive answer to the Oswald puzzle will not be provided by this study. Still, the macroeconomic evidence on the positive association between homeownership and unemployment is not supported by most of the evidence at the micro level. The body of evidence suggests that homeowners tend to become unemployed less often, and, moreover, tend to leave unemployment earlier on average than renters do. The evidence in this study does help to indicate in what directions the solution should be sought—and which directions could be discarded. As the evidence of the impact of housing tenure at the individual level is fairly robust, the solution should be sought in aggregate effects and the interaction between the housing and labour markets. Oswald offers a few suggestions related to the impact of housing market inefficiencies on general welfare in the economy. To this we added the idea that government subsidies to promote homeownership could be a possible cause of inefficiencies as well. Finally, Dohmen (in Chapter 1) hints at the possibility that composition effects might offer a clue to the Oswald puzzle. Also in that case one should go beyond the individual characteristics and look at the underlying mechanisms that explain both housing tenure choice and labour market behaviour. This study serves as a significant first step in the right direction and as a source of inspiration for further contributions in this highly relevant research area.

References

Belot, M., and Ederveen, S. (2005), 'Indicators of cultural and institutional barriers in OECD countries', CPB Memorandum (The Hague).

Glaeser, E. L., and Shapiro, J. M. (2002), 'The benefits of the home mortgage interest deduction', NBER Working Paper no. 9284.

Graaff, T. de, and Van Leuvensteijn, M. (2007), 'The impact of housing market institutions on labour mobility: a European cross-country comparison', CPB Discussion Paper no. 82 (The Hague).

Green, R., and Hendershott, P. (2001), 'Home-ownership and unemployment in the US', *Urban Studies*, 38/9, 1509–20.

Hendershott, P. H., and White, M. (2000), 'The rise and fall of housing favored investment status', *Journal of Housing Research*, 11/2, 257–75.

Oswald, A. J. (1996), 'A conjecture on the explanation for high unemployment in the industrialized nations: part I', Warwick Economic Research Paper 475.

―― (1999), 'The housing market and Europe's unemployment: a non-technical paper', mimeo, University of Warwick. Reproduced as Ch. 2 below.

Van Ewijk, C., Jacobs, B., and De Mooij, R. (2007), 'Welfare effects of fiscal subsidies on home ownership in the Netherlands', *De Economist*, 155/3, 323–62.

Van Ommeren, J., and Van Leuvensteijn, M. (2005), 'New evidence of the effect of transaction costs on residential mobility', *Journal of Regional Science*, 45/4, 681–702.

Part I

Theory and Empirics

1

Housing, Mobility, and Unemployment[*]

Thomas J. Dohmen

1.1. Introduction

Much of the puzzle of high European unemployment is still unresolved despite substantial effort and remarkable theoretical progress. Blanchard and Katz (1997, p. 52) conclude that 'while many suspects have been identified, none has been convicted'. Nickell (1997) shows empirically that key factors of prominent models—including labour market rigidities, the treatment of the unemployed, taxes, union coverage, union and employer coordination in wage bargaining—do not provide a satisfactory explanation for cross-country differences in unemployment rates. Although Nickell (1997) mentions that lack of mobility potentially affects labour market outcomes adversely—an idea that is at least as old as the concept of the natural rate of unemployment[1]—and despite a growing body of evidence of a positive correlation between rates of homeownership and unemployment (e.g. Oswald 1996), he neglects regional mobility as an explanatory factor in his empirical analysis of equilibrium unemployment.[2] When Nickell (1998) adds the proportion of homeownership to the regression, its fit improves considerably. The R2 rises from 0.76 to 0.82. The coefficient estimate implies that a 10 per cent point rise in the owner-occupation rate is associated with an additional 1.3 percentage points of the unemployment rate.

This paper develops a model that explains the links between housing tenure, regional mobility, and unemployment.[3] Few theoretical models focus on the interaction between regional mobility and unemployment. Oswald (1997) predicts that higher homeownership rates lead to more unemployment, and

[*] I thank Andrew Oswald, Gerard Pfann, and Ben Kriechel for fruitful discussions and very useful remarks on earlier drafts of the paper. Comments by two anonymous referees and the editor have improved the paper.

Reprinted from *Regional Science and Urban Economics*, 35 (2005), 305–25, with permission from Elsevier.

that unemployment is concentrated among homeowners. The latter prediction is contradicted, however, by the empirical fact that renters have lower employment rates.[4]

This paper develops a model that is consistent with the stylized facts about unemployment, housing tenure, and regional mobility. It shows why higher aggregate rates of homeownership are associated with higher unemployment rates, although unemployment might not be concentrated among homeowners. It explains why high-skilled workers are more mobile than low-skilled workers given the choice of housing tenure. The model illustrates that increased aggregate homeownership rates are associated with reduced search intensity, diminished attractiveness of job offers, and with higher unemployment. If mobility and search behaviour are partly determined by conditions in the housing market, the wage pressure variable in models of the Layard and Nickell type (see Layard *et al.* 1991) or the search effectiveness parameter in matching models (e.g. Pissarides 2000) become a function of housing market conditions. Consequently, interventions in the housing market affect labour market outcomes. This has important policy implications.

The remainder of the paper is organized as follows. The following section discusses links between housing and labour markets and reports some stylized facts that motivate the model of housing, mobility, and unemployment that is introduced in Section 1.3. Section 1.4 discusses how shocks affect mobility and unemployment. Section 1.5 refines the model. Section 1.6 extends the model to analyse interactions between search and moving costs. Section 1.7 focuses on policy implications. Section 1.8 concludes.

1.2. Links between housing and labour markets—stylized facts and empirical evidence

The model is built to study the link between the choice of housing tenure, regional mobility, and employment status. It generates predictions that are consistent with a broad pattern of empirical results and with the following set of stylized facts.[5]

1. Job flows in the labour markets are immense.[6]
2. Most of the cross-country differences in unemployment rates can be ascribed to variations in long-term unemployment, and most of the rise in European unemployment can be attributed to an increase in the duration rather than a higher inflow rate into unemployment.[7]
3. The outward shift of the Beveridge curve suggests that it has become harder to match workers and firms, possibly because workers are less prepared to move regions and spend less effort on search across regions.[8]
4. Aggregate rates of homeownership are positively correlated with unemployment.[9]

5. Private renters move relatively more than owners.[10]
6. High-skilled workers experience fewer and shorter spells of unemployment.
7. Skilled workers migrate more.[11]
8. High-skilled workers also search more and prefer employed search.[12]
9. Regional migration is higher during economy-wide booms and is lower during recessions.[13]
10. Migration rates are affected by asymmetric regional shocks. Net migration from depressed regions largely comprises high-skilled workers, but there is no correlation between regional employment growth and low-skilled worker net migration.[14]

Variations in regional unemployment rates do not stimulate migration of low-skilled workers unless there is geographic wage flexibility. High relative wages stimulate in-migration.[15] Homeowners also do not appear to move from high unemployment areas to regions with lower unemployment.[16] Therefore, high-skilled renters respond most to asymmetric shocks and are the first to leave a depressed region.

Taking into account that labour markets are characterized by large gross job flows (stylized fact (1)), a model is developed next that explains stylized facts (2) to (10).

1.3. A simple model

This section introduces a simple model that is consistent with the empirical regularities: that higher rates of homeownership are associated with higher rates of unemployment (stylized fact (4)), that private renters move relatively more than owners (stylized fact (5)), and that high-skilled workers migrate more and are less often unemployed than low-skilled workers (stylized facts (6) and (7)). While these implications are not too surprising, the model generates the novel result that unemployment does not need to be concentrated among homeowners to explain the positive correlation between aggregate homeownership rates and aggregate unemployment rates. In fact, unemployment among the group of homeowners might be lower than among renters. The model demonstrates under which conditions regional mobility among homeowners is higher than among renters. This implication of the model is of great consequence for empirical work, as it calls attention to the importance of controlling for the expected income of workers when estimating the effect of the type of housing tenure on regional mobility. The model is based on the following assumptions:

1. There are two identical regions, East and West. Hence, the size of the regions and the number of jobs in both regions are the same.

2. Workers must live where they work (unemployed can live anywhere). To accept a job offer outside the home region, a worker must move and incur the fixed moving costs k^m.

3. Workers are either homeowners or renters. The fixed moving costs k^m equal k^o for owners and k^r for renters. Moving is more expensive for owners, i.e. $k^o > k^r$.

4. There are two types of workers: high-skilled workers who earn a wage $W = H$ and low-skilled workers who earn $W = L$, where $H > L$.

5. High-skilled workers only receive job offers for high-skilled jobs, and low-skilled workers only receive offers for low-skilled jobs.

6. Jobs last for one period. At the beginning of a period, each worker receives one job offer. The offer comes from a firm in West with probability q and from a firm in East with probability $(1 - q)$. Workers who reject become unemployed for one period and get another job offer at the beginning of the next period.[17]

7. In the absence of asymmetric shocks, q is assumed to equal 0.5.

8. The unemployed receive benefits B, with $B < L$. Benefits are net of any costs of unemployment, C, including mental costs.[18]

9. The discount factor is equal to δ, $0 < \delta < 1$.

10. Workers' lives are infinite.[19]

Because wages exceed benefits associated with unemployment for any worker type (by assumptions 4 and 8), every worker always accepts a job offer in his home region. Reluctance to migrate in order to accept a job offer outside the home region initiates unemployment. Since workers migrate only if they satisfy the condition

$$W - B > k^m \tag{1.1}$$

(see Appendix A), regional mobility—and hence unemployment—depends on wages relative to moving costs and unemployment benefits. A rise in net benefits, B, or an increase in moving costs, k^m, makes workers less likely to migrate, and therefore more likely to become unemployed. Condition (1.1) implies that renters have *ceteris paribus* a higher propensity to migrate than homeowners, as they incur lower moving costs (assumption 3).[20] An increase in the home-ownership rate raises aggregate moving costs and consequently leads to a fall in the job offer acceptance rate, so that unemployment rises.

High-skilled workers are more likely to migrate than low-skilled workers for a given choice of housing tenure. High-skilled renters are most likely, and low-skilled owners least likely, to migrate. Corroborating evidence is provided by Böheim and Taylor (2002), who estimate the probability of interregional mobility conditional on *inter alia* income, education, age, and employment status. They find that income and education raise interregional mobility, and that private renters are most likely to move between regions when income and education are held constant. The model predicts that an increase in the proportion of low-skilled (high-skilled) owners unambiguously has an adverse effect on employment if moving regions is optimal not for low-skilled (high-skilled) owners but for low-skilled (high-skilled) renters. High-skilled owners are even more mobile than low-skilled renters if $H - L > k^o - k^r$.[21] Not conditioning on income, homeowners might be more mobile on average if high-wage earners are more likely to be homeowners. This indicates that econometric specifications in empirical studies of the determinants of regional mobility must be carefully specified to control fully for moving costs and expected gains from moving.[22]

1.4. The effects of shocks

Next, it is analysed how shocks affect mobility and unemployment rates for the different types of workers. Predictions are derived that are consistent with stylized facts (9) and (10). Asymmetric shocks reduce employment opportunities in the depressed region (say East) and increase job offers and employment opportunities in the booming region (West). This is modelled as a rise in q. Temporary random asymmetric shocks, in which q changes for one period only, and persistent asymmetric shocks, are considered. Adverse symmetric shocks are modelled as a fall of the job offer arrival rate. In particular, it is assumed that workers receive a job offer every second period rather than every period. Analogously, a positive symmetric shock is modelled as an increase in the job offer arrival rate.

1.4.1. Asymmetric shocks

Proposition 1. *A temporary random asymmetric shock tends to increase the number of workers moving to the booming region (West) and tends to lower the number of workers moving to the depressed region (East).*

Proof of Proposition 1. If the shock is temporary, i.e., lasts one period, the moving constraint is still given by condition (1.1) because the income stream from the next future period onwards is not affected by the region of residence. However, as the asymmetric shock increases q, a bigger fraction of workers in East is offered a job in West, while fewer workers in West are offered a job in East. Since those who do not satisfy condition (1.1) become unemployed, unemployment rises in East and falls in West. Unemployment remains concentrated among immobile workers.

Proposition 2. *A persistent asymmetric shock makes workers in the depressed region more likely to leave and workers in the booming region more likely to stay. Because* *the effect is bigger the longer the shock is expected to persist, serially correlated shocks have a bigger impact on mobility than random shocks. High-skilled renters are the first to leave a depressed region while the low-skilled workers, especially low-skilled homeowners, might not move at all.*

Proof of Proposition 2. If differences in job offer arrival rates between regions persist throughout the next future period, the moving constraint for a worker in East changes to

$$W - B > k^m - \delta(2q - 1) \max[k^m; W - B], \tag{1.2}$$

while the moving constraint for a worker in West changes to

$$W - B > k^m + \delta(2q - 1) \max[k^m; W - B]. \tag{1.3}$$

Since $2q - 1 > 0$, the moving condition becomes more likely to be satisfied compared to condition (1.1) for workers in East and less likely to be satisfied for workers in West. For a proof of the effect of serially correlated shocks, see Appendix B.

The bigger δ, i.e. the more workers value the future, and the bigger q, i.e. the more intense the shock is, and the longer it persists (see Appendix B), the more attractive moving becomes for workers in East and the more attractive staying becomes for workers in West. High-skilled renters are predicted to be the first to leave a depressed region, while low-skilled owners are the last to leave. These predictions are consistent with the evidence reported by McCormick (1997) and Henley (1998). A comparison of Eqns. (1.1) and (1.2) and of Eqns. (1.1) and (1.3) shows that the asymmetric shock changes the moving condition most for workers earning higher wages. High-skilled workers in the depressed region become more likely to move regions in response to the shock than low-skilled workers do. Interestingly, it is possible that high-skilled owners are induced by the shock to move between regions while low-skilled renters remain immobile even if their moving probability in absence of the shock had been the same. Suppose, for example, that $H - B - k^o = L - B - k^r < 0$, so that both groups of workers would not move in the absence of the shock, then an asymmetric shock could make moving profitable for the high-skilled owner but not for the low-skilled renter. This surprising result, which to the author's knowledge has not been derived in theoretical work, could be tested in future empirical work. The differential mobility responses of high-skilled and low-skilled workers suggest that regional differences in unemployment rates are much more persistent in the low-skilled labour market. These theoretical predictions are corroborated by the empirical results of Evans and McCormick (1994). They distinguish between manual and non-manual workers and find that manual workers have low levels of gross migration and that variations in regional unemployment persist in the manual labour market. In contrast, non-manual labour markets are characterized by similar regional unemployment rates and by net migration towards regions with low unemployment and relatively high rates of regional mobility.

In addition, the model implies that this effect is magnified if there is uncertainty about the length of the shock. To appreciate this argument, assume that shocks either persist three periods or one period and that both scenarios are equally likely so that the expected length of a shock is two periods. Suppose that there is a group of workers for whom migration is optimal only if the shock lasts at least for three periods. Given an expected duration of two periods, it is *ex ante* never optimal for them to move, although in half of the cases migrating is optimal *ex post*. When workers learn about the true type of the shock (say after one period), the remaining duration of the shock is too short to make migration profitable. The moving constraint (1.2) might remain binding for some workers while unemployment in the depressed region is increasing.[23] This is consistent with Evans and McCormick (1994) finding that relative demand shocks do not stimulate out-migration from the depressed region unless local wages fall.

Although migration rates for some workers seem not to respond to higher unemployment rates, a higher unemployment level that creates downward wage pressure has an (indirect) effect on regional mobility if wages are flexible such that wages in East fall to W^E, while wages in West equal W^W, $W^W > W^E$. Moving away from the depressed region, East becomes more attractive as relative wages in the booming region rise.[24] To illustrate, consider the moving constraint of a worker in East who is offered a job in the booming region. If the shock lasts for one future period, after which relative wages are equal to 1, moving is preferred if[25]

$$
W^W - B > k^m - \delta\Big\{ q\big(W^W - \max\big[W^W - k^m; B\big]\big) \\
+ (1 - q)\big(W^E - \max\big[W^E - k^m; B\big]\big)\Big\}.
\tag{1.4}
$$

In all three cases—(i) workers satisfying $W^E - B > k^m$, (ii) workers not satisfying $W^E - B < k^m < W^W - B$, and (iii) workers satisfying $W^E - B < k^m$—the moving constraint (1.4) is eased more the higher the wage in the booming region W^W and the larger the shock q is.[26]

1.4.2. Symmetric shocks

An adverse symmetric shock that affects both regions in the same way does not alter the moving condition (1.1), given that wages remain unchanged. Moreover, the length of the recession does not affect the moving decision either (see Appendix C). The shock, however, does raise the level of unemployment, because everybody enters the unemployment pool after an employment spell.

The expected unemployment duration is exactly one period for mobile workers (those who satisfy condition (1.1)) but exceeds one period for immobile workers. Consequently, the unemployment rate is higher among immobile workers.

Proposition 3. *An adverse symmetric shock results in a higher level of unemployment but does not affect regional mobility.*

Proof of Proposition 3. See argument above and Appendix C.

Proposition 3 documents an important result that should guide empirical research because it highlights the importance of controlling for changes in relative labour market demand conditions (e.g. relative vacancy inflow and vacancy filled rates) rather than for absolute changes therein when estimating regional mobility rates. It should be noted, however, that mobility is reduced during economy-wide downturns if wages fall during recessions because the moving constraint (1.1) is then less likely to become satisfied. This enlightens Pissarides and Wadsworth's (1989, p. 750) conclusion 'that higher overall unemployment reduces (1) the likelihood that unemployed workers will migrate and (2) the effectiveness of the incentives to migrate provided by vacancy differentials'.

Positive symmetric shocks cause jobs to last longer than the period between two job offers. Here, it is assumed that employment lasts for t periods, $t \in N$ and $t > 1$. Workers must fulfil their contract and receive a job offer either when their job ends or after each period of unemployment.[27]

Proposition 4. *A positive symmetric shock raises mobility and reduces unemployment. The effect is stronger the stronger the boom.*

Proof of Proposition 4. If the shock is temporary, say lasts for one period such that only jobs accepted in the first period last for two periods, the moving constraint alters to

$$W - B > k^m - 0.5\delta \left(W - \max\left[W - k^m; B \right] \right). \tag{1.5}$$

The moving barrier is reduced by $0.5\delta(W - \max\left[W - k^m; B\right])$. For immobile workers (i.e. for whom $W - k^m < B$), this reduction is larger the higher the wage and the lower unemployment benefits are.

If employment lasts t periods, a permanent positive symmetric shock alters the moving constraint for workers who satisfy $W - k^m > B$ to

$$W - B > k^m - \frac{0.5(\delta - \delta^t)}{1 - \delta^t} k^m. \tag{1.6}$$

Since $[(\delta - \delta^t)/(1 - \delta^t)] > 0$, moving becomes more attractive. This is because a longer employment duration reduces the number of expected future moves. The coefficient $[(\delta - \delta^t)/(1 - \delta^t)]$ is increasing in t.[28] Thus, the stronger the boom, the more mobile workers become.

The moving barrier is reduced more during a temporary boom than during a permanent boom for all workers (compare (1.5) and (1.6) and note that $\delta > [\delta/(1+\delta)]$). Opportunity costs of not moving are higher during a temporary boom. Workers who do not satisfy condition (1.1) but condition (1.6) become mobile and will therefore not become unemployed. Workers who do not satisfy condition (1.6) become unemployed when their job ends. Yet, they are still better off after the shock because they are employed more often in their home region as jobs last twice as long. That regional mobility is positively correlated with the business cycle squares nicely with the evidence reported in the literature (e.g. Jackman and Savouri 1992; Pissarides and Wadsworth 1989; Vanderkamp 1968).

1.5. Refinements of the simple model

So far, it has been assumed that only wages differ for high-skilled and low-skilled workers. There is ample evidence, however, that high-skilled workers receive more wage offers. Moreover, employment spells for workers with firm specific skills and workers in high-wage industries last longer than for those in low-skilled jobs. Heterogeneity with respect to job offer arrival rates and employment duration is considered next.

Proposition 5. *The higher the job offer arrival rate, the lower are moving barriers and the lower is the risk of becoming unemployed.*

Proof of Proposition 5. See the proofs of previous Propositions.

Because high-skilled workers are more likely to receive job offers at a higher rate, high-skilled workers are more mobile, less frequently unemployed, and more often observed to move in the data. Proposition 5 also highlights the importance of controlling for occupation-specific job offer arrival rates in econometric models of regional mobility.

Proposition 6. *The longer the expected length of an employment spell is, the more mobile a worker is and the less likely he is to become unemployed.*

Proof of Proposition 6. See the Proof of Proposition 4.

23

Workers with longer expected employment relationships are more prepared to move in order to accept a job offer outside their home region. Therefore, they are less likely to become unemployed than low-skilled workers.

It is more realistic to assume that wage offer distributions are not degenerate, as has been assumed so far (see assumption 4). Suppose that H and L are the respective mean wages of the wage offer distribution functions $f(w)$ for high-skilled workers and $g(w)$ for low-skilled workers with cumulative distribution functions $F(w)$ and $G(w)$. Defining the wage required to make moving optimal as w^o for homeowners and w^r for renters, with $w^o > w^r$, the probabilities that workers who receive a job offer from a firm in the other region accept the offer and move are given by $1 - F(w^r)$ for high-skilled renters, $1 - F(w^o)$ for high-skilled owners, $1 - G(w^r)$ for low-skilled renters, and $1 - G(w^o)$ for low-skilled owners. Renters are more likely to migrate than owners because $w^o > w^r$ so that $1 - F(w^r) > 1 - F(w^o)$ and $1 - G(w^r) > 1 - G(w^o)$ because $F(w^r) < F(w^o)$ and $G(w^r) < G(w^o)$. High-skilled renters are more mobile than low-skilled renters if $F(w^r) < G(w^r)$, while high-skilled owners are more mobile than low-skilled owners if $F(w^o) < G(w^o)$.[29] The latter two conditions are always satisfied if $f(w)$ and $g(w)$ differ only in the mean such that $F(w) < G(w)$ for any w in the support.

Proposition 7. *Everything else equal, a rise in the mean of the wage distribution increases the probability of receiving a wage offer that makes moving optimal.*

Proof of Proposition 7. See the argument above.

Proposition 8. *An increase in the variance of the wage offer distribution raises mobility if the wage required to make moving optimal exceeds the expected offer wage.*

Proof of Proposition 8. If $f(w)$ and $\tilde{f}(w)$ (with respective cumulative distribution functions F and $\tilde{F}$) differ only with respect to the variance which is bigger for $\tilde{f}(w)$, then $\tilde{F}(w) < F(w)$ for values exceeding the mean $\bar{w}$. Since $w^m > \bar{w}$ by assumption, such that $\tilde{F}(w^m) < F(w^m)$, acceptable job offers from outside the home region arrive more often.

Proposition 8 therefore implies that mobility rates tend to be lower, *ceteris paribus*, in countries with more compressed wage distributions. It is likely that the variance of an individual's wage offer distribution is positively related to his skills.[30] A straightforward way to integrate this idea into the model is to assume that workers can either have a 'good' job paying $(1 + h)H$ or a 'bad' job paying $(1 - h)H$, $h > 0$. Similarly, low-skilled workers can either earn $(1 + l)L$ or $(1 - l)L$, $l > 0$. The moving constraint for a high-skilled worker being offered a 'good' job is then given by $H - B + hH > k^m$; for those being offered a 'bad' job, it is $H - B - hH > k^m$; and similarly, the respective moving constraints for low-skilled workers become $L - B + lL > k^m$ and $L - B - lL > k^m$.[31] High-skilled workers who are offered a 'good' job are most likely to move for a given choice of housing tenure as long as $l < [(1 + h)H - L]/L$. It is possible that they are the only type of workers who move in absence of any shocks if in addition $(1 + h)H > k^m + B > (1 - h)H$.

1.6. Interactions between search and moving costs

So far, it has been assumed implicitly that search is costless because workers automatically receive a job offer at given intervals. Relaxing this assumption, the model generates novel results concerning the interaction between fixed moving costs and job search. For this purpose, the simple model of Section 1.3 is altered in two ways. First, a worker becomes unemployed for one period after his employment contract expires. In each of the following periods, he receives a job offer free of charge. Secondly, a worker can search for a job while employed in order to generate one job offer at a fixed cost, s; i.e. on-the-job search is more expensive than search from unemployment.[32]

Beyond the obvious effect that higher search costs have a negative impact on search effort and hence employment, the current model predicts—consistent with empirical findings in the literature (e.g. Pissarides and Wadsworth 1994)— that high-skilled workers search more and prefer on-the-job search. Higher opportunity costs make it more profitable for high-skilled workers to engage in costly on-the-job search activity so that they are less likely to become unemployed.[33] The model also implies that immobile workers would concentrate their search activity locally if this was possible. This is likely to lead to inefficient matching. The result that moving costs have a negative impact on employment continues to hold.[34] A new result is, however, the model's prediction that the type of housing tenure influences search behaviour.

Proposition 9. *High-skilled workers are more likely to search on-the-job than low-skilled workers and are less likely to experience unemployment. Renters are ceteris paribus more likely to search on-the-job. The more expensive moving becomes, the less likely are mobile workers to search.*

Proof of Proposition 9. See Appendix D.

A worker, who would move even if on-the-job search was not possible, always prefers on-the-job search if

$$W - B > + \frac{1 + \delta}{\delta} s + 0.5 k^m \qquad (1.7)$$

(see Appendix D), which is more likely to be satisfied, the higher W. A fall in δ, a rise in search costs s, and higher moving costs k^m all increase the right-hand side of Eqn. (1.7) and therefore reduce search activity of workers who are prepared to move. A worker who optimally rejects a job outside his home region, searches on-the-job if

$$W - B > +\frac{\delta + 2}{\delta}s \tag{1.8}$$

(see Appendix D). Again, an increase in search costs and a higher discount rate, i.e. lower δ, make searching less attractive.

Search costs are more important for immobile workers—the coefficient on search costs in Eqn. (1.8) is bigger than the one in Eqn. (1.7)—since workers who are not prepared to migrate accept only half of the job offers they generate, and their search effort is obsolete half of the time. However, the excess amount of income over benefits, $W - B$, that is required to make search attractive is lower for immobile workers if $k^m > 2s/\delta$ which is always satisfied if $[(1 + \delta)/\delta]s + 0.5k^m > W - B > [(\delta + 2)/\delta]s$.[35] Thus, higher moving costs, lower search costs, and a lower discount rate δ make mobile workers less likely to search relative to immobile workers. The less a worker values the future, the lower is search intensity, and the higher is unemployment. However, the unemployment rate of non-searching mobile workers is lower than the unemployment rate of searching immobile workers because the expected duration of unemployment is longer for immobile workers.[36]

An increase in moving costs affects search effort via two channels that lead to reduced employment. First, it reduces the net gain of search for mobile workers, tending to diminish their search activity. Secondly, it increases the proportion of immobile workers. Although this tends to increase overall search activity, fewer matches will be formed in the aggregate because immobile workers who accept only half of the offers search less effectively. Although the inflow rate into unemployment might fall—some non-searching mobile workers might become searching immobile workers in response to higher moving costs—outflow rates fall even more. The unemployment rate rises because unemployment duration increases. These theoretical results are consistent with the combination of two stylized facts: (1) homeownership rates have risen in OECD countries between 1960 and 1990 (Oswald 1996), while at the same time, (2) the Beveridge curve has shifted outwards, meaning that vacancies are filled less efficiently; that is, it has become harder to match workers and firms. Workers can belong to one of the following four groups:

i. If they satisfy condition (1.7) and the moving condition (D.1), which is given in Appendix D, they will search, accept any offer, and will never become unemployed.

ii. Workers might satisfy the search condition but do not find it optimal to migrate. Proportion q of them will become unemployed, where q is the probability of receiving a job offer in the other region.

iii. Workers who are mobile but do not search experience a spell of unemployment that lasts exactly one period. Thereafter, they accept a job offer in any region.

iv. Workers who neither move nor search will become unemployed, and the expected duration of unemployment is two periods.

1.6.1. Implications of shocks

Random temporary shocks do not impact on search behaviour when workers decide to search before a shock is revealed.[37] Things are different if workers expect a shock to persist in the future. If q, the probability of getting a job offer in West exceeds 0.5 throughout the next future period, workers take the higher employment prospects in West into account. Searching becomes less attractive for workers in the depressed region and more attractive in the booming region. For mobile workers in the depressed (booming) region, the expected benefit from searching falls (rises) by $\delta(q - 0.5)k^m$, whereas the expected gain from searching falls (rises) by $\delta(q - 0.5)(W - B)$ for immobile workers. Workers in the depressed region become not only more likely to migrate if the shock persists for longer, as shown in Section 1.4, but their value of search increases because searching raises the chances of finding employment in the booming region early, which is more attractive because it makes future moves less frequent.

1.7. Policy implications

The model implies that policies that raise moving costs reduce mobility and thereby increase unemployment. The analysis of asymmetric shocks indicates that higher moving costs slow the adjustment process as unemployment among immobile workers in the slump region remains high for a prolonged period. Additional interactions between moving costs and job search behaviour reinforce the adverse effects of such policies. These interactions are largely neglected in the theoretical and empirical literature but explain the correlation between homeownership rates and the level of unemployment.

Subsidizing moving costs, for example, by making them tax deductible or by offering some other form of tax benefit, increases mobility and thereby reduces the level of unemployment. However, when a policy favours a particular type of housing tenure, substitution effects have to be considered. For example, a subsidy for buying or building a home reduces moving costs for those who decide to move into owned property. However, it also makes owning more attractive, so that more workers are lured into homeownership. This has negative effects on future job mobility. Such a policy is especially bad if the subsidy is paid only once upon becoming a homeowner, because it raises aggregate moving costs in future periods after the homeownership rate has—induced by the policy—risen.

Subsidies to the renting sector have to be evaluated carefully as well. At first sight, rent control would probably be judged to be beneficial for renters, as it is designed to keep rents low. However, rent control reduces landlords' return on their investment in renting property, triggering a reduction of supply, either because property is sold off or simply due to attrition. Therefore, renters become constrained in their housing consumption.[38] This makes owning more attractive, so that some workers leave the renting sector.[39] Aggregate moving costs rise so that unemployment increases. Whether unemployment rises more among owners is ambiguous, because the most mobile renters leave the private renting sector first as the costs of additional immobility are smallest for them.[40] An increase in the proportion of homeowners therefore decreases average mobility in the renting sector. It would therefore not be surprising to see a higher unemployment rate among renters after the homeownership rate has risen in response to the subsidy.

1.8. Conclusion

The model explains the empirical regularity that higher owner-occupation rates are associated with higher aggregate unemployment rates. For an individual, regional mobility, and hence unemployment, depends on the difference between moving costs and forgone income during unemployment. Any rise in the value of unemployment relative to the value of employment, e.g. an increase in unemployment benefits or a reduction in wages, reduces mobility and causes unemployment to rise. Because forgone earnings during unemployment are larger for high-skilled workers, the latter are more willing to move regions to accept a job than low-skilled workers given the same choice of housing tenure. Conditional on the earnings potential, regional mobility is lower for homeowners than for renters. However, high-wage homeowners are more mobile than low-wage renters if the differential income loss associated with a spell of unemployment exceeds the difference in moving costs associated with owning versus renting a home. Failing to fully control for expected income (losses), it is consequently possible to find empirically that homeowners are more mobile than renters. On the one hand, this result indicates that econometric models in empirical studies of the determinants of regional mobility must be carefully specified. On the other hand, this theoretical finding helps us in reconciling the seemingly paradoxical findings that a higher homeownership rate is associated with a higher equilibrium level of unemployment although homeowners have lower unemployment rates on average.

Higher moving costs and lower mobility raise unemployment. If the private renting sector shrinks, e.g. because of government intervention or a change in preferences, more mobile workers are likely to leave the renting sector first, causing average mobility in the renting sector to fall. If the average wage among workers leaving the renting sector is lower than the average wage among home-owners, mobility also falls in the owner-occupied sector. A higher rate of owner occupation is therefore associated with more unemployment.

Economy-wide booms raise mobility of all workers but affect the most high-wage workers that move most often in absence of shocks. Economy-wide recessions reduce regional mobility. Asymmetric shocks increase migration to the booming region and reduce the number of workers leaving the booming region. Asymmetric shocks affect mobility of high-wage workers most, so that they are the first to leave a depressed region.

The type of housing tenure also affects search behaviour and hence job matching because workers search less effectively for new jobs; the higher are their moving costs, the lower is the income loss associated with unemploy-ment. Because search effectiveness is an increasing function of mobility, a reduction in mobility leads to less efficient matching of unemployed workers to vacancies, as is observed in many European countries. The choice of hous-ing tenure and its effect on regional mobility is likely to prove an important step towards explaining the puzzle of European unemployment.

The possibility of commuting increases workers' opportunities and raises their mobility. To account for commuting and the importance of distance, elements from gravity models might be integrated with the kind of mod-elling suggested in this paper. Additional aspects that could be integrated in a more general model include the consumption and investment characteristics of housing which affect mobility through adjustments of housing prices.

APPENDIX A

MOVING CONDITION IN SIMPLE MODEL

Proof. Suppose a worker receives a job offer in the other region. If he accepts and moves, his expected income, Y^a, is given by

$$Y^a = W - k^m + \frac{0.5\delta}{1-\delta} \left(W + \max\left[W - k^m; B \right] \right).$$

His expected income when rejecting, Y^r, and staying is given by

$$Y^r = B + \frac{0.5\delta}{1-\delta} \left(W + \max\left[W - k^m; B \right] \right).$$

(Note that q equals 0.5 by assumption 7). Hence, a worker migrates if

$$W - B > k^m; \quad \text{which proves Eqn. (1.1).}$$

PERSISTENT ASYMMETRIC SHOCKS

To prove that moving to the booming region (West) becomes more attractive the longer the boom is expected to persist, suppose it is optimal for a worker in East not to move to West if the asymmetric shock persists only in the next future period; that is, the worker does not satisfy $W - B < k^m - \delta(2q - 1)(W - B)$ (condition (1.2)). If the shock persists for another period, it is never optimal to move in the second period after not having moved in the first. If the shock persists for the next two periods, not accepting a job offer in West yields an expected income of

$$B + \delta \left\{ (1 - q) W + qB \right\} + \delta^2 \left\{ (1 - q) W + qB \right\} + \delta^3 V,$$

where V is the expected stream of income discounted to period 3 which is the same in expectation for movers and non-movers. The income when accepting can be calculated by backward induction and is given by

$$W - k^m + \delta \left\{ qW + (1 - q) B \right\} + \delta^2 \left\{ qW + (1 - q) B \right\} + \delta^3 V$$

because $W - B < k^m - \delta(2q - 1)(W - B)$ and $W > B$. Hence a worker will move if

$$W - B > k^m - \delta(2q - 1)(W - B) - \delta^2(2q - 1)(W - B) \tag{B.1}$$

When the shock persists for just one more future period, the moving constraint was given by condition (1.2):

$$W - B > k^m - \delta(2q - 1)(W - B).$$

Comparing (B.1) with (1.2) it is obvious that moving becomes more likely because the additional term, $\delta^2(2q - 1)(W - B)$, in (B.1) is positive.

1.8.1. *Serially correlated shocks*

If the shock is serially correlated, the moving condition is given by

$$W - B > k^m - 2\delta\rho\sigma k^m,$$

where ρ is defined as the correlation coefficient, and σ is a measure of the shock with $0 < \sigma < 0.5$ and $0 < \rho < 1$. This is derived as follows. A worker in the depressed region who accepts a job offer in the booming region and who will always move, has an expected income of

$$W - k^m + \delta \left(W - 0.5k^m + \rho\sigma k^m \right) + \delta^2 \left(W - 0.5k^m + \rho^3\sigma^3 k^m \right) + \dots$$

Somebody who rejects, but would move in the second period, receives

$$B + \delta(W - 0.5k^m - \rho\sigma k^m) + \delta^2(W - 0.5k^m + \rho^3\sigma^3 k^m) + \ldots$$

Notice that the expected income from the second period onwards is the same, because the probability of being in the booming region is the same.

ADVERSE SYMMETRIC SHOCKS

Assume that workers receive a job offer every second period, while a job lasts for one period, such that all workers whose job ends become unemployed for at least one period. We derive the moving constraint for those who receive a job offer outside their home region. At the time the moving decision has to be made, i.e. in the second period, the expected income from accepting the job offer equals

$$W - k^m + \frac{\delta}{1 - \delta^2} B + \frac{0.5\delta^2}{1 - \delta^2} \left(W + \max\left[W - k^m; B \right] \right),$$

whereas rejecting the offer yields an income of

$$B + \frac{\delta}{1 - \delta^2} B + \frac{0.5\delta^2}{1 - \delta^2} \left(W + \max\left[W - k^m; B \right] \right),$$

so that a worker accepts the job offer and moves if

$$W - B > k^m; \quad \text{which is identical to condition (1.1).}$$

APPENDIX D

MOBILITY AND SEARCH

The moving condition in the absence of search differs from (1.1) as a non-searching worker becomes unemployed every second period, which lowers the net benefit from moving. The discounted stream of income for somebody who is offered a job in the other region and moves is given by

$$
W - k^m + \frac{\delta}{1 - \delta^2} B + \frac{0.5\delta^2}{1 - \delta^2} \left(W + \max\left[W - k^m; B\right]\right),
$$

while expected income when rejecting the offer equals

$$
B + \frac{0.5\delta}{1 - \delta^2} \left(W + \max\left[W - k^m; B\right]\right) + \frac{\delta^2}{1 - \delta^2} B,
$$

so that it is optimal to move if

$$
W - B > k^m + \frac{0.5\delta}{1 + \delta} \left(W + \max\left[W - k^m; B\right]\right) - \frac{\delta}{1 + \delta} B.^{41} \tag{D.1}
$$

Consider now the search decision of workers satisfying (D.1). Their expected income when searching only in the first period is given by

$$
W - s + \frac{\delta}{1 - \delta^2} W - \frac{0.5\delta}{1 - \delta^2} k^m + \frac{\delta^2}{1 - \delta^2} B,
$$

while not searching yields an expected income of

$$
W + \frac{\delta}{1 - \delta^2} B + \frac{\delta^2}{1 - \delta^2} W - \frac{0.5\delta^2}{1 - \delta^2} k^m.
$$

Hence, search is optimal if

$$
W - B > \frac{1 + \delta}{\delta} s + 0.5 k^m. \tag{D.2}
$$

A worker satisfying (D.1) will always search on-the-job because his expected income when always searching is given by

$$
W - s + \frac{\delta}{1 - \delta} W - \frac{\delta}{1 - \delta} s - \frac{0.5\delta}{1 - \delta} k^m.
$$

Always searching is hence preferred to never searching if

$$
W - B > +\frac{1 + \delta}{\delta} s + 0.5 k^m, \quad \text{which gives Eqn. (1.7).}
$$

The present value of income of workers who optimally reject a job offer outside the home region is given by

$$W - s + \delta\,(0.5W + 0.5B) + \delta^2\,[0.5B + 0.5\,(0.5W + 0.5B)]$$
$$+ \delta^3\,[0.25B + 0.75\,(0.5W + 0.5B)] + \ldots$$

when searching only in the first period; while the present value of future income when not searching is given by

$$W + \delta B + \delta^2\,(0.5W + 0.5B) + \delta^3\,[0.5B + 0.5\,(0.5W + 0.5B)] + \ldots$$

Search is hence profitable if

$$W - B > \frac{\delta + 2}{\delta}s, \quad \text{which gives Eqn. (1.8).}$$

Notes

1. Friedman (1968) already explained: 'The natural rate of unemployment is the level which would be ground out by the Walrasian system of general equilibrium equations, provided that there is imbedded in them the actual structural characteristics of the labor and commodity markets, including market imperfections, stochastic variability in demands and supplies, the cost of gathering information about job vacancies and labor availabilities, the cost of mobility, and so on.'
2. Evidence for a positive correlation between rates of homeownership and unemployment is also provided by Green and Hendershott (2001), Partridge and Rickman (1997), and Pehkohnen (1999). See also n. 9 below.
3. The model is concerned with regional mobility. Böheim and Taylor (2002, p. 370) find in an analysis of data from the British Household Panel Survey (BHPS) that '[A] desire to move motivated by employment reasons has the single largest effect on the probability of moving between regions' and that it is the unemployed who are most likely to move, particularly between regions. Gardner *et al.* (2001) also find that joblessness stimulates mobility, in data from both the BHPS and the National Child Development Study.
4. In a sample, in which 75 per cent are homeowners, Böheim and Taylor (2002) find that over 50 per cent of the unemployed live in rented accommodation, while less than 20 per cent of those in work are renters.
5. The idea that housing and labour markets are linked is not new. Research by Hughes and McCormick (1981, 1985b, 1987) focuses on the private and public renting sector, and concludes that council housing restricts labour mobility and hence raises unemployment. Bover *et al.* (1989) argue that regional house price/earnings differentials are important elements in wage and unemployment equations, as well as in vacancy equations.
6. See Davis *et al.* (1996), Contini and Revelli (1997), and OECD (1996), ch. 5.
7. See Nickell (1997).
8. In most countries, the number of unemployed has risen relative to the number of vacancies, indicating that vacancies are filled less efficiently.
9. Oswald (1996) finds that the gradient of unemployment to owner occupation is roughly 0.2 in different datasets including cross-sections of OECD countries, UK regions, US states, regions of France, Sweden, and Italy, and a panel dataset of UK regions. This empirical regularity is buttressed by the fact that nations with the fastest growth of homeownership rates experienced the strongest unemployment growth. A 10 percentage point increase in the rate of owner occupation is associated with an increase in the unemployment rate of approximately 2 percentage points. Henley's (1998) findings also suggest that homeownership reduces mobility. Pehkohnen (1999) confirms Oswald's results using Finnish data. Green and Hendershott (2001) find evidence for a positive correlation between rates of homeownership and unemployment in US data for the middle age (35–64) classes. However, see also n. 22 below.
10. Böheim and Taylor (2002) estimate that private renters are most likely to move between regions when controlling *inter alia* for income, education, age, and employment status.

11. Evans and McCormick (1994) find that non-manual workers have much higher gross rates of interregional mobility. Pissarides and Wadsworth (1989) report that the likelihood of migration rises with educational attainment. See also Hughes and McCormick (1987) and McCormick (1997).

12. Hughes and McCormick (1985a) find that education increases the probability of job search, and Pissarides and Wadsworth (1994) provide evidence that skilled workers search more and prefer employed search.

13. See Jackman and Savouri (1992), Pissarides and Wadsworth (1989), and Vanderkamp (1968).

14. Evans and McCormick (1994), Hughes and McCormick (1985b, 1994), and McCormick (1997) all find little evidence that manual workers migrate to low-unemployment markets, whereas absolute net migration rates are much higher for non-manuals.

15. McCormick (1997) reports that workers migrate to regional markets with high relative wages. See also Hughes and McCormick (1994) and Pissarides and Wadsworth (1989).

16. See Henley (1998).

17. A fixed length of employment spell is assumed for simplicity despite the awareness that there is great variation in the length of employment spells (Farber 1999).

18. Gross benefits include any payment or subsidy an unemployed worker receives as well as the monetary value of additional leisure time or self-employment he enjoys. Let M be the monetary value of gross benefits and C the monetary value of any cost associated with unemployment, then $B = M - C$.

19. An infinite horizon facilitates the algebra and exposition, but the important implications of the model can be derived with finite lives.

20. This is confirmed empirically by Böheim and Taylor (2002).

21. In this simple model setting low-skilled renters either always or never move. Lowering moving costs has no impact on mobility over some range, but causes discrete jumps in mobility rates once the moving condition is met by a particular group of workers. These results disappear if we, more realistically, assume either continuous wage offer distributions for different types of workers or a continuum of mobility costs.

22. Coulson and Fisher (2002) find, for example, that homeowners typically earn significantly higher wages than do renters and are more mobile. Green and Hendershott (2001) point out that selection issues are important. For example, those who expect to have more stable employment (and thus can amortize the sunk costs associated with owning over a longer period) are likely to have lower user costs of owning, and are consequently more likely to become homeowners. Although the partial equilibrium analysis takes the housing choice as given, the model implies that a higher job offer arrival rate and a lower job destruction rate reduce the need for moving regions for job reasons. Green and Hendershott (2002) deal with some of the issues of selectivity and aggregation. Flatau et al. (2003) analyse Australian data and point out that empirical results conflicting with Oswald's findings (Oswald 1996) stem from (1) highly leveraged owners having a greater incentive to stay employed and search hard to become re-employed quickly after job loss and from (2) public house tenants paying below market rents and thus having reduced incentives to move for job reasons.

23. Note that the unemployment rate rises in the depressed region among immobile workers because fewer of them receive a job offer in their home region.
24. This is consistent with the findings of Hughes and McCormick (1994), McCormick (1997), and Pissarides and Wadsworth (1989).
25. A worker's expected discounted future income when moving to West is given by

$$W^W - k^m + \delta \left\{ qW^W + (1-q) \max \left[W^E - k^m; B \right] \right\} + \frac{0.5\delta^2}{1-\delta} \left\{ W + \max \left[W - k^m; B \right] \right\}$$

the present value of staying is given by

$$B + \delta \left\{ (1-q) W^E + q \max \left[W^W - k^m; B \right] \right\} + \frac{0.5\delta^2}{1-\delta} \left\{ W + \max \left[W - k^m; B \right] \right\}$$

26. For more details see Dohmen (2000).
27. The alternative assumption that a job offer arrives in each period irrespective of the employment status complicates analysis. An employed worker would optimally accept a job offer in his home region, quitting the current job to be employed for another $t-1$ periods in his home region, but he would reject an offer from the other region and rather fulfil his current contract waiting for the job offer he gets after his current contract will have expired.
28. The first derivative with respect to t is given by $(-\delta t/(1 - \delta t)) \ln \delta$ which is positive because $0 < \delta < 1$.
29. The condition that makes high-skilled owners more mobile than low-skilled renters is given by $1 - F(w^o) > 1 - G(w^r)$ $F(w^o) < G(w^r)$.
30. The skewed aggregate wage distribution observed in reality provides support for the hypothesis that the variance of the offer distribution is positively related to income (and hence skills).
31. If there are as many 'good' as 'bad' jobs, $h_2 H_2$ and $l_2 L_2$ are the variance of the job offer distribution for high-skilled and low-skilled workers, respectively. If $l = h$; that is, if remuneration of 'good' jobs is $2h$ per cent higher than that of 'bad' jobs for both types of workers, the wage offer distribution for workers with a higher mean income also has a larger variance.
32. The assumption that search from unemployment is free of charge is a result of scaling costs such that on-the-job search is more costly, so that s can be interpreted as the excess cost of employed over unemployed search. This assumption is reasonable, because unemployed often receive additional support from employment agencies; furthermore, employed workers have to take time off to search and, unlike unemployed, incur a loss of income.
33. In fact, opportunity costs impact on the decision to search on-the-job. Workers whose wage largely reflects firm-specific skills face higher opportunity costs than workers with more general skills and are therefore less likely to search and migrate.
34. It should be noted that the assumptions about the length of the periods of employment and unemployment are not crucial to derive these implications. In principle, the longer expected employment becomes relative to the period between two job offers, the more likely a worker becomes to search and migrate. The length of the periods chosen facilitates the illustration of the main implications of the model.
35. This is because it implies that $k^m > [(2+\delta)/(\delta - 0.5\delta2)]s$. Hence, $k^m > (2s/\delta)$ because $[(2 + \delta)/(\delta - 0.5\delta2)] > (2/\delta)$.

36. For non-searching mobile workers, the expected duration of unemployment is one period, while the expected duration for searching immobile workers is two periods.

37. A negative (positive) symmetric shock increases (reduces) unemployment among immobile workers. An asymmetric shock increases (decreases) unemployment in the region that is negatively (positively) affected because it reduces (increases) job offers for immobile workers. Although the shock has no impact on the employment status of mobile workers, mobile workers in the depressed region are worse off as they become more likely to incur the moving costs. Mobile workers in the booming region gain because the risk of having to incur the moving costs falls.

38. A shrinking private renting sector limits choices of those who are remaining in the renting sector even further if landlords reduce supply at a higher rate than the exit rate from the renting sector.

39. Note that they are worse off than without controlled rents, because they preferred renting when their consumption opportunity was not limited. The loss in utility is reflected in lower mobility.

40. Moreover, those with higher incomes are more mobile and more likely to be able to afford ownership. In Britain, workers on lower incomes have opted to leave the private renting sector for council housing. Mobility of council tenants is lower than mobility of private renters (see Hughes and McCormick 1981). Council tenants wishing to migrate have to obtain council housing in their destination region, and that process does not seem to work well. Hughes and McCormick (1987) argue that council tenants are no less likely than owner-occupiers to wish to migrate but merely less successful in fulfilling their intentions.

41. Notice that the term $[(0.5\delta)/(1 + \delta)](W + \max[W - k^m; B]) - [\delta/(1 + \delta)]B$ is always positive, confirming that moving in this setting is generally less attractive than in the simple model.

References

Blanchard, O. J., and Katz, L. F. (1997), 'What we know and do not know about the natural rate of unemployment', *Journal of Economic Perspectives*, 11, 51–72.

Böheim, R., and Taylor, M. P. (2002), 'Tied down or room to move? Investigating the relationships between housing tenure, employment status and residential mobility in Britain', *Scottish Journal of Political Economy*, 49, 369–92.

Bover, O., Muellbauer, J., and Murphy, A. (1989), 'Housing, wages and UK labour markets', *Oxford Bulletin of Economics and Statistics*, 51, 97–136.

Contini, B., and Revelli, R. (1997), 'Gross flows vs. net flows in the labour market: what is to be learned?', *Labour Economics*, 4, 245–63.

Coulson, E. N., and Fisher, L. M. (2002), 'Tenure choice and labour market outcomes', *Housing Studies*, 17, 35–49.

Davis, S. J., Haltiwanger, J. C., and Schuh, S. (1996), *Job Creation and Destruction* (Cambridge, MA: MIT Press).

Dohmen, T. J. (2000), 'Housing, mobility and unemployment', IZA Discussion Paper 210.

Evans, P., and McCormick, B. (1994), 'The new pattern of regional unemployment: causes and policy significance', *Economic Journal*, 104, 633–47.

Farber, H. S. (1999), 'Mobility and stability: the dynamics of job change in labor markets', in O. C. Ashenfelter and D. Card, (eds.), *Handbook of Labor Economics* (Amsterdam: North-Holland), iiiB. 2439–83.

Flatau, P., Forbes, M., Hendershott, P. H., and Wood, G. (2003), 'Homeownership and unemployment: the roles of leverage and public housing', NBER Working Paper 10021.

Friedman, M. (1968), 'The role of monetary policy', *American Economic Review*, 58/1, 1–17.

Gardner, J., Pierre, G., and Oswald, A. J. (2001), 'Moving for job reasons', mimeo, University of Warwick, Department of Economics.

Green, R. K., and Hendershott, P. H. (2001), 'Home-ownership and unemployment in the US', *Urban Studies*, 38/9, 1509–20.

———— (2002), 'Homeownership and the duration of unemployment: a test of the Oswald hypothesis', paper presented at AREUEA Annual Meetings, January 2002.

Henley, A. (1998), 'Residential mobility, housing equity and the labour market', *Economic Journal*, 108, 414–28.

Hughes, G. A., and McCormick, B. (1981), 'Do council housing policies reduce migration between regions', *Economic Journal*, 91, 919–37.

———— (1985a), 'An empirical analysis of on-the-job search and job mobility', *Manchester School*, 53/1, 76–95.

———— (1985b), 'Migration intentions in the UK', *Economic Journal*, 95, 113–23 (Conference Papers Supplement).

———— (1987), 'Housing markets, unemployment and labor market flexibility in the UK', *European Economic Review*, 31/3, 615–41.

———— (1994), 'Did migration in the 1980s narrow the North–South divide?', *Economica*, 61/244, 509–27.

Jackman, R., and Savouri, S. (1992), 'Regional migration in Britain: an analysis of gross flows using NHS center register data', *Economic Journal*, 102/415, 1422–50.

Layard, R., Nickell, S. J., and Jackman, R. (1991), *Unemployment: Macroeconomic Performance and the Labour Market* (Oxford: Oxford University Press).

McCormick, B. (1997), 'Regional unemployment and labour mobility in the UK', *European Economic Review*, 41/3–5, 581–9.

Nickell, S. J. (1997), 'Unemployment and labor market rigidities: Europe versus North America', *Journal of Economic Perspectives*, 11/3, 55–74.

—— (1998), 'Unemployment: questions and some answers', *Economic Journal*, 108/448, 802–16.

OECD (1996), *Employment Outlook* (Paris: OECD).

Oswald, A. J. (1996), 'A conjecture on the explanation for high unemployment in the industrialized nations: part I', Warwick Economic Research Paper 475.

—— (1997), 'Theory of homes and jobs', mimeo, University of Warwick.

Partridge, M., and Rickman, D. (1997), 'The dispersion of US state unemployment rates: the role of market and nonmarket equilibrium factors', *Regional Studies*, 31, 593–606.

Pehkohnen, J. (1999), 'Unemployment and home-ownership', *Applied Economics Letters*, 6, 263–5.

Pissarides, C. A. (2000), *Equilibrium Unemployment Theory*, 2nd edn. (Cambridge, MA: MIT Press).

——and Wadsworth, J. (1989), 'Unemployment and the inter-regional mobility of labour', *Economic Journal*, 99/397, 739–55.

————(1994), 'On-the-job search: some empirical evidence from Britain', *European Economic Review*, 38/2, 385–401.

Vanderkamp, J. (1968), 'Interregional mobility in Canada: a study of the time pattern of migration', *Canadian Journal of Economics*, 1/3, 595–608.

2

The Housing Market and Europe's Unemployment: A Non-technical Paper[*]

Andrew Oswald

2.1. Introduction

This paper argues that the housing market lies at the heart of the European unemployment problem. It describes a practical suggestion to reduce joblessness in Europe's nations—that our continent should revive private renting and try to make the housing market function more smoothly. We can put Europe back to work, the essay argues, by reducing homeownership. It is worth beginning with three background facts. Of the major industrial nations

- Spain has the highest unemployment, and also the highest rate of homeownership.
- Switzerland has the lowest unemployment, and the lowest rate of homeownership.
- In the 1950s and early 1960s, the United States had the highest unemployment, and at that time had the highest rate of homeownership.

The underlying argument in the paper is that an economy's 'natural rate' of unemployment depends on the ease with which its citizens can move around to find jobs. Fluid societies have efficient economies. Although Milton Friedman pointed this out in his famous American Economic Association address of 1967, few European economists have thought hard about labour mobility and different forms of accommodation. Yet we know the housing market is likely to have an influence on the degree of labour mobility.

By making it expensive to change location, high levels of homeownership foster spatial mismatch between workers' skills and the available jobs.

---

[*] This chapter was written in 1999 and is being reprinted here.

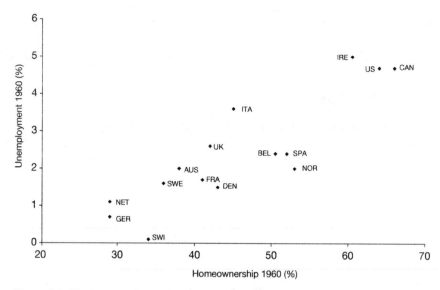

Figure 2.1. Homeownership and unemployment rates forty years ago: the countries of North America and Europe in 1960

Notes: The unemployment rates are from the OECD and are as close as can be obtained to standardized data for that era. I have omitted Finland from the figure because I have doubts about the reliability of its data: it has the lowest male employment/population ratio in the sample while recording ostensibly low unemployment. I have omitted the Communist bloc because data are not available. The homeownership rates are so-called 'owner-occupation' proportions from national censuses, and were generously provided by Francis Castles of the Political Science Program, RSSS, Australian National University, Canberra.

Friedman does not mention the housing market in his address. However, the data in Figure 2.1 for 1960, suggesting a remarkable correlation between ownership and unemployment levels, were available when he was preparing his lecture. If Milton Friedman had stumbled upon the graph, and published it in his AEA address paper, it is possible European history would have been different.

With the exception of Switzerland (which has had lower unemployment than almost all other Western countries), the nations of Europe have, by conscious design, seen strong growth in homeownership since the 1950s. Spain is a good example: it now has a homeownership rate of 80 per cent compared to less than 40 per cent after the Second World War. European governments today continue to offer subsidies to try to persuade their people to give up rental housing and become owner-occupiers. The evidence in this paper, however, raises doubts about the wisdom of providing tax breaks to those who own homes.

2.2. The main ideas and evidence

Economies need to be adaptable. In an ever-changing world, countries require workers to be able to move around to find new jobs. Private rental housing helps. Renting allows people to be mobile: it provides a way for a square peg in Zurich to drop into a square hole in Geneva.

In the period from 1950 to 1960, most European nations had low owner-occupation rates and low unemployment rates. The United States then had relatively high owner occupation of 60 per cent. At that time—this fact tends to be forgotten by young economists—the US had the highest unemployment rate in the industrialized world. Americans gazed in wonder at the low jobless-ness across the Atlantic and pondered if they too should aim for a generous welfare state and strong trade unions. Since then, US homeownership has been constant through the years (like the trend in its unemployment). All the other industrialized nations except Japan and Switzerland have witnessed a large increase in homeownership.

Unemployment rates have risen most quickly in the nations with the fastest growth in homeownership.

The figures provide an informal look at the evidence. Figures 2.2 and 2.3 illustrate the current position: nations where many people rent have less

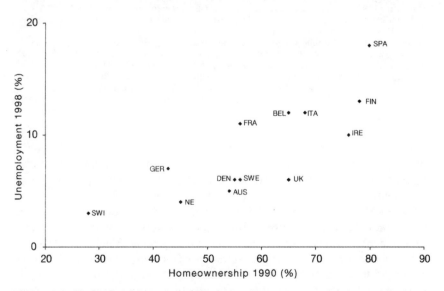

Figure 2.2. Unemployment rates and owner-occupation rates: the main European nations in the 1990s

Notes: The unemployment data are the latest OECD numbers, and the owner-occupation rates are as recent as possible and are taken from UN census or similar sources.

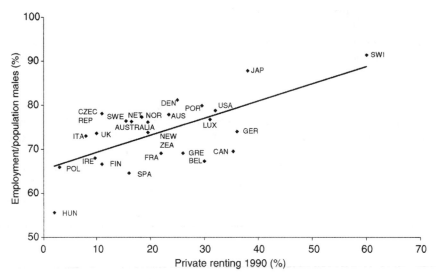

Figure 2.3. The relationship between countries' employment rates and the size of their private rented housing markets: 25 industrial nations in the 1990s

Notes: The vertical axis is the male employment rate, expressed as a proportion of population. This is for men of ages 15–65. These data are for *circa* 1992 and come mostly from the OECD Employment Outlook, July 1995, Table A, 1992 column, p. 204. For the Czech Republic, Hungary, and Poland, the data are for 1993, and come from Table B, p. 164, of OECD Employment Outlook, July 1997.

The horizontal axis is the proportion of people who rent. The data on housing are principally from Table 1.12, p. 11, of *Housing Policy in Europe*, ed. Paul Balchin (London and New York: Routledge, 1996). For the Czech Republic, Hungary, and Poland, the data come from the later pages of Balchin, including p. 286. For New Zealand and Australia, the data are taken from p. 184 of *From Public Housing to the Social Market*, ed. J. Kemeny (London and New York: Routledge, 1995). Marion Steele of the University of Guelph provided helpful information about Canada. Japanese and US data were imputed by making a small adjustment to (1 − homeownership rate), calculated from UN census data.

Technical note: this graph is not greatly influenced by outliers. Omitting the two most favourable observations, Switzerland and Hungary, alters the gradient to 0.26 with a well-defined *t* statistic.

joblessness than nations where homeownership is the norm. According to the slope in Figure 2.3, a rise of 10 percentage points in the extent of private renting is associated with a rise of 4 percentage points in the proportion of men working (statistics on females' work are a less reliable indicator because they are influenced by national cultures). Figures 2.4 and 2.5 show that similar patterns are found even inside countries. The link between housing and jobs appears to hold across space within a country as well as across different countries.

This relationship can be found in many nations' regions, but only two are presented here. Figure 2.4 is for the cantons of Switzerland. It is included because it might be thought this is the least likely country where the paper's ideas would fit the data. Figure 2.5 is for the United States and is included here for a similar reason, and to show that the mechanisms run deeper than being specific to Europe's institutions.

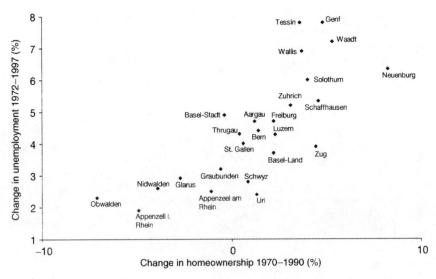

Figure 2.4. The correlation between the growth of homeownership and unemployment across the cantons of Switzerland from the 1970s to the 1990s

Notes: Each diamond is a Swiss canton. The horizontal axis gives the twenty-year change for home-ownership, that is, the 1990 figure minus the 1970 figure. The vertical axis is the change in the unemployment rate from 1972 to 1997.

The data sources are BFS and BWA.

The axes are in percentage points; thus a canton that went from 2 per cent to 3 per cent unemployment and from 40 per cent homeownership to 46 per cent homeownership would appear as (6, 1).

2.3. What are the likely mechanisms?

The processes behind these correlations are not fully understood, but there are five likely links in the chain. First, there is a direct effect from home-ownership. Selling a home and moving is expensive. For this reason, indeed, many homeowners who lose their jobs are willing to commute long distances to find work. Hence owner-occupiers are less mobile than renters, and therefore more vulnerable to economic downturns in their region. Nevertheless, this probably cannot be the whole story. If we look at countries like Spain and the UK, a key part of the problem is young unemployed people living at home, unable to move out because the rental sector hardly exists.

Therefore, second, part of the difficulty is not that unemployed people are themselves the homeowners; it is that unemployed men and women cannot move into the right places. High homeownership levels block young people's ability to enter an area to find a job. Those without capital to buy are at a

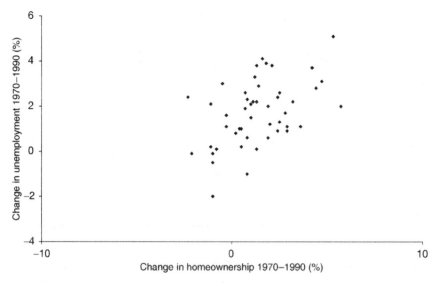

Figure 2.5. The correlation between the growth of homeownership and unemployment across the states of the USA: 1970 to 1990

Notes: Each diamond is a state of the US. These are twenty-year changes, that is, the 1990 figure minus the 1970 figure. There are forty-nine observations, one for each of the mainland states of the USA (Hawaii and Alaska are omitted) plus DC. The axes are in percentage points; thus a state that went from 4 per cent to 6 per cent unemployment and from 40 per cent homeownership to 48 per cent homeownership would appear as (8, 2). The data are from the BLS and the Statistical Abstract of the US.

particular disadvantage in a world where ownership is the dominant form of housing tenure.

Third, in an economy in which people are immobile, workers do jobs for which they are not ideally suited. This inefficiency is harmful to everyone: it raises costs of production and lowers real incomes in a country. Prices thus have to be higher, and real wages lower, than in a more mobile society. Jobs get destroyed—or more precisely priced out of existence—by such inefficiencies.

Fourth, areas with high homeownership levels may act to deter entrepreneurs from setting up new operations. Planning laws and restrictions on land development, enforced by the local political power of groups of homeowners, may discourage business start-ups.

Fifth, we know from survey data that homeowners commute much more than renters, and over longer distances, and this may lead to transport congestion that makes getting to work more costly and difficult for everyone. Technically speaking, this acts like higher unemployment benefits, because it reduces the gain from having a job. If getting to work is more expensive, that has the same net effect as raising the attractiveness of not working.

2.4. Comparing the strength of the homeownership theory with other explanations

Economists have tried for a long time to understand why OECD joblessness has risen from around 2 per cent in the 1950s to approximately 10 per cent today. The standard explanations are that trade unions have become too powerful, unemployment benefits are now too generous, and labour markets are too highly taxed and not sufficiently flexible. It is probable these ideas have some role to play in the whole answer. However, if we look in detail at nations, the data do not provide much support for these otherwise plausible ideas. Those countries with the worst unemployment problems, for example, do not have especially high unemployment benefits or strong unions. Conventional wisdom is more the result of theoretical preconception than a weighing of hard evidence.

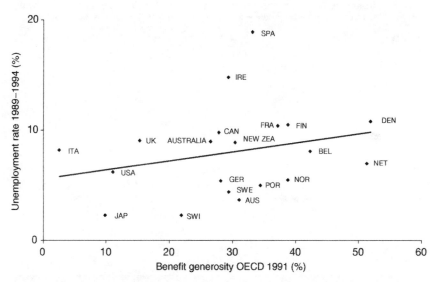

Figure 2.6. Countries with more generous unemployment benefits have only slightly more unemployment

Notes: Each diamond is a country. The unemployment data are standardized OECD rates and average over the years 1989–94. The benefit generosity variable is taken from the OECD Database on Unemployment Benefit Entitlements and Replacement Rates. It is a summary measure of benefit entitlement before tax as a percentage of previous earnings before tax. It thus combines a country's amount and length of benefits, because the data are averages over different earnings levels, length of unemployment spells, and family situations.

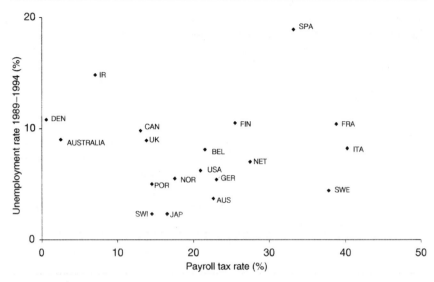

Figure 2.7. Countries which tax labour highly do not have more unemployment

Notes: Each diamond is a country. The unemployment data are standardized OECD rates, and the payroll tax data were generously provided by Steve Nickell of the London School of Economics. Fitting a line through the scatter produces a horizontal slope. The R-squared is less than 0.01.

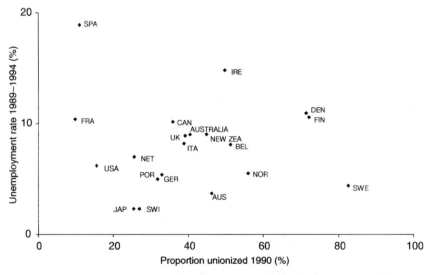

Figure 2.8. Countries with high trade union density do not have more unemployment

Notes: Each diamond is a country. The unemployment data are standardized OECD rates, and the unionized proportion variable is the proportion of workers in the country who are members of trade unions, which was generously provided by Steve Nickell. Fitting a line through the scatter produces a negative slope. The R-squared is less than 0.01.

Figures 2.6, 2.7, and 2.8 provide an informal illustration of the empirical difficulty faced by orthodox arguments. There is a little evidence that high-benefits countries have slightly greater unemployment (in Figure 2.6), but the size of the effect is not large. The other two graphs show the correlations between unemployment and labour taxes, and unemployment and unionism. Both are weak.

On a final and more technical point, it is straightforward to estimate so-called fixed effects and random-effects models on large panels of European countries and panels of regions within countries, to use micro data, and to do further more complex checks. These regressions hold constant other variables (including the proportion of women working, age structure of the population, and the so-called Layard–Nickell variables). Housing variables continue to have large estimated effects and to be statistically significant at normal confidence levels. Allowing for interest-rate and other macroeconomic effects also leaves the correlations unaffected.

It might be thought, finally, that reverse causality is a possibility—that high levels of unemployment lead to large amounts of homeownership. Apart from the intrinsic implausibility of this kind of argument, it can be shown using two-stage least squares methods that there are reasons to doubt such a view. All this technical material is omitted.

2.5. Conclusion

Although much remains to be learned, the housing market may contain the key to a puzzle that has defied us for a long time. We can put Europe back to work, this essay suggests, by reducing homeownership.

Renting worked in the 1950s and can work again. Europe can too.

3

Homeownership, Social Renting, and Labour Mobility across Europe

Thomas de Graaff, Michiel van Leuvensteijn, and Casper van Ewijk

3.1. Introduction

> The dominant adjustment mechanism is labor mobility, rather than job
> creation or job migration. Labor mobility, in turn, appears to be primarily a
> response to changes in unemployment, rather than in consumption wages.
>
> (Blanchard and Katz 1992, p. 52)

This quote stipulates the importance of residential mobility regarding both individual labour market status and aggregate unemployment levels. Indeed, individuals find jobs easier when willing to move residence, and national employment levels are positively correlated with national migration rates.

The probability of moving residence differs widely across countries. Oswald (1997) regards this as one of the fundamental reasons for European unemployment levels being structurally higher than unemployment levels in the United States. Moreover, countries differ as well in the various transaction costs which enter the housing market—whether they are monetary, social, or psychological. Some of these transaction costs are explicit, such as transaction taxes for homeowners, which can be as high as 13–15 per cent of the residential property values for countries such as Belgium and Italy. Other transaction costs are less explicit, such as cultural, ethnic, and religious differences within countries, but may nevertheless hamper free migration between local labour markets. Especially since the seminal working papers of Oswald (1997, 1999), the impact of these transaction costs on being a homeowner have been extensively studied. Although the impact of homeownership on unemployment is still somewhat controversial, the impact of homeownership on residential mobility is not. Compared with private renters, homeowners are considerably less mobile in the housing market; in Europe, they move residence on average four to five times less than private renters.

However, renters who rent from a public, municipal, voluntary, or non-profit agency—henceforth, social renters—face substantial moving costs as well. Usually, social renters have accumulated certain rights to rent residential property below market rents which are not transferable across municipalities or local labour markets. Thus, when moving to a new local labour market, i.e. to accept a job offer, social renters lose (the option value of) these rights, and, as a consequence, these add up to the transactions costs of moving residence.

In contrast to homeownership, not much research has been done on the relationship between social renting and labour market behaviour. Moreover, because the institutional framework regarding the housing market differs across countries—which accounts both for social renting and for homeownership—empirical research into the impact of transaction costs embodied by social renting and homeownership should focus on country-specific effects. Therefore, the main objective of this chapter is to look into the impact of social renting and homeownership on labour market mobility across Europe.

We do so by looking at the exit rates of workers to another job, unemployment, and non-participation. For exit rates out of unemployment by homeowners and renters under rent control we refer to Svarer *et al.* (2005), and Chapter 4 below, which have looked into this for the case of Denmark and, for homeowners, to Van Leuvensteijn and Koning (Chapter 8 below) and Van Vuuren and Van Leuvensteijn (2007) for the case of the Netherlands. The specific contribution of this paper to the literature is twofold: namely, (i) it takes a European perspective and performs cross-country analysis for most countries in Western Europe, and (ii) it includes data on the issue of social renting as well and analyses its impact on mobility. This chapter is explorative in nature; it considers the differences in homeownership and social renting institutions between the various countries, but we do not aim to develop a structural model explaining the differences in labour market effects.[1] Neither do we take differences in commuting time—between countries and between residential tenure types—into account. We refer to the Appendix for an overview of the differences in housing market institutions across Western European countries.

The remainder of this chapter is organized as follows. The next section provides a survey of the literature. Because the literature on the impact of social renting is rather limited, the section emphasizes the impact of homeownership. However, one might argue that, theoretically, the process is to some extent similar, because they both involve residential transaction costs as a barrier to mobility. The third section deals with the data and provides an overview of some preliminary facts regarding residential mobility, homeownership, and social renting across fourteen countries in Western Europe. Thereafter we continue with the econometric specification followed by a discussion of the results for both homeowners and social renters in Europe. Although the results are presented in a descriptive manner, the discussion provides an interpretation as well. The last section concludes.

3.2. Theory and literature

The impact especially of homeownership but also of social renting on residential transaction costs has already been well established in the literature. Moreover, it is also well established that transaction costs hamper mobility in the housing market, and, as a consequence, in the job market. However, high residential transaction costs do not seem necessarily to entail high probabilities of becoming unemployed. The following subsection therefore first argues why—for *individual* workers—the theoretical impact of reduced mobility on the probability of becoming unemployed is *ex ante* not clear. Thereafter, it reviews both the micro- and macroeconomic literature concerning the impact of homeownership and social renting on labour market mobility.

3.2.1. *Theoretical impact of reduced mobility on labour market behaviour*

Higher transaction costs on the housing market clearly reduce residential mobility. Munch *et al.* (Chapter 4 below) show in a search theoretical framework that is *ex ante* not clear what sign the impact of a reduced residential mobility has on unemployment. This depends on the labour market behaviour of the worker herself and the characteristics of the labour market. Basically, there are two competing hypotheses:

1. Workers who face higher transaction costs on the housing market, such as social renters and homeowners, are inclined to decline more job offers: usually, because some of these job offers originate from different regional labour markets and are therefore not acceptable (if commuting fails to be an option) or because social renters and homeowners demand higher wages to compensate the transaction costs to move residence. Therefore, social renters or homeowners may search longer and have longer unemployed spells or enter unemployment faster than, e.g., private renters who are more inclined to move residence to accept a suitable job offer.

2. Or those workers are—*ceteris paribus*—more committed to their current job as long as it is within their specific local labour market. They have more to lose when forced to move residence, especially when the transaction costs are sunk (for homeowners) or when the transaction consists of losing substantial benefits or a large option value (for social renters). Such job commitment could manifest itself in longer (unpaid) working hours, lower reservation wages, and higher productivity levels. This also entails that they leave unemployment faster, because their reservation wages for job offers in the local labour market are lower. Thus, compared with private renters, their job spells are longer, and their unemployment spells are shorter.

Although both homeowners and social renters are affected by transaction costs, the impact may differ empirically because of the size of the transaction costs. Apart from that there are several other possible reasons why the outflow into unemployment is different between homeowners and social renters.

First of all, there are external effects associated with homeownership and social renting. As Dietz and Haurin (2003) have shown, most external effects of homeownership that are not directly related to labour market behaviour are beneficial. Homeowners are, e.g., more attached to their residence than others, and therefore willing to invest more in their residential property and the surrounding neighbourhood. For social renters, higher attachment to the residence has not been reported, but is likely to be less than for homeowners. Disregarding for the moment selection effects amongst workers to the social renting sector, it might even be that social renting causes a negative external effect because social renters are, e.g., usually not responsible for the maintenance of the residence.

Secondly, there may be social security or fiscal reasons for homeowners or renters to avoid unemployment as much as possible. Subsidies or unemployment benefits may be lower for homeowners than for renters. For example, several Western European countries still allow (partly) for mortgage interest deduction from income taxation. When homeowners enter unemployment, monthly mortgage payments increase substantially.

Finally, landlords may be more forgiving in terms of monthly payments than mortgage providers, especially when homeowners are highly leveraged.

Which of the two hypotheses above is correct is mainly an empirical question, both for homeowners and for social renters. The next subsection first reviews the mostly empirical literature considering the effects of owning a home on labour mobility. Subsequently, it looks into the smaller empirical literature concerning the effect of social renting and rent control.

3.2.2. Previous literature

The theoretical literature on the relationship between homeownership on the one hand and job mobility and unemployment on the other hand does not predict a clear *ex ante* outcome with respect to the direction of this relationship. From a macro perspective, Green and Hendershott (2001*b*), e.g., offer three additional explanations for the fact that homeownership may cause reduced labour market mobility. First, when the economy is in a downturn, housing becomes a very illiquid asset, causing homeowners to be reluctant to sell their homes and search for appropriate jobs outside their local labour market. Secondly, high interest rates may cause homeowners to be locked in as well, with similar consequences for residential mobility. And finally, high transaction costs usually associated with homeownership may also cause reduced residential mobility.

Dohmen (Chapter 1 above) looks at the consequences of homeownership in a microeconomic theoretical framework with search and moving costs and derives, *ceteris paribus*, that homeowners are less mobile than renters. However, *high-skilled* homeowners may be more mobile than *low-skilled* renters if the income loss associated with unemployment exceeds the income loss associated with moving house. Along the same line of thought, Van Vuuren and Van Leuvensteijn (2007) analyse the relationship between expected labour market outcomes and the housing market in a search theoretical framework, and argue that the empirically often observed negative relation at the micro level between unemployment durations and housing tenure boils down to an unobserved heterogeneity problem: namely, workers only become homeowners when expectations on the labour market (e.g. within their current job) are favourable. And the researcher usually observes realized outcomes instead of expectations.

Regarding the individual relation between residential and job mobility, several modelling frameworks exist, mostly in the context of job search theory (see, e.g., the study of Van den Berg and Gorter 1997). Theoretical predictions for the impact of residential mobility on job mobility are less ambiguous than for the impact of housing tenure. If workers face substantial (monetary) costs in changing residence, job mobility is severely hampered. These moving costs often result from particular types of housing tenure, but may also stem from household characteristics (like coordination problems in two-earner households in combination with higher commuting costs, as in Van Ommeren 1996).

Thus, because of the theoretical ambiguity, the relationship between homeownership and labour mobility and unemployment is mainly an empirical issue. Unfortunately, macroeconomic and microeconomic empirical analyses show contradicting outcomes. On a macroeconomic level, most contributions show that homeownership increases unemployment. Nickell (1998) analyses the relationship between homeownership and unemployment, using a panel of twenty OECD countries, from 1989 to 1994. With these data, Nickell shows that the unemployment rate is (seemingly) positively correlated with the homeownership rate, with an elasticity of 0.13. Green and Hendershott (2001b) estimate an elasticity of 0.18, using aggregated data for the different states of the United States for the period 1970–90. This estimate is close to the estimate of Oswald (Chapter 2 above), with an elasticity equal to 0.2. He analyses the relationship between homeownership and unemployment, using panel time series data for nineteen OECD countries, from 1960 to 1990. He actually found this relationship not only between countries, but also between the regions of France, Italy, Sweden, Switzerland, the US, and the UK as well. In line with these results, Murphy *et al.* (2006) show that strong housing market conditions can prevent movement since expensive housing can deter migrants and make commuting more attractive as an alternative to moving residence.

Contrary to the findings presented above, several microeconomic contributions show that homeownership actually diminishes the probability of becoming unemployed. Van Leuvensteijn and Koning (Chapter 8 below) and Munch *et al.* (Chapter 4 below) have analysed the effect of homeownership on job mobility and unemployment for, respectively, the Netherlands and Denmark. They find no effects on job mobility but identify a small negative effect on the probability of acquiring a job outside the local area. Van der Vlist (2001) studied the Dutch situation, and concludes that homeownership has a small positive effect on changing jobs. Barcelo (2003) analysed for five major European countries the effects of homeownership on unemployment and found that owners are more reluctant to move than renters. Interestingly, for the Australian situation, Flatau *et al.* (2003) found as well that homeowners become less unemployed than renters. However, this accounts only for homeowners with mortgages which supports the hypothesis that workers who are leveraged are more committed to their jobs. Finally, using US household data, Green and Hendershott (2001a) found that unemployed homeowners indeed find jobs at a slower rate than renters, but with an impact of only an eighth of what is found for aggregate data.

Following Dietz and Haurin (2003), the conclusion from the above literature is that the empirical results concerning the effect of homeownership on labour market mobility are ambiguous. It seems that, in general, studies using micro data tend to reject the Oswald hypothesis—i.e. homeownership increases unemployment—while studies using macro data tend to support it. This might point to the existence of a spurious relation or aggregation effects at the macro level or omitted variables at the micro level (as Van Vuuren and Van Leuvensteijn (2007) suggest).

The theoretical literature on the relationship between social renting and labour market behaviour is very much in line with that of homeownership. Like homeowners, social tenants receive an implicit subsidy through lower rental prices and their place on the waiting list. The size of the subsidy depends in most countries (like Denmark and the Netherlands) on the age of the rental home, or the length of the tenure, the location of the residence (rural or urban), and the distance to the city centre. This subsidy or the place on the waiting list is diminished or lost if a social renter moves to another residence. This opportunity cost thus limits the labour mobility of social renters living in residences under rent control.

Basically, there are two strands of literature. The first is primarily a UK literature which reports both a reduced residential mobility of social renters and an increased probability of becoming unemployed amongst social renters (Hughes and McCormick 1987; Minford *et al.* 1988). More recently, Flatau *et al.* (2003) found as well that social renters (and those living rent-free) are more likely than private renters to become unemployed.

The second is a Danish literature which focuses on rent control. Munch and Svarer (2002) show that tenancy mobility is severely reduced by rent control. For a typical household in the private rental sector, tenancy duration is found to be six years longer if the apartment belongs to the 10 per cent most regulated units than if it belongs to the 10 per cent least regulated units. Svarer *et al.* (2005) find that rent control benefits reduce housing mobility and hence labour mobility. Furthermore, they find that renters subject to rent control are more likely to accept job offers in the local market than job offers in the non-local market.

The empirical evidence for social renters and rent control schemes is clearly mixed—at least more than the empirical evidence for homeownership—and probably depends upon country specific effects, such as type of social renting, institutions on the labour and housing market, and the national probability of migrating across regional labour markets.

3.3. Data and stylized facts

The dataset used in this chapter is derived from the European Community Household Panel (ECHP). The ECHP survey is based on a standardized questionnaire that involves annual interviewing of a representative panel of households and individuals in various European countries.[2] The questionnaire covers a wide range of topics like income, health, education, housing, demographics, and employment characteristics, which makes the database especially suitable for a micro-econometric analysis of differences in residential and labour mobility between countries. The ECHP covers the period 1994 to 2001. In the first wave, i.e. in 1994, a sample of some 60,500 nationally representative households were interviewed in the twelve member states at that juncture, which equals approximately 130,000 adults aged 16 years and over. Austria, Finland, and Sweden joined the project in respectively 1995, 1996, and 1997.[3]

The ECHP accommodates several types of residential ownership: namely, homeownership, private and social renting, and accommodation that is provided rent-free (occupants do not have to pay rent; this happens predominantly when renting from family and friends). To be more precise, homeownership is defined in the ECHP as owner-occupied housing, and social renting is defined as when the accommodation is rented from a public, municipal, voluntary, or non-profit agency.[4]

Table 3.1 looks into the distribution of the various types of residential ownership across the various European countries in the ECHP. The percentages have been calculated by summing up the residential ownership types of all observations. Note that we thus assume that there is no selection in attrition from the panel. In other words, social renters and homeowners have the same

Table 3.1. Percentage of homeowners and various types of renters across Europe during 1994–2001

	Homeowners	Renting		
		Private	Social	Rent-free
Germany	0.44	0.32	0.21	0.03
Netherlands	0.61	0.04	0.34	0.01
France	0.63	0.18	0.15	0.05
Austria	0.68	0.12	0.14	0.06
Sweden	0.69			
Denmark	0.71	0.12	0.17	0.00
Portugal	0.72	0.14	0.04	0.10
UK	0.74	0.06	0.18	0.02
Belgium	0.74	0.17	0.06	0.03
Luxembourg	0.76	0.21	0.00	0.03
Finland	0.77	0.09	0.12	0.01
Italy	0.78	0.11	0.06	0.06
Greece	0.83	0.13	0.01	0.03
Spain	0.84	0.08	0.02	0.05
Ireland	0.88	0.03	0.08	0.01
Total	0.71	0.14	0.11	0.04

probability of leaving the panel. Because the Swedish Living Conditions survey does not provide information about specific characteristics when the accommodation is rented, we leave them out of the analysis, although we include them in the table for completeness.

Clearly, owner-occupied housing is the dominant form of housing across Europe. More than 70 per cent of the households in our sample report that they own their home. The percentage homeownership is smallest in Germany and highest in Spain and Ireland. However, during our sample years percentage homeownership has grown in all countries (for some countries, such as France and Denmark, even by more than 10 per cent).

Renting is divided into private, social renting, and rent-free renting, and the shares of various renting types differs considerably across Europe. Social renting is most prevalent in the Netherlands, Germany, the UK, Denmark, France, and Austria and seems to be completely absent in Greece, Spain, and Luxembourg—and to a lesser extent in Portugal and Italy. Obviously, the number of social renters in a country coincides with the geographical location (the north-western part of Europe) and the pervasiveness of the welfare state.

With its average of 4 per cent, rent-free accommodation seems to be a relatively minor issue in Europe. It occurs mostly in countries such as Portugal, Austria, and Italy, and to a certain degree it seems to correlate negatively with the presence of social renting within a country.

It is now insightful to look at the country-specific residential mobility for each of the various types of housing. We specify residential mobility here as one when a household has moved residence in the year prior to the interview and average this over countries. This residential mobility can be seen as a proxy for a household's probability of moving, but is most likely an underestimation because households can move residence multiple times during a year. A household's probability of moving is not identical to an individual's probability of moving—especially because most individuals' residential moves coincide with a change in household composition. Table 3.2 presents residential mobility across Europe.

Clearly, European private renters move residence most. And European homeowners move residence the least of all. So, countries that have high percentages of homeowners in Table 3.1, such as Ireland, Spain, Greece, and Italy, have low percentages of households moves. Households in Finland, Denmark, the UK, and France move the most, which clearly leads to a North–South divide again in terms of residential mobility.

Private renters move much more than homeowners (up to four to five times). Especially private renters in the UK, Ireland, Denmark, and Finland are mobile. However, social renters move much less than their private counterparts. Indeed, although social renters move more than twice as much as homeowners, they also move almost half as much as private renters.

Obviously, those are descriptive statistics and do not reveal much about possible causal impacts of transaction costs of owner-occupied or socially rented houses, especially because two possible sources of selection effects are present. First of all, households may select themselves out over types

Table 3.2. Percentage of households that moved residence in the year prior to the interview

	Total	Type of housing		
		Owner	Social renter	Private renter
Ireland	0.02	0.01	0.03	0.26
Austria	0.03	0.01	0.04	0.08
Greece	0.03	0.02	0.09	0.10
Italy	0.03	0.02	0.02	0.08
Portugal	0.04	0.03	0.05	0.06
Spain	0.04	0.03	0.06	0.12
Netherlands	0.05	0.05	0.06	0.12
Belgium	0.06	0.03	0.09	0.16
Sweden	0.06	0.03		
Luxembourg	0.06	0.04	0.08	0.12
Germany	0.07	0.03	0.07	0.11
France	0.08	0.04	0.10	0.21
UK	0.08	0.06	0.09	0.36
Denmark	0.10	0.06	0.15	0.26
Finland	0.10	0.05	0.25	0.34
Total	0.05	0.03	0.08	0.14

of housing. Individuals who expect to settle down, such as to start families, may opt for homeownership, while people who expect large life-cycle changes, such as students or singles, may opt for private renting. And, of course, those individuals who (initially) need housing assistance choose social renting if possible. However, one might argue that this selection effect is partly caused by the existence of transaction costs. If households settle down, they are willing to pay large sunk costs as investments in their housing career. Households that are uncertain about their future are not prepared to invest those costs.

A second source of selection may be attributed to the accommodation itself. It might well be that the characteristics of owner-occupied houses are different from those of social or private rented houses. Differences may occur in quality, neighbourhood, and (lot) size of the house. This may result in larger attachments to owner-occupied housing than to private rented housing.

As argued above, and as Figure 3.1 shows clearly, homeowners do face large transaction costs when buying a residence. These transaction costs consist not only of taxation on moving residence, but also of real estate agent fees, notary fees, and the like. Especially, homeowners in Italy, Belgium, Portugal, and Greece seem to have paid large sunk costs to buy their home. This surely makes them less mobile than if they had rented privately.

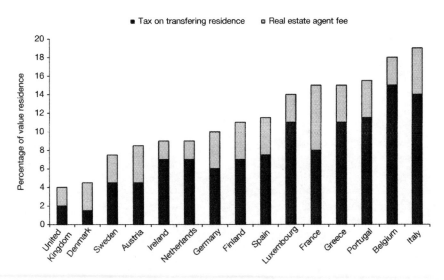

Figure 3.1. Taxation on moving residence and real estate agent fees for several European countries. *Source*: Belot and Ederveen (2005)

Social renters do not face transaction costs as such, but instead a loss of subsidies or a loss of the option on subsidies when on a waiting list. Thus, social renting normally involves some kind of subsidy associated with the dwelling and not with the household. Households in general are not inclined to move when this entails a loss of (the option on) their subsidy. However, this loss of (the option on) subsidy usually occurs only when moving between municipalities. This is in contrast to formal transaction costs for homeowners, which always occur when moving residence. Obviously, because institutions, finance of social dwellings, and supervision differ across European countries, the impact of social renting on labour mobility should be researched in a country-specific manner (for a detailed analysis of the institutional setting of social housing in the Netherlands, France, Belgium, Germany, the UK, Sweden, and Denmark, see Priemus and Boelhouwer 1999).

3.4. Estimation strategy

To study the impact of private renting, social renting, and homeownership on cross-country labour market mobility differences, we focus on the probability of leaving a job for various exit destinations. We assume that workers only end their current job for three possible reasons. First, they may find another job (whether more suited to the worker or not). Secondly, workers may become unemployed. And thirdly, workers may leave the labour force altogether because of retirement, to raise a child, to look after disabled family members, for study purposes, and so on. If labour mobility is hampered, this may show up in two ways. First, a worker may remain longer in his or her current job and move at a slower rate to a new one. This indicates that a worker is hampered in his or her upward career mobility. Secondly, a worker may end up faster in unemployment or leave the labour force faster. This happens when workers face difficulties in finding a job in the local labour market and when it is too costly to move to a different regional labour market with more attractive job opportunities.

The model we construct consists of a competing risk duration framework for the various exit rates of employment in combination with a discrete choice model for the probability of buying or renting—privately or socially—a house. The fundamental assumption we make is that the decision about the type of housing is correlated with labour market behaviour through observed and unobserved factors. First, as mentioned above, we allow labour market mobility to be directly related to housing tenure, by incorporating type of housing in the job duration model. This entails a direct test of whether homeowners or social renters are more or less mobile on the labour market relative to renters.

Simultaneously, we allow for unobserved heterogeneity to control for those unobserved factors that drive both job mobility and housing tenure. In our case, unobserved heterogeneity may occur because of unobserved skills and job commitment. For example, workers with short-term contracts are less likely to buy a house compared to workers with tenure. And workers who have diminished prospects on the labour market may end up earlier in social housing.

The modelling approach we adopt in this paper is a direct extension of De Graaff and Van Leuvensteijn (2007), and closely resembles that of Van Leuvensteijn and Koning (Chapter 8 below) and Munch *et al.* (Chapter 4 below) as well, so little attention is spent on technical details. The first subsection deals with the econometric model. Subsequently, we pay some attention to the issue of identification. The last subsection combines all components and specifies the complete likelihood function to be estimated.

3.4.1. *The econometric model*

To model the probability of leaving a job we use a duration analysis framework. The basic concept in duration analysis is the hazard rate θ, which is defined here as the rate at which workers leave their current job in the time interval $[T, T + dt]$ given that these workers occupy their job at least up to T. The probability that someone leaves employment within an interval dt after t can be denoted as $\Pr(T < t < T + dt \mid t \geq T)$ (see e.g. Lancaster 1990). Dividing this probability by dt, we get the average probability of leaving employment per unit time period:

$$\theta_b(t) = \frac{\Pr(T < t < T + dt \mid t \geq T)}{dt}, \tag{3.1}$$

where the subscript $b \in \{e, u, o\}$ indicates the exit destination, which in our case can be employment (e), unemployment (u), and out of the labour force (o). Note that if $dt \to 0$, we have an instantaneous rate of leaving per unit time period at t.

We use a proportional hazard rate specification, indicating that we assume that the impact of individual characteristics is proportional to the impact of the elapsed time of the job spell. Further, each destination-specific hazard is a function of a set of observed characteristics, such as age, sex, being married, and educational attainment, which may vary over time, $\mathbf{X}_t$, a time-varying indicator for housing tenure; h_t, a function which measures duration dependence for a specific exit destination; $\lambda_b(t)$, and unobserved characteristics, v_b. Thus, the hazard rate of a specific destination may be written as:

$$\theta_b(t \mid \mathbf{X}_t, h_t, v_b) = \exp\left(\mathbf{X}_t \beta_b + \lambda_b(t) + \gamma_b h_t + v_b\right). \tag{3.2}$$

Often, $\lambda_b(t)$ is also referred to as the baseline hazard. We adopt here a non-parametric flexible specification in the form of a piecewise constant specification. So, duration dependence is assumed to be constant within duration intervals.

We assume that the dichotomous—homeowners versus renters and social versus private renters—housing tenure variable h_t conforms to the following logit specification:

$$\Pr(h_t = 1|\mathbf{Y}_t, \mu_h) = \frac{\exp(\mathbf{Y}_t\delta_h + \mu_h)}{1 + \exp(\mathbf{Y}_t\delta_h + \mu_h)},$$
$$\Pr(h_t = 0|\mathbf{Y}_t, \mu_h) = 1 - \Pr(h_t = 1|\mathbf{Y}_t, \mu_h), \qquad (3.3)$$

where h is 1, if the worker owns or socially rents his current residence, and zero if the worker rents it socially or rents it privately, respectively. $\mathbf{Y}_t$ denotes a set of variables that characterizes the particular choice of housing tenure. Note that the set of variables $\mathbf{Y}_t$ may partly overlap with the set of variables $\mathbf{X}_t$, which is used to model job duration spells. Finally, to account for unobserved heterogeneity, we incorporate an additional unobserved random component, denoted by μ_h.

In contrast to regression models, unobserved heterogeneity causes an estimation bias in duration modelling. Therefore, several modelling approaches have been developed to control for unobserved heterogeneity. We adopt here the often used non-parametric approach proposed by Heckman and Singer (1984). Basically, this boils down to the assumption of a discrete distribution, denoted G, with a pre-specified number (say K) of mass points. In addition, we assume v_e, v_u, v_o, and μ_h to be correlated. Together with K mass points, this leaves us with 4^K possible combinations between the K mass points, each with a separate probability, which has to be estimated simultaneously. When using constant terms, the distribution is identified by normalizing the first point of support to $\{0,0,0,0\}$, so that the number of mass points to be estimated reduces to $(K-1) \times 4$.[5]

As shown above, our model consists of two parts: the housing model and the job duration model. If not for the correlation between the unobserved heterogeneity components, these two parts can be estimated separately. Allowing for correlation creates a mixture model which has to be integrated over the entire distribution of unobserved variables, $G\{v_e, v_u, v_o, \mu_h\}$ (see Van den Berg 2001 for more details on the application of mixture distributions in duration models).

3.4.2. Identification

A key issue in the literature on the relationship between housing tenure and labour market mobility is the identification of the causal effect. Housing tenure may cause a change in labour market mobility, but the reverse relation is, a priori, just as likely. Those workers who have good prospects of long job spells (or lower probabilities of ending up unemployed) are the ones most likely to buy a house, and those workers who have high probabilities of entering unemployment are the ones most likely to opt for social housing. The literature distinguishes two approaches to deal with this endogeneity. The first uses instrumental variables, where variables that affect housing tenure but not labour market mobility are incorporated in the housing model to control for endogeneity. Van Leuvensteijn and Koning (Chapter 8 below) proposed using regional homeownership as an instrument, while Munch et al. (Chapter 4 below) used homeownership of the parents in 1980 and the proportion of homeowners in the municipality where the individual was born. Usually, however, the impact of these instrumental variables is rather low, indicating that these models are already fairly well identified or that the performance of the chosen instruments is rather weak.

We choose a second approach by using multiple spells for identification (cf. Van Vuuren and Van Leuvensteijn 2007 and Munch et al. (Chapter 4 below))—the latter pay much attention to the intuition for this strategy (see Abbring and Van den Berg 2003 for a formal argumentation for this identification strategy). To summarize their arguments, it is not difficult to see that making repeated observations of one individual removes all interpersonal variation.[6] Thus, if there are multiple job spells available to a specific individual, and if her housing tenure status varies as well over these spells, then the effect of housing tenure on labour market mobility is theoretically identified.[7] Identification is then based on a sub-sample with multiple spells and changes in housing tenure status, where the existence of multiple spells ensures that the unobserved heterogeneity components capture the 'within person' effects (Chapter 4 below).

3.4.3. The log-likelihood function

To construct the log-likelihood, we introduce some additional notation. As in Lancaster (1990), let there be B binary destination vectors d_b, where d_b is such that there is a transition to state b and zero otherwise. Because we do not observe all job duration spells as ending, we model right-censored job duration spells as well. We do this by treating right-censoring theoretically as an additional dummy state. Thus, the set of possible destination vectors B now consists of employment, unemployment, out of the labour force, and censoring.[8] Thus, given that individuals have an elapsed duration time T and job exit destination b, and conditional on their observed characteristics, housing tenure, and mass point v_b, the log-likelihood for job durations may be written as:

$$\ell\ell_T(\phi_b|T, b, \mathbf{X}_t, h_t, v_b) = \sum_{b=1}^{B} \left[d_b \ln \theta_b(T) - \int_0^T \theta_b(t)\mathrm{d}t \right], \qquad (3.4)$$

where ϕ_b is shorthand notation for the parameter vector $\{\beta_b, \lambda_b(t), \gamma_b\}$. Note that the first part of Eqn. (3.4) displays the hazard rate of the transition to destination b, while the second part denotes the probability of survival of the job spell until time T.

The log-likelihood of choice of housing tenure h_t during the total length of the job spell conditional on the observed characteristics and country-specific housing market variables follows immediately from the logit Eqn. (3.3), and is given by:

$$
\ell\ell_h(\phi_h|h_t, \mathbf{X}_t, \mathbf{Y}_t, \mu_h) = \sum_{t=1}^{T} h_t \ln(\Pr(h_t = 1|\mathbf{X}_t, \mathbf{Y}_t, \mu_h))
$$
$$
+ (1 - h_t) \ln\left(\Pr(h_t = 0|\mathbf{X}_t, \mathbf{Y}_t, \mu_h)\right), \qquad (3.5)
$$

where ϕ_h denotes the parameter vector $\{\beta_h, \delta_h\}$. The joint log-likelihood is now formed by multiplying the likelihoods of (3.4) and (3.5)—given the discrete unobserved heterogeneity distribution—and integrating over the entire distribution of mass points $G\{v_e, v_u, v_o, \mu_h\}$. Allowing for the presence of multiple job spells, the joint log-likelihood for the contribution of an individual i can be written as:

$$
\ell\ell_{Th,i} = \ln \iiiint \prod_{j=1}^{N_j} \exp\left[\ell\ell_{T_j}(\phi_b) + \ell\ell_{h_j}(\phi_h)\right] dG\{v_e, v_u, v_o, \mu_h\}, \qquad (3.6)
$$

where, j ($j \in \{1,\ldots,N_j\}$) stands for spell j, and N_j for the total number of job spells of individual i. The log-likelihood in (3.6) basically states that the log-likelihood of job duration, as in (3.4), and the log-likelihood of housing tenure, as in (3.5), has to be integrated over the distribution of mass points, which raises an additional difficulty, in that we have to optimize not over a set of parameters, but over a probability distribution as well. To do this, we apply an expectation-maximization (EM) algorithm to solve for the parameters of Eqn. (3.6) that we are interested in (see De Graaff and Van Leuvensteijn 2007 for more details).

3.5. Estimation results

We have monthly information about each worker's status and yearly information on all other characteristics. Thus, job tenure is measured in months, and housing tenure in years. In terms of exit destinations, we denote a job move when a worker changes job or apprenticeship, a job exit to unemployment only when the next activity is labelled unemployment, and entry into the out-of-labour force when a worker becomes retired, spends his or her time in (unpaid) housework activities, is doing community or military service, or ends up in other activities that are economically inactive.

We use individual and household characteristics to control as much as possible for individual, household, and life-cycle effects that might influence the event of leaving the current job spell apart from residential mobility effects. First, we use age cohort dummies as age controls for life-cycle effects that might cause, e.g., individuals to enter an out-of-labour force status. Secondly, gender is included to control for the fact that females have a higher probability of looking after children and thus may leave a current job spell faster to become economically inactive. The same accounts for the dummy variables that control for the presence of children of different ages within the household. We include education—measured as low, medium, and high—to control for the fact that more educated workers earn higher wages and therefore show higher homeownership rates. Here, medium education denotes secondary level, and high education a university degree or above. Having a partner in the household and whether the partner earns an income is included, as these households usually have higher probabilities of owning a house as well. Finally, housing tenure is included to test the impact of reduced housing mobility at an individual level.

Identification is done by using the availability of multiple spells. A fair amount of multiple spells is present in the data. More than 30 per cent of the observed workers show two or more employment spells.

All variables are measured at the moment the worker leaves his or her current job. As mentioned above, to control for duration dependence, we adopt a non-parametric flexible specification. Here, duration dependence is assumed to be constant within the following duration intervals: within one year, between one and three years, between three and five years, and above five years. A specific approach to incorporate such a non-parametric specification is shown in Lancaster (1990).

Finally, we set the number of mass points (K) at two, which—in theory—leaves us with sixteen probabilities to be estimated. However, experiments with sub-samples show that a smaller number of these probabilities make computation not only considerably faster, but give (almost) the same estimation results as well. We therefore only use four of these probabilities.

3.5.1. *The impact of homeownership*

To analyse the impact of homeownership on labour mobility, we distinguish between homeowners and private renters. Because our dataset contains in total more than 200,000 employment spells, we use a 10 per cent random sample to reduce computing time, resulting in a total of 19,482 employment spells. Table 3.3 displays the estimation results of the joint model of being a homeowner and leaving the current employment spell for three possible exit destinations.

Table 3.3. Joint estimation of owning a home and competing risk model (standard errors given in parentheses)

Variable	Homeowner	$\theta_b(t)$		
		Employment	Unemployment	Non-participation
Constant	−0.300 (0.05)			
Age dummies (baseline: age < 25)				
Age 25–34	−0.190 (0.05)	−0.569 (0.04)	0.100 (0.06)	−0.864 (0.05)
Age 35–44	0.254 (0.06)	−0.974 (0.05)	−0.197 (0.07)	−1.674 (0.07)
Age > 45	1.090 (0.06)	−1.089 (0.04)	−0.245 (0.07)	−0.973 (0.06)
Female	−0.164 (0.04)	0.254 (0.03)	0.163 (0.04)	0.617 (0.04)
Education dummies (baseline: education = low)				
Education medium	−0.047 (0.04)	−0.012 (0.03)	−0.261 (0.04)	−0.019 (0.04)
Education high	0.050 (0.05)	−0.254 (0.04)	−0.557 (0.06)	−0.008 (0.05)
Spouse employed	0.287 (0.05)	−0.137 (0.04)	−0.157 (0.05)	−0.213 (0.05)
Living with partner	−0.680 (0.06)	−0.119 (0.04)	−0.275 (0.06)	0.051 (0.06)
Children within the household (baseline: no children ≤ 18)				
Children < 11	0.345 (0.04)	−0.001 (0.03)	0.052 (0.05)	0.082 (0.05)
Children 12–15	0.420 (0.07)	−0.015 (0.05)	0.252 (0.06)	−0.031 (0.06)
Children 16–18	0.759 (0.07)	0.230 (0.04)	0.162 (0.06)	0.261 (0.06)
Homeowner		−0.219 (0.03)	−0.275 (0.04)	0.027 (0.04)
Baseline hazard				
0–1 year		−2.951 (0.04)	−4.048 (0.06)	−4.037 (0.06)
1–3 years		−4.985 (0.05)	−5.862 (0.08)	−5.623 (0.07)
3–5 years		−4.994 (0.07)	−6.160 (0.10)	−5.670 (0.08)
> 5 years		−5.007 (0.06)	−5.557 (0.08)	−5.287 (0.08)
Unobserved heterogeneity distribution				
Mass point	1.820 (0.04)	0.646 (0.03)	0.701 (0.04)	0.448 (0.04)
Probabilities				
$\Pr(G = \{0, 0, 0, 0\})$	0.192			
$\Pr(G = \{1, 0, 0, 0\})$	0.588			
$\Pr(G = \{0, 1, 1, 1\})$	0.073			
$\Pr(G = \{1, 1, 1, 1\})$	0.147			
Mean log-likelihood	−3.690			
No. of spells	19,482			

Most estimated coefficients of the competing hazard rate model are significant, conforming with intuition and previous research. Our main variable of interest, whether someone is a homeowner, reduces the probability of changing jobs significantly (risk reduction 20 per cent, which can be calculated as exp(−0.219)). Further, homeownership ensures that workers face smaller probabilities of becoming unemployed (risk reduction of 24 per cent) and a (insignificant) higher risk of leaving the labour force (risk increase 3 per cent). These results are very similar to outcomes of previous microeconomic studies (see e.g. Van Leuvensteijn and Koning (Chapter 8 below) and Munch *et al.* (Chapter 4 below)).[9] Basically, this confirms the hypotheses of, e.g., Dietz and Haurin (2003) and Van Leuvensteijn and Koning (Chapter 8 below), that homeowners have larger job commitment than private renters. This can partly be explained by the substantial monetary transaction costs when forced to sell their house because of, e.g., unemployment (De Graaff and Van Leuvensteijn 2007).

The remaining coefficients for the housing model are as might be expected. Age tends to increase the probability of homeownership, just as being male, having received higher education, and having an employed spouse. Living together with an (unemployed) partner reduces homeownership, while having (older) children increases this probability again. The latter is probably a proxy for a life-cycle effect, where household heads have a smaller probability of being a homeowner when households are relatively recently formed.

The hazard rate for job-to-job transitions is found to decline with age, which is understandable, because younger workers are more mobile on the labour market searching for a suitable job. The same accounts for the probability of entering unemployment. However, hazard rates into non-participation seem to rise again for older workers (with age above 45). Females have in general higher hazard rates out of employment than males; in particular, females have a high risk of ending up as non-participants in the labour market (their risk of non-participation is about 85 per cent higher than that for males). Higher educational levels result in smaller hazards with respect to job changes or unemployment, although education does not affect the probability of becoming a non-participant significantly. Having an employed spouse or living with a partner diminishes the risk of changing jobs, becoming unemployed, or leaving the labour force altogether, although living with a partner does not significantly affect the latter. Finally, having older children increases the probability of changing jobs, becoming unemployed, or leaving the labour force. This might again point to a life-cycle effect.

The piecewise constant specification for duration dependence gives consistent and intuitively appealing outcomes. After the first year, all hazard rates out of employment drop significantly and continue falling with the worker's job duration.

Finally, we turn to the unobserved heterogeneity distribution. All mass points are positive and very significant. Most probability is assigned to the combination with a low exit rate out of current employment and a high probability of owning a home. Interestingly, only a small part of our population—around 22 per cent—face higher exit rates out of their current job. The current estimation, where four segments are used, show that two segments account for almost 80 per cent of all individuals.[10] The actual allocation of the probabilities to the segments depends upon the number of segments and the initial starting point of the algorithm, but experiments show that all combinations converge to the same log-likelihood, and that the largest group is usually the segment that contains all favourable mass points (thus the one denoted here as $G = \{1, 0, 0, 0\}$).

As mentioned above, European countries differ widely in their institutional setting, the functioning of the labour and housing market, and the general tendency of the population to move house. Therefore, it is insightful to look

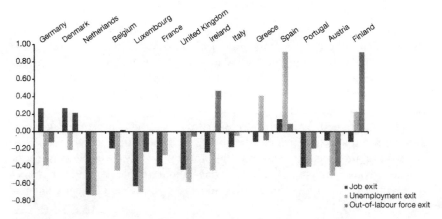

Figure 3.2. Impact of homeownership on labour mobility across Europe

at the impact of owning a home on labour market behaviour for each European country separately. Figure 3.2 displays for each country in our dataset the impact that homeownership has on the *probability* of leaving the current job for another job, unemployment, or leaving the labour market altogether.

Unsurprisingly, there is a large amount of country-specific variation present. This is primarily caused by the countries' institutional differences in both the labour and the housing market. Overall, homeownership seems to diminish the probability of leaving the current job. The notable exceptions—Ireland, Greece, Spain, and Finland—all occur in countries with high percentages of homeownership. And for Greece, Spain, and Finland it truly does seem that homeownership does not impede residential mobility such that it hampers labour market behaviour; homeowners enter unemployment faster than renters. Thus, in Spain, Greece, and Finland private renters are doing better on the labour market than homeowners.

However, in most other European countries, such as the UK, the Netherlands, Germany, Belgium, France, and Portugal, homeowners seem to stay longer in their current jobs than non-homeowners. Assuming that our analysis has corrected sufficiently for self-selecting, then at least for these countries homeownership causes a higher job commitment than non-homeownership. A possible reason for this is that homeowners grow attached to their homes (and the surrounding neighbourhood) through both monetary and psychological investments.

The next subsection presents the empirical results for social renters and investigates whether being tied to a social home causes social renters as well to increase their job commitment.

3.5.2. The impact of social renting

To analyse the impact of social renting on labour mobility, we distinguish in this subsection between private and social renters. There are in total 72,292 employment spells in our database which can be attributed to renters. Analogously to Table 3.3, Table 3.4 displays the estimation results of the joint model of being a social renter and leaving the current employment spell for three possible exit destinations.

Again, most coefficients from the social renting and competing risk model are significant and conform to intuition. Most importantly, whether someone is a social renter seems to increase the probability of leaving the current job (versus private renters). Social renters have about a 3 per cent higher chance of leaving the current job for another job and a 12 per cent higher chance of

Table 3.4. Joint estimation of social renting and competing risk model (standard errors given in parentheses)

Variable	Social renter	$\theta_b(t)$		
		Employment	Unemployment	Non-participation
Constant	−0.978 (0.02)			
Age dummies (baseline: age < 25)				
Age 25–34	−0.138 (0.02)	−0.630 (0.02)	0.066 (0.03)	−0.829 (0.03)
Age 35–44	0.114 (0.03)	−1.011 (0.02)	−0.068 (0.03)	−1.407 (0.03)
Age > 45	0.484 (0.03)	−1.285 (0.02)	−0.339 (0.03)	−0.873 (0.03)
Female	0.016 (0.02)	0.067 (0.01)	0.001 (0.02)	0.469 (0.02)
Education dummies (baseline: education = low)				
Education medium	−0.212 (0.02)	0.060 (0.01)	−0.130 (0.02)	0.167 (0.02)
Education high	−0.629 (0.03)	−0.223 (0.02)	−0.391 (0.03)	0.295 (0.03)
Spouse employed	−0.219 (0.02)	−0.083 (0.02)	−0.188 (0.03)	−0.118 (0.03)
Living with partner	−0.152 (0.02)	−0.030 (0.02)	−0.014 (0.03)	−0.006 (0.03)
Children within the household (baseline: no children ≤ 18)				
Children < 11	0.507 (0.02)	−0.012 (0.02)	0.171 (0.02)	0.132 (0.02)
Children 12–15	0.428 (0.03)	0.029 (0.02)	0.072 (0.04)	−0.159 (0.04)
Children 16–18	0.145 (0.03)	0.202 (0.02)	0.158 (0.04)	0.203 (0.03)
Social renter		0.034 (0.01)	0.113 (0.02)	−0.022 (0.02)
Baseline Hazard				
0–1 year		−2.732 (0.02)	−4.120 (0.03)	−3.987 (0.03)
1–3 years		−4.806 (0.02)	−5.962 (0.04)	−5.736 (0.04)
3–5 years		−4.888 (0.03)	−6.080 (0.05)	−5.743 (0.04)
> 5 years		−4.838 (0.03)	−5.533 (0.04)	−5.281 (0.04)
Unobserved heterogeneity distribution				
Mass point	1.534 (0.02)	0.109 (0.01)	0.094 (0.02)	0.07 (0.02)
Probabilities				
$Pr(G = \{0, 0, 0, 0\})$	0.414			
$Pr(G = \{1, 0, 0, 0\})$	0.215			
$Pr(G = \{0, 1, 1, 1\})$	0.195			
$Pr(G = \{1, 1, 1, 1\})$	0.175			
Mean log-likelihood	−3.977			
No. of spells	72,292			

ending up in unemployment. The lower probability of leaving the labour force is not significant. Thus, the mobility costs associated with social renting seem to hamper labour market performance in terms of the probability of leaving employment. Job-to-job mobility, however, is higher for social renters than for private renters.

The other coefficients for the social renting model are as might be expected. Being a low-educated, older, single person with children increases the probability of ending up in the social renting sector. Living with a working partner increases the chance of renting in the private sector, just as being more highly educated does.

As might be expected, the coefficients for the competing risk model are, in a qualitative sense at least, rather similar to those in Table 3.3, although the absolute values change of course because of the different sample selection (only renters). The unobserved heterogeneity distribution is, however, rather different. Where the results in Table 3.3 show a clear, almost bimodal distribution, the results in Table 3.4 show a more homogeneous distribution. Especially, there does not seem to be much unobserved heterogeneity present in the labour market. There is a clear group who seem to leave the current job 10 per cent faster for whatever reason; but this is not as strong as presented in Table 3.3.

This does not entail that results are homogeneous across countries as well. Again, because European countries differ widely in their institutional setting, we distinguish the impact of social renting on each country separately in our dataset in Figure 3.3.

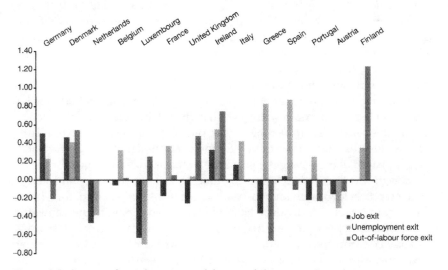

Figure 3.3. Impact of social renting on labour mobility across Europe

When comparing Figure 3.3 with Figure 3.2 it is obvious that social renting has a less homogeneous impact on labour market behaviour then homeownership. In general, social renting seems to increase the probability of changing jobs, especially for countries such as Germany, Denmark, Ireland, Italy, and France. In countries such as Belgium, France, the UK, and to a lesser extent Portugal, social renting causes employees to change jobs less frequently. More distinctly, however, social renters have higher probabilities of entering unemployment than private renters, except for countries such as the Netherlands, Austria, and Luxembourg. Social renting in these countries even decreases the overall probability of ending a job spell. Note that of these countries there is a sizeable social renting sector only in the Netherlands and Austria.

Thus, overall one can conclude that social renting does not increase job commitment, or at least not to the extent that homeownership does. This might be because social renters do not invest—both monetarily and psychologically—as much as homeowners in their residence. Usually there is a landlord who maintains the dwelling (see as well the appendix for Western European cross-country differences in social renting institutions). This might cause social renting to hamper labour market performance in the sense that a larger social renting sector increases aggregate unemployment.

3.6. Conclusion

This chapter has dealt with the impact of homeownership and social renting on labour market behaviour. We have argued that homeownership and social renting both increase transaction costs and therefore should both have an impact on labour market behaviour. To what extent social renting and home-ownership increase transaction costs or affect labour market behaviour differs widely across European countries. Thus, the main goal of this chapter was to distinguish between various European countries in our analysis, to control for the various national institutional settings.

In general, residential transaction costs hamper individual mobility because they limit individual choices. However, it is difficult to make *ex ante* predictions about the impact on (un)employment probabilities. For higher residential transaction costs may as well increase job commitment or lower reservation wages instead of increasing the probability on, e.g., unemployment.

Indeed, previous research such as that of Van Leuvensteijn and Koning (Chapter 8 below) and Munch *et al.* (Chapter 4 below) find that homeownership benefits individual labour market behaviour in the sense that homeowners change jobs less frequently but leave unemployment faster. This chapter confirms those findings for most countries in Europe. Exceptions are countries with a high level of aggregate homeownership, such as Spain and Greece.

The results for workers in the social renting sector are less clear, in that they vary much more across European countries. However, overall we can say that social renters display a worse labour market performance than private renters, except for countries such as the Netherlands (note that the amount of private renting is rather low in the Netherlands compared with social renting), Luxembourg, and Austria.

Therefore, we may conclude that although both social renting and home-ownership increase residential transaction costs, only social renting increases individuals' probabilities of entering unemployment. A possible reason might be that homeowners invest more then social renters—both monetarily and psychologically—in their houses and neighbourhoods. If true, then one might also hypothesize that homeowners will make larger commutes than social renters: for they may be willing to sacrifice leisure time to commuting time to avoid paying residential transaction costs. Another consequence would be that homeowners are willing to accept lower wages than private renters, where social renters would be more hesitant to do so. Or, alternatively, homeowners are willing to work more hours for the same (monthly) wage.

Apart from this, it would be interesting as well to look at the impact of transaction costs on the individual outflow of unemployment. Although this has already generated a large literature, it has never been done on a micro level (except for the study of Barcelo 2003) for a variety of European countries. Moreover, the impact of social renting on unemployment deserves more attention, together with the need for more information on the various forms of social renting across Europe and the institutions that drive them.

HOUSING MARKET CHARACTERISTICS IN EUROPE

A.1. Homeownership in European countries

Table 3.5 presents some selected characteristics of homeownership throughout Europe. The percentage of homeowners is the mean of 1994–2001 data found in the European Community Household Panel by Eurostat. Property transfer taxes (usually paid by the buyer), real estate agent fees (these vary somewhat), and mean duration of transactions are taken from Belot and Ederveen (2005).

Typical loan-to-value ratios and average typical terms are found in IMF (2008) and are more recent. The former figure is known to have increased in most countries in the last decade as mortgage requirements became less strict.

Finally, the last two columns represent the possibility of interest tax deduction and a taxation on the property itself (Wolswijk 2005). Both characteristics are known to vary quite a bit, as legislation changed drastically in most European countries during the 1990s and 2000s. For example, Sweden abolished interest tax deduction at the marginal tariff (of 70 per cent) but only allowed deduction at the tariff of 30 per cent in 1991. A similar change occurred in Finland in 1993.

A.2. Social renting in European countries

Table 3.6 presents some selected characteristics of social renting in Europe. Because social renting and its associated institutions vary significantly across Europe, a direct comparison of the characteristics in Table 3.6 should be made very carefully. In this table social renting is defined as renting from a public, municipal, voluntary, or non-profit agency.[11] Unfortunately, we only have information about social renting in a limited number of countries. As source of information we have used Eurostat (ECHP) and Whitehead and Scanlon (2007).

As Table 3.6 clearly shows, social renting varies hugely across European countries. Social renting seems to be especially prevalent in the north-western part of Europe. Moreover, who may rent where seems to be especially decided at a local (municipal) level. If taken into account that most people are eligible for social housing, that rents usually do not increase when income increases, and that for most social housing there is a significant waiting list (Whitehead and Scanlon 2007), then—clearly—large transaction costs can be associated with social renting.

Table 3.5. Characteristics of homeownership in Europe in the late 1990s and early 2000s

Country	Percentage homeowners (mean 1994–2001)	Property transfer tax (%)	Real estate agent fees (%)	Duration of transaction (weeks)	Typical loan-to-value ratio (%)	Average typical term (years)	Interest tax deductibility (yes/no)	Wealth tax on housing (yes/no)
Germany	0.44	4.3–4.7	3–5		70	25	no	no
Netherlands	0.61	6	1.5–3	4–6	90	30	yes	no
France	0.63	4.89	5–10	6–13	75	15	no	yes
Austria	0.68	4.5	3–5		60	25	no	no
Sweden	0.69	1.5	0.5–5	4–6	80	25	yes	yes
Denmark	0.71	0.6	3	6	80	30	yes	no
Portugal	0.72	10	3–5	6–8			no	no
UK	0.74	1	1–3	12	75	25	no	no
Belgium	0.74	12.5	3–5		83	25	yes	yes
Luxembourg	0.76	9	3				yes	yes
Finland	0.77	4	4–8		75	17	yes	yes
Italy	0.78	11	3–8		80	15	yes	no
Greece	0.83	9.5–11.5	4		75	17	yes	no
Spain	0.84	6.5	3–5		70	20	no	yes
Ireland	0.88	6	1.75		70	20	no	no

Table 3.6. Social renting in Europe in the late 1990s and early 2000s

Country	Percentage social renting (%)	Ownership municipality/housing association (%)	Eligible at entry (% of population)	Happens when income exceeds limit	Determines eligibility	Assigns household
Germany	0.21		<20	rent unchanged	local government	landlord
Netherlands	0.34	1	40	rent unchanged	landlord	landlord
France	0.15	36	30–80	small supplement	landlord	landlord
Austria	0.14	40	80–90	rent unchanged	local government and landlord	local government and landlord
Sweden		100	100	NA	landlord	landlord
Denmark	0.17	5	100	NA	local government and landlord	local government and landlord
Portugal	0.04					
UK	0.18	54	100	NA		
Belgium	0.06					
Luxembourg	0.00					
Finland	0.12					
Italy	0.06					
Greece	0.01					
Spain	0.02					
Ireland	0.08	88	restricted	rent rises	local government	landlord

Notes

1. For an explanation of the differences between the impact of homeownership on labour market mobility we refer to De Graaff and Van Leuvensteijn (2007).
2. The countries involved in the ECHP are Germany, the Netherlands, France, Austria, Sweden, Denmark, Portugal, the UK, Belgium, Luxembourg, Finland, Italy, Greece, Spain, and Ireland.
3. The data for Sweden have been derived from the Swedish Living Conditions Survey and transformed into ECHP format.
4. The term 'public housing' is used as well for this particular tenure type. However, public housing is usually associated with government authorities, whereas social housing can also be provided by other organizations, e.g. by the church.
5. Note that this leaves the maximum number of probabilities still to be estimated as 4^K.
6. However, as one referee rightfully observed, this is true only if unobserved individual heterogeneity is constant over time. Because in our case of job and housing mobility this assumption may be a bit strong, we incorporate as many variables as we can in models (3.2) and (3.3) that might reflect changes in preference structures, i.e. because of life-cycle effects.
7. That is, apart from possible changes in her preference structure, which may well arise if, e.g., life-cycle effects are not properly accounted for by the exogeneous variables.
8. To avoid confusion, we do not model censoring as another competing risk. In other words, transitions to state b do not include censoring, while the destination vector d_b does include censoring.
9. The cited risk into the out-of-labour force is somewhat inconsistent across studies. In our case, the coefficient is (marginally) significantly positive. Van Leuvensteijn and Koning (Ch. 8 below), e.g., find for the Netherlands that the coefficient is insignificantly positive as well. In any case, the coefficient is small, pointing to the limited effect of homeownership on leaving the labour force.
10. Actually, estimations with only two segments—one with all mass points and one with no mass points—result in almost the same log-likelihood and coefficient estimates.
11. Opposed to definitions that are concerned with who constructed the dwelling, whether rents are below market levels, or what the relevant funding or income streams are.

References

Abbring, J., and Van den Berg, G. (2003), 'The non-parametric identification of treatment effect in duration models', *Econometrica*, 71, 1491–517.

Barcelo, C. (2003) 'Housing tenure and labour mobility: a comparison across European countries', CEMFI Working Paper no. 0302.

Belot, M., and Ederveen, S. (2005), 'Indicators of cultural and institutional barriers in OECD countries', CPB Memorandum (The Hague).

Blanchard, O. J., and Katz, L. R. (1992), 'Regional evolutions', *Brookings Papers on Economic Activity*, 11, 1–75.

De Graaff, T., and Van Leuvensteijn, M. (2007), 'The impact of housing market institutions on labour mobility: a European cross-country comparison', CPB Discussion Paper no. 82 (The Hague).

Dietz, R. D., and Haurin, D. R. (2003), 'The social and private micro-level consequences of homewnership', *Journal of Urban Economics*, 54, 401–50.

Dohmen, T. J. (2005), 'Housing, mobility, and unemployment', *Regional Science and Urban Economics*, 35, 305–25. Reproduced as Ch. 1 above.

Flatau, P., Forbes, M., Hendershott, P. H., and Wood, G. (2003), 'Homeownership and unemployment: the roles of leverage and public housing', NBER Working Paper 10021.

Green, R. K., and Hendershott, P. H. (2001a), 'Homeownership and the duration of unemployment: a test of the Oswald hypothesis', Working Paper, University of Aberdeen.

____ ____ (2001b), 'Homeownership and unemployment in the US', *Urban Studies*, 38/9, 1509–20.

Heckman, J. J., and Singer, B. (1984), 'A method for minimizing the impact of distributional assumptions in econometric models for duration data', *Econometrica*, 52, 271–320.

Hughes, G., and McCormick, B. (1987), 'Housing markets, unemployment and labour market flexibility in the UK', *European Economic Review*, 31/3, 615–45.

IMF (2008), *World Economic Outlook: Housing and the Business Cycle* (Washington: IMF).

Lancaster, T. (1990), *The Econometric Analysis of Transition Data* (Cambridge: Cambridge University Press).

Minford, P., Ashton, P., and Peel, M. (1988), 'The effects of housing distortions on unemployment', *Oxford Economic Papers*, 40, 322–45.

Munch, J. R., and Svarer, M. (2002), 'Rent control and tenancy duration', *Journal of Urban Economics*, 52, 542–60.

____ Rosholm, M., and Svarer, M. (2006), 'Are homeowners really more unemployed?', *Economic Journal*, 116, 991–1013. Reproduced as Ch. 4 below.

Murphy, A., Muellbauer, J., and Cameron, G. (2006), 'Housing market dynamics and regional migration in Britain', Nuffield College, UK.

Nickell, S. (1998), 'Unemployment: questions and some answers', *Economic Journal*, 108/448, 802–16.

Oswald, A. J. (1997), 'The missing piece of the unemployment puzzle: an inaugural lecture', mimeo, University of Warwick.

____ (1999), 'The housing market and Europe's unemployment: a non-technical paper', mimeo, University of Warwick. Reproduced as Ch. 2 above.

Priemus, H., and Boelhouwer, P. (1999), 'Social housing finance in Europe: trends and opportunities', *Urban Studies*, 36, 633–45.

Svarer, M., Rosholm, M., and Munch, J. R. (2005), 'Rent control and unemployment duration', *Journal of Public Economics*, 89, 2165–81.

Van den Berg, G. (2001), 'Duration models: specification, identification and multiple durations', in *Handbook of Econometrics* (Dordrecht: Elsevier), 3381–453.

____ and Gorter, C. (1997), 'Job search and commuting time', *Journal of Business & Economic Statistics*, 15, 269–81.

Van der Vlist, A. J. (2001), *Residential Mobility and Commuting*, Thela Thesis, Tinbergen Institute Research Series 248 (Amsterdam).

Van Leuvensteijn, M., and Koning, P. (2004), 'The effect of homeownership on labor mobility in the Netherlands', *Journal of Urban Economics*, 55, 580–96. Reproduced as Ch. 8 below.

Van Ommeren, J. N. (1996), *Commuting and Relocation of Jobs and Residences: A Search Perspective*, Thela Thesis, Tinbergen Institute Research Series 130 (Amsterdam).

Van Vuuren, A. P., and Van Leuvensteijn, M. (2007), 'The impact of homeownership on unemployment in the Netherlands', CPB Discussion Paper no. 86 (The Hague).

Whitehead, C., and Scanlon, K. (2007), *Social Housing in Europe* (London: LSE).

Wolswijk, G. (2005), 'On some fiscal effects on mortgage debt growth in the EU', Working Paper, European Central Bank, no. 526.

Part II

Country Studies: Unemployment and Homeownership

4

Are Homeowners Really More Unemployed?[*]

Jakob Roland Munch, Michael Rosholm, and Michael Svarer

4.1. Introduction

Homeownership may influence labour market outcomes in several ways, but, in particular, one link between homeownership and unemployment has been emphasized recently. Oswald (1996) presents evidence that unemployment rates and the proportion of homeowners are positively correlated for a number of countries and regions. The proposed mechanism suggests that homeowners are much less mobile than renters due to costs associated with the buying and selling of their homes, and so they are relatively inflexible in the labour market. Thus, if the proportion of homeowners is high, then the work force is more immobile, which tends to result in higher structural unemployment due to an insufficient supply of labour. In his original work, Oswald presents evidence showing that countries or regions with a 10 percentage point higher share of homeowners have a two percentage point higher unemployment rate.

Homeowners in most Western countries receive favourable tax treatment of the capital invested in their homes (see Hendershott and White 2000), which, *ceteris paribus*, tends to raise the proportion of homeowners. In light of this, it is not surprising that Oswald's hypothesis—that homeownership causes unemployment—has received considerable attention, and has been investigated more thoroughly in subsequent studies. Nickell and Layard (1999) show in an analysis of 20 OECD countries that when other explanatory covariates are included (such as unionization rate, coverage rate, degree of wage coordination, replacement rate of UI benefits, duration of UI benefits), the effect of homeownership is reduced from 2 to around 1.3 percentage points. In addition, Green and Hendershott (2001a) conduct an extended analysis for

[*] This article was published in *The Economic Journal*, 116, 991–1013, Blackwell Publishing, 2006, © Royal Economic Society, 2006.

states in the US and find that the relationship only holds for households with middle-aged individuals. In the present study, we also present aggregate data for Danish regions that support the Oswald hypothesis to some extent.

The studies mentioned above all use aggregate data to draw inferences concerning individual behaviour. In order for their conclusions to prevail, the positive association between ownership and unemployment should be established on individual data, which is the subject of this paper. Specifically, we investigate whether the positive correlation found between aggregate unemployment and homeownership arises from a positive correlation between unemployment duration and homeownership on the individual level, which is the hypothesized cause of the correlation in aggregate data.

The main innovation of our analysis is the recognition that while homeownership may reduce geographical mobility and the willingness to move for jobs, there is a countervailing effect; in order to avoid having to move, individuals will set lower reservation wages for accepting jobs in the local labour market. This is likely to increase the transition rate into employment locally, and lower the transition rate into employment outside the local labour market. The net effect on unemployment depends on the empirical magnitudes of each of these two effects. We demonstrate this in a stylized job search model. The theoretical finding that homeowners are less inclined to be geographically mobile and therefore have longer spells of unemployment is the main mechanism proposed behind the Oswald hypothesis. In empirical work, the lesson from the theoretical model emphasizes the importance of distinguishing between jobs found in the local labour market (not involving a change of residence) and in distant labour markets (where a change of residence would be necessary). Using a very rich register-based dataset of Danish workers' event histories, we test the theoretical predictions in a competing risks duration model with two different employment destinations from unemployment: local jobs and jobs outside the local labour market.

We are not the first to look at this issue from a micro data perspective, but there are only a few recent studies that have done so, and none of them consider competing risks. Coulson and Fisher (2002) test the hypothesis on PSID data from the US that owners have poorer labour market outcomes than do renters. Both in terms of unemployment duration and wages, they find that this is *not* the case. On the contrary, they find that homeowners fare much better than do renters in the labour market. Coulson and Fisher (2002), however, can be criticized on one major point. They do not consider the potential selection bias issue that is present. This selection bias can arise because some households are inherently less mobile than others (e.g. they could have a preference for stability), and such households are more likely to choose owner occupation, as the fixed costs associated with buying and selling a house are amortized over a longer period, and so user costs are lower. In the event of unforeseen unemployment, these households might be less willing to move for a job, but this is not because of their choice of housing. Rather, it should be attributed to the household's preference for stability. In other words, tenure choice is endogenous to the process that describes individual labour market transitions and failure to take that into account can result in inconsistent estimates of the effect of ownership on the escape rate from unemployment.

A number of studies have addressed the potential selection bias issue. Green and Hendershott (2001*b*) (also using US PSID data) and Brunet and Lesueur (2003) (using French micro data) use a modified version of Heckman's selection model to purge the empirical model of endogeneity. Specifically, they estimate the probability of being a homeowner and use the predicted value in a duration model for spells of unemployment. Both studies obtain estimates that support the Oswald hypothesis. A concern in these studies is the way in which they try to correct for selectivity bias. This is acknowledged by Brunet and Lesueur (Chapter 6 below), who state that their procedure does not incorporate a rigorous statistical correction for selectivity bias. A rigorous statistical procedure to correct for selectivity bias is applied by Van Leuvensteijn and Koning (Chapter 8 below). They consider different mechanisms to explain the Oswald hypothesis, and analyse the duration of job spells in the Netherlands, while explicitly controlling for selection bias by simultaneously estimating a binary choice equation for the selection into homeownership and transitions in the labour market. The selection into homeownership is allowed to be correlated with the duration of employment by specifying a bivariate distribution for two unobserved variables, one of which affects the selection process and the other the duration of employment spells. They suggest that the negative correlation between homeownership and unemployment could be attributed to owners' lower job mobility and their increased risk of becoming unemployed. After correcting for self-selection into homeownership, they find that homeownership has no significant impact on job-to-job mobility and that employed homeowners have a lower probability of becoming unemployed, i.e. they find no empirical support for these alternative mechanisms underlying the hypothesis.

We address selection bias in a model that is similar to Van Leuvensteijn and Koning (Chapter 8 below). The selection into homeownership is allowed to be correlated with the duration of unemployment by specifying a bivariate distribution for two unobserved variables, one of which affects the selection process and the other the hazard rate into employment.

As mentioned above, to accommodate for the theoretical predictions in our empirical framework, we estimate a competing risks duration model with two destination-specific hazard rates for the transitions from unemployment to employment locally or employment in a geographically distant labour market. In line with the hypothesis, homeownership should have a negative effect on the transition rate from unemployment to jobs involving geographical mobility.

We also investigate whether the overall effect of homeownership on unemployment duration is positive, since this is what the correlations found in aggregate data suggest. According to our search model, the effect of homeownership on the local job hazard rate should be positive, so the negative effect on the 'mobility' hazard should dominate the positive effect on the local job hazard.

Our findings suggest that homeownership indeed lowers the propensity to move geographically for jobs while unemployed. Also in line with expectations, homeownership is shown to have a positive effect on the probability of finding employment in the local labour market. However, this positive effect on the hazard rate out of unemployment in the local labour market dominates the negative effect on the mobility hazard, such that the overall hazard rate is higher for homeowners. Our empirical findings thus contradict the so-called Oswald hypothesis, even if support is found for the main mechanism behind the hypothesis, namely that homeownership hampers mobility. The theoretical model suggests an explanation for the negative overall correlation between homeownership and unemployment duration; in countries where geography, history or culture facilitate/necessitate higher geographical mobility for reasons unrelated to homeownership (think of the US vs. continental European countries), it is possible that the effect on the 'mobility' hazard dominates in the overall effect of homeownership on unemployment duration, whereas the opposite may be the case in countries with low 'innate' geographical mobility. This line of argument also illustrates how the macro data correlation found in some of the above-mentioned studies may reflect spurious correlation rather than causality: if innate geographical mobility is high, the proportion of homeowners will be low. At the same time, when mobility is high, geographical mismatches in labour demand and supply are more easily accommodated, and hence unemployment may be low.

The rest of the paper is organized as follows. The next section presents the theoretical search model. Section 4.3 describes data and briefly characterizes the Danish labour and housing markets. Section 4.4 specifies the empirical model, Section 4.5 presents the estimation results, and Section 4.6 provides conclusions.

4.2. Theoretical model

In this section, a two-region job search model is set up in order to present the main idea of the paper formally. There are two labour markets, a local labour market and a national labour market, excluding the local market. We assume that the two regions are geographically separated, so workers must live and work in the same region, i.e. commuting is not possible. Let the arrival rate for job offers in the local labour market be α_l and denote the arrival rate for job offers in the national labour market as α_n. The wage offer distribution, $F(w)$, is taken to be identical for the two regions. Unemployed workers receive unemployment insurance (UI) benefits, b, and the discount rate is ρ. Jobs are assumed to last forever, implying that the asset value of employment with wage rate w is

$$V^E(w) = w/\rho. \tag{4.1}$$

Consider first a situation where the unemployed can move residence between the two regions without incurring any moving costs. Think of this as living in rented housing.[1] Following standard search theory, the expected discounted lifetime income for an unemployed person, V^U, can be expressed as the solution to the asset pricing equation

$$\rho V^U = b + (\alpha_l + \alpha_n) \int_{w^*}^{\overline{w}} \left(\frac{w}{\rho} - V^U \right) dF(w), \tag{4.2}$$

where w^* is the reservation wage. The reservation wage is the solution to an optimization problem, where the worker maximizes the expected present discounted value of future income streams. Such an optimal reservation wage exists because the value of employment increases in the wage, w, whereas the value of unemployment does not; i.e. employment is more favourable than continued search for wages above w^*. Since the reservation wage is defined by $w^* = \rho V^U$, it can be expressed as

$$w^* = b + \frac{\alpha_l + \alpha_n}{\rho} \int_{w^*}^{\overline{w}} (w - w^*) dF(w). \tag{4.3}$$

Clearly, in this simple setup, an unemployed worker living in rental housing is indifferent regarding whether to accept a job locally or in a geographically distant region, and hence the reservation wage is the same for accepting a job offer in the two labour markets.

Now, if the unemployed worker lives in owner-occupied housing, accepting a job offer outside the local labour market involves costs associated with selling the house and buying a new one (or finding a rental apartment), c, since the worker must migrate to the new region.[2] In this case, the expected discounted lifetime income becomes

$$\rho \tilde{V}^U = b + \alpha_l \int_{w_l^*}^{\overline{w}} \left(\frac{w}{\rho} - \tilde{V}^U \right) dF(w) + \alpha_n \int_{w_n^*}^{\overline{w}} \left(\frac{w}{\rho} - c - \tilde{V}^U \right) dF(w), \tag{4.4}$$

where the reservation wage for the local labour market is defined by $w_l^* = \rho \tilde{V}^U$, while the reservation wage for jobs outside the local labour market is defined by $w_n^* = \rho \tilde{V}^U + \rho c$. Thus, the reservation wage for jobs outside the local labour market is larger than the reservation wage for local jobs, since the unemployed person must be compensated for the costs of moving.

To determine the size of w^* relative to w_l^* and w_n^*, Eqn. (4.4) is rewritten as

$$w_l^* = b + \frac{\alpha_l}{\rho} \int_{w_l^*}^{\overline{w}} (w - w_l^*)\, dF(w) + \frac{\alpha_n}{\rho} \int_{w_n^*}^{\overline{w}} (w - (w_l^* + \rho c))\, dF(w). \qquad (4.5)$$

Consider first the sign of $w^* - w_l^*$. After rearranging terms, we obtain

$$w^* - w_l^* = \frac{\alpha_l + \alpha_n}{\rho} \left[\int_{w^*}^{\overline{w}} (w - w^*)\, dF(w) - \int_{w_l^*}^{\overline{w}} (w - w_l^*)\, dF(w) \right]$$
$$+ \frac{\alpha_n}{\rho} \int_{w_l^*}^{w_n^*} (w - w_l^*)\, dF(w) + c\alpha_n \left(1 - F\left(w_n^*\right)\right). \qquad (4.6)$$

Now assume $w_l^* \geq w^*$. The term in square brackets is then positive since the option value of search is declining in the reservation wage. The other terms are positive as well, so by contradiction we must have $w_l^* < w^*$.

We can write w_n^* in the following way:

$$w_n^* = \rho c + b + \frac{\alpha_l}{\rho} \int_{w_l^*}^{\overline{w}} (w - (w_n^* - \rho c))\, dF(w) + \frac{\alpha_n}{\rho} \int_{w_n^*}^{\overline{w}} (w - w_n^*)\, dF(w). \qquad (4.7)$$

Consider now the differential $w_n^* - w^*$:

$$w_n^* - w^* = \rho c + \frac{\alpha_l + \alpha_n}{\rho} \left[\int_{w_n^*}^{\overline{w}} (w - w_n^*)\, dF(w) - \int_{w^*}^{\overline{w}} (w - w^*)\, dF(w) \right]$$
$$+ \frac{\alpha_l}{\rho} \int_{w_l^*}^{w_n^*} (w - w_l^*)\, dF(w) + c\alpha_l \left[1 - F\left(w_n^*\right)\right]. \qquad (4.8)$$

Assume that $w_n^* \leq w^*$. Again the term in square brackets is then positive, and the other terms are positive as well, so by contradiction we must have $w_n^* > w^*$. That is, we now have the following result:

Proposition 1. $w_l^* < w^* < w_n^*$.

Homeowners' reservation wage for jobs outside their local labour market is higher than is the reservation wage of renters, because homeowners have to cover their moving costs. Since fewer job offers from outside their local labour markets are acceptable, homeowners try to avoid having to move by reducing their reservation wage for jobs in the local labour market.

To see how moving costs associated with owner-occupied housing affect individual transitions from unemployment, we first state the hazard rate out of unemployment to a job in the local labour market, θ_l, and the hazard rate to jobs involving geographical mobility, θ_n, for renters with no moving costs:

$$\theta_l = \alpha_l(1 - F(w^*)) \quad \text{and} \quad \theta_n = \alpha_n(1 - F(w^*)). \tag{4.9}$$

The exit rate from unemployment is the product of the arrival rate of job offers and the probability that the offer is accepted. For owners, the relevant hazard rates for exit to a new job in the local labour market and the national labour market, respectively, are

$$\tilde{\theta}_l = \alpha_l(1 - F(w_l^*)) \quad \text{and} \quad \tilde{\theta}_n = \alpha_n(1 - F(w_n^*)). \tag{4.10}$$

It follows trivially that $\tilde{\theta}_l > \theta_l$ and $\tilde{\theta}_n < \theta_n$, so unemployed workers in owner-occupied housing have higher transition rates into employment in the local labour market, while they have lower transition rates into jobs in regions outside the local labour market.

Oswald's hypothesis states that homeownership causes the observed positive correlation between homeownership rates and unemployment in aggregate data. In our framework, this implies that the overall hazard rate out of unemployment should be higher for renters than for owners, or $\theta_l + \theta_n > \tilde{\theta}_l + \tilde{\theta}_n$. However, according to the model, it is easy to see that the validity of this claim depends on the relative size of α_l and α_n, and the relative sizes of $F(w_l^*) - F(w^*)$, and $F(w_n^*) - F(w^*)$, which is an empirical question. It is clear that factors such as the geographical layout of a country, the spatial distribution of industries, cultural and linguistic differences between regions, etc. are expected also to affect geographical mobility and therefore the offer arrival rate α_n.

A natural extension of the model is to allow for on-the-job search. In the most simple case, where the job offer arrival rates are identical in employment and unemployment we would have that $w^* = w_l^* = b$, and $w_n^* = b + \rho c$.[3] Then, since $\theta_l = \tilde{\theta}_l$ and $\theta_n > \tilde{\theta}_n$, it would always be the case that $\theta_l + \theta_n > \tilde{\theta}_l + \tilde{\theta}_n$ and owners would clearly have longer unemployment spells on average than renters. There is, however, a rather substantial empirical literature that has estimated the job offer arrival rates for unemployed and employed persons. These studies find consistently that the job offer arrival rate for search on-the-job is much lower than the job offer arrival rate of unemployed job searchers, see e.g. Flinn (2002) and Rosholm and Svarer (2004) and the references therein. Extending the model with different arrival rates for employed and unemployed complicates the model, but does not affect the qualitative predictions of the model. The reason why a homeowner has a lower reservation wage locally is that his option value of continued search is lowered by moving costs. Likewise, his reservation wage for non-local jobs is higher due to the direct effect of the realized moving costs if he decides to accept the job offer. This is still the case after introduction of on-the-job search with different arrival rates.

Another extension of the model would be to let b be lower for homeowners than it is for renters, because owning is essentially an investment with high initial costs, such that owners have higher disutility of 'losing the home'. The implication is that the reservation wage for owners in the local labour market will still be lower than that for renters, while the reservation wage for jobs outside the local labour market may now be higher or lower for owners than for renters depending on the relative order of magnitude of moving costs versus the disutility. It would also depend on whether those who move would become owners or renters in their new locations, hence the theoretical model would be more complex. As the theoretical model here is mainly to be viewed as a framework for interpretation of our empirical results, we have not modelled this case. In addition, it could be argued that the more likely response of homeowners to moving costs would be to increase their search intensity locally. However, the implication for the hazard rates would be similar. Moreover, the hazard rates are the focus of the empirical part of this paper, in which we do not investigate wage differences between owners and renters.

Of course there may be other effects of homeownership on the labour market. First, the willingness to commute, and hence realized commuting distance, could be greater for unemployed workers who are homeowners. In a related model, Manning (2003) shows that the reservation wages increase with commuting distance if higher commuting distance is associated with a loss of utility. However, to introduce commuting distance into the model presented here would be beyond the scope of the paper. Nevertheless, it is clear that commuting is another mechanism, that implies that homeowners may have higher job finding rates locally than do renters; if owners face higher costs of mobility, they would be willing to commute longer, giving them a higher local job offer arrival rate (because their local labour market is larger). This would tend to give them a higher job finding rate for local jobs and a lower job finding rate for jobs outside the local labour market (because the non-local labour market has shrunk in size). Hence, commuting would tend to generate the same outcomes as those posited in our model. Since we have no available data on commuting, we are unable to distinguish between the two mechanisms. The potential effect of commuting however should be kept in mind when interpreting the results.

Second, by setting a lower reservation wage for local jobs, unemployed workers accept matches with lower productivity (lower wages). This implies an efficiency loss for the economy as a whole. Moreover, it implies that employed individuals in owner-occupied housing units will conduct more on-the-job search, *ceteris paribus*, because they have more to gain from doing so. However, it is beyond the scope of this paper to analyse these effects in depth.

4.3. Data and the Danish labour and housing markets

The Danish labour market is characterized by having a high turnover rate, which is due to weak employment protection and high unemployment benefit replacement rates. At the same time, the labour market is highly unionized and the wage structure is very compressed. Also, active labour market measures play an important role, and in a review of active labour market policies in Europe, Kluve and Schmidt (2002) find that the extent of participation in active labour market programmes in Denmark stands out. The geographical mobility of both employed and unemployed workers is modest, and regional migration rates are at the low end compared to other continental European countries, cf. OECD (2002) and Danish Economic Council (2002). For the unemployed, 50 per cent of migration costs can be reimbursed if they move to get a job, but the lack of mobility is illustrated by the fact that only twenty-six applications for reimbursement were accepted in the first quarter of 2002. Furthermore, since 1994, regional migration rates have declined somewhat even though regional unemployment disparities have been constant or rising.

The Danish housing market is comprised of four different main segments. The largest part is owner-occupied housing, including somewhat more than 50 per cent of all housing units. Private rental housing and social housing each constitute almost 20 per cent and cooperative housing accounts for 6 per cent of the housing market. The alternative to being an owner is to rent, and of particular relevance here is that the markets for private rental housing, social housing and cooperative housing are heavily regulated by rent controls. For the private rental market, Munch and Svarer (2002) show that rent control seriously distorts mobility, as tenancy duration is longer the more regulated the rent of the dwelling is.

To investigate the causes behind mobility of unemployed workers in Denmark, a very rich dataset, which is drawn from administrative registers, is employed. The dataset is a flow sample of all unemployment spells beginning between 1997 and 2000 for individuals in a 10 per cent random sample of the Danish population. The sample is restricted to include only the inflow to unemployment of workers in the age group 19–66 years. The duration of each unemployment spell is known in weeks, and the subsequent destination state (new job locally, new job in another geographic area, other states than employment and unemployment) is known as well. In addition, there is access to information on a number of demographic and socio-economic variables for each individual.

The local labour markets between which migration takes place are so-called commuting areas, which are defined such that the internal migration rate is 50 per cent higher than the external migration rate, cf. Andersen (2000). The commuting areas are based on geographically connected municipalities, and the 275 municipalities in Denmark are merged into 51 such commuting areas. An unemployed worker is then defined to be geographically mobile if he or she gets a job and moves to another commuting area up to 8 weeks before and 52 weeks after the beginning of the job spell.[4] This definition is based on the fact that the majority of all moves take place within this interval, reflecting that workers typically first accept a new job and then search for a permanent new residence. Gregg *et al.* (2003) find a similar pattern for the UK.

In the dataset, there are 75,806 persons with at least one unemployment spell and altogether there are 208,775 unemployment spells. Of these spells, 30 per cent end with employment locally, 1.2 per cent end with employment in a distant labour market, 29 per cent end with a return to latest employer, 25 per cent terminate with non-participation, and 15 per cent are uncompleted. Thus among all spells that are completed with employment, 2 per cent end with employment in another local labour market.[5] Table 4.1 reports descriptive statistics for the individual characteristics behind the spells.

The explanatory variables used in the econometric analysis contain first of all an indicator concerning homeownership. This variable is allowed to vary over time according to the present homeowner status of the unemployed. Other variables are the age of the worker, gender, number of dependent children

Table 4.1. Descriptive statistics

Variables	Mean	Stdv.
Homeownership	0.5708	0.495
Age 19–24	0.1436	0.3507
Age 25–29	0.155	0.3619
Age 30–39	0.279	0.4485
Age 40–49	0.21	0.4073
Age 50+	0.2124	0.409
Female	0.5618	0.4962
Children 0–17 years	0.3642	0.4812
Two adults	0.6172	0.4861
Non-OECD country	0.026	0.159
Copenhagen	0.2829	0.4504
Large city	0.2845	0.4512
Small city	0.4326	0.4954
Basic schooling	0.4084	0.4915
Vocational education	0.3721	0.4834
High school	0.0803	0.2718
Higher education	0.1392	0.3461
Non-insured	0.1403	0.3473
UI replacement rate	0.7043	0.2907
Number of observations	208,775	

Note: Means are averages over spells. The mean UI replacement rate is reported for members of UI funds.

(aged 0–17), whether the person lives in a two-adult household, whether or not the person is an immigrant from a non-OECD country, the size of the municipality, the educational level of the worker, whether or not the person is a member of an unemployment insurance fund, and finally, if so, the UI replacement rate.

4.3.1. Proportion of homeowners and level of unemployment

The Oswald hypothesis is based on the positive correlation between the proportion of homeowners in a given country or region and the corresponding level of unemployment found in various aggregate datasets. Before we investigate the hypothesis on micro data, we take a look at some aggregate data for Denmark. In Table 4.2, we show the Pearson coefficient of correlation between the share of homeowners in each municipality in Denmark (there are 275 different municipalities) and the regional level of unemployment. We do not have access to rates of unemployment on the municipal level. Instead, we use a measure of regional unemployment constructed by the Institute for Local Government Studies in Denmark. The measure gives the unemployment rate in an area around the municipality. The area is defined by how far an individual living in a given municipality can commute without having a daily cost associated with commuting that exceeds DKK 60 (corresponds to approximately 9 euros in 1987 prices). The data are available in the period between 1987 and 2000.[6]

Table 4.2. Coefficient of correlation: homeowner and unemployment

Year	Correlation	P-value
1987	0.1437*	0.0171
1988	0.1854*	0.0020
1989	0.1840*	0.0022
1990	0.1915*	0.0014
1991	0.1815*	0.0025
1992	0.1239*	0.0400
1993	0.1423	0.0182
1994	0.0620	0.3052
1995	−0.0153	0.7998
1996	−0.0096	0.8740
1997	−0.0064	0.9157
1998	0.0406	0.5016
1999	0.0838	0.1655
2000	0.1083	0.0729

Note: *indicates a significant parameter estimate (5% level).

From 1987 to 1993, our aggregate data support the finding in Oswald (1996) and Nickell and Layard (1999). After 1993, the relationship is not significant. In the observation period of the micro data, 1997–2000, the correlation is either zero or positive, albeit not significantly positive. In 2000, the correlation is positive and significant at the 10 per cent level. Thus, this pattern of correlations is roughly in accordance with analyses of the aggregate datasets that have been used to support the Oswald hypothesis. To investigate whether the pattern reflects causality or is 'spurious', we now turn to an analysis of the patterns actually found in the micro data.

4.3.2. Non-parametric hazard functions

A first impression of the association between homeowner status and unemployment duration is obtained by plotting different Kaplan–Meier estimates of the escape rate from unemployment. In Figure 4.1, we show the non-parametric single risk hazard functions for moving from unemployment to employment. We distinguish between owners and non-owners.

As can be seen, owners have a consistently higher escape rate from unemployment than do non-owners. This first picture is at odds with the Oswald hypothesis. The picture is, however, in line with Coulson and Fisher (2002), who show—based on US micro data—that homeowners have better labour market outcomes than do renters. Compared to Brunet and Lesueur (Chapter 6 below), who investigate the same issue on French micro data, the results are not consistent. In the French labour market, owners experience unconditionally longer unemployment periods than do non-owners. We will not discuss the diverging results any further at this stage. Instead, we present Kaplan–Meier estimates of the competing risks hazard functions. Figure 4.2 shows the hazard functions for moving from unemployment to a job in the local labour market.

Once more, it is clear that owners have a higher escape rate than do non-owners, which is in clear accordance with the theoretical model presented in Section 4.1. In Figure 4.3, we show the hazard functions for finding employment in geographically distant labour markets. In this case, the non-owners have a higher escape rate. This picture is in accordance with both the theoretical model and also with the main proposal of the Oswald hypothesis, namely that owners experience a higher degree of unemployment because they are less geographically mobile. The difference between the two hazard functions beyond twelve months is not statistically significant.

In the remainder of this paper, we take a closer look at the relationship between homeownership and unemployment duration. Specifically, we investigate whether homeownership is endogenous with respect to the unemployment process, and if so, if this is the reason behind the observed negative association between homeownership and unemployment duration in the raw data.

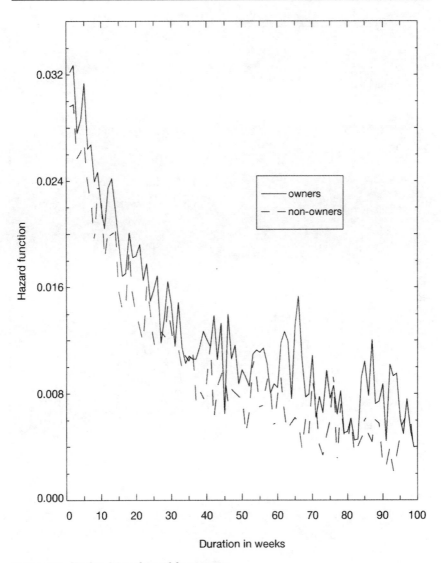

Figure 4.1. Kaplan–Meier hazard functions

4.4. Econometric model

In order to investigate the effect of homeownership on unemployment duration we apply an empirical model that is quite similar to that used by Van
Leuvensteijn and Koning (Chapter 8 below). The part of the model that

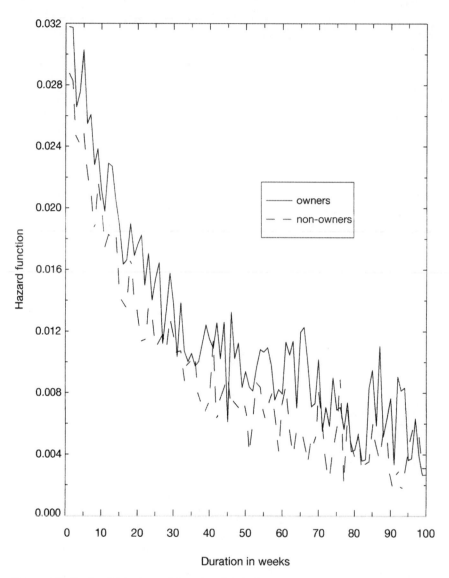

Figure 4.2. Kaplan–Meier hazard function: local jobs

describes transitions in the labour market is specified as a competing risks mixed proportional hazard model. Two transition rates out of unemployment are modelled: the unemployed can leave unemployment for a (new) job locally (*l*) or for a job in another local labour market by being mobile (*n*). All other

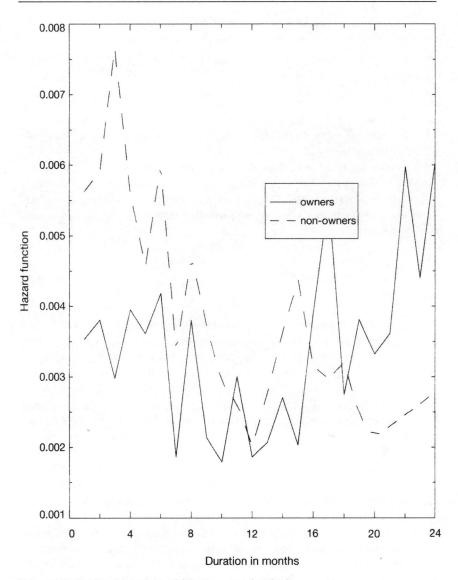

Figure 4.3. Kaplan–Meier hazard function: non-local jobs

destinations (e.g. out of the labour force and recall to last employer) are treated as right censored observations.[7] Each destination-specific hazard $j = l, n$ is the product of the baseline hazard, which captures the time dependence in the hazard rate and a function of observed characteristics, x, a time varying indicator

99

for ownership status, z_t, and unobserved characteristics, v_j

$$\theta_j(t|x, z_t, v_j) = \lambda_j(t) \cdot \exp(\beta_j'x + \gamma_j z_t + v_j), \qquad (4.1)$$

where $\lambda_j(t)$ is the baseline hazard and $\exp(\beta_j'x + \gamma_j z_t + v_j)$ is the systematic part of the hazard. The baseline hazards are specified flexibly, as both $\lambda_l(t)$ and $\lambda_n(t)$ have a piecewise constant specification, such that they are constant within duration intervals.

To account for possible endogeneity of the homeownership variable, z_t, we simultaneously model the probability of being a homeowner and the transition rates out of unemployment. The probability of being a homeowner depends on explanatory variables, x, and an unobserved component, v_h, and is specified as a logit model

$$P(x, v_h) = P(z_t = 1|x, v_h) = \frac{\exp(\beta_h'x + v_h)}{1 + \exp(\beta_h'x + v_h)}. \qquad (4.2)$$

We assume that all sources of correlation between the two processes—beyond those captured by the observed explanatory variables—can be represented by the individual-specific heterogeneity terms. These terms are assumed to be time-invariant and hence constant across replications of the same process for the individual. Due to multiple occurrences of both unemployment spells and ownership status for the individuals, we can exploit the multiple spell feature of our data to identify the effect of homeownership on the exit rate from unemployment, as suggested by identification results for duration models with multiple spells; cf. Honoré (1993). This identification approach has been used in a series of papers by Lillard and coauthors (see e.g. Panis and Lillard 1994, Lillard et al. 1995, and Upchurch et al. 2002). Identification requires that we—for at least a subset of individuals—observe unemployment spells both when the individual is a homeowner and when the individual is a renter. The intuition for identification is spelled out in Panis (2004). In terms of our application, his argument goes as follows: suppose we observe only one respondent over a long period of time during which he switches homeowner status. With a sample of one, there is no heterogeneity and no correlation across equations, such that the equations are independent. The effect of homeowner status on exit rates from unemployment is identified because of repeated observations on unemployment spells and variations in homeowner status. More generally, conditional on heterogeneity, the equations are independent and identification rests on repeated outcomes with intraperson variation in homeowner status.[8] In terms of intraperson variation in homeowner status 16 per cent of the individuals in the sample are observed both as renters and as homeowners.

The contribution to the likelihood function from an individual in our model is

$$
\mathcal{L} = \prod_{m=1}^{M} \left\{ \begin{array}{c} \iiint P(x_m, v_h)^{z_{tm}}(1 - P(x_m, v_h))^{1-z_{tm}} \\ \theta_l(t|x_m, z_{tm}, v_l)^{d_{tm}} \theta_n(t|x_m, z_{tm}, v_n)^{d_{nm}} \\ \exp\left(-\int_0^t \theta_l(s|x_m, z_{sm}, v_l)\, ds - \int_0^t \theta_n(s|x_m, z_{sm}, v_n) ds\right) \end{array} \right\} dG(v_l, v_n, v_h),
$$

$$(4.3)$$

where d_l and d_n are destination indicator variables for the unemployment hazard rates (thus also taking into account censoring of the duration variable), M is the number of unemployment spells the individual experiences in the sample period, and $G(v_l, v_n, v_h)$ is the joint cdf of the unobservables. We use a flexible and widely applied specification of the distribution of the unobservables; it is assumed that v_l, v_n and v_h each can take two values, where one of the support points in each destination-specific hazard is normalized to zero (i.e. $v_{l1} = 0$ and $v_{n1} = 0$), because the baseline hazard acts as a constant term in the hazard rates. Thus, there are eight possible combinations of this trivariate unobserved heterogeneity distribution, each with an associated probability. For more details on this class of mixture distributions in duration models, see e.g. Van den Berg (2001).

4.5. Results

This section first presents estimation results of a simplified version of the duration model, where no distinction is made between finding employment locally and finding employment by being mobile (i.e. a single risk duration model), but where the selection into homeownership is accounted for. The first two columns in Table 4.3 show estimated coefficients and their standard errors of the unemployment hazard, while columns three and four contain parameter estimates and standard errors of the selection equation.

With respect to explanatory variables in the selection into homeownership, it appears that older workers and households with two adults are more likely to be homeowners, as expected. Also, individuals living outside Copenhagen are more likely to own their homes and individuals with vocational education are more often homeowners than are individuals in other education groups. Uninsured workers are less inclined to own, while UI fund members are less likely to be homeowners the higher the benefit replacement rate they have. Since the UI system has a quite low ceiling, this basically means that the wage is positively correlated with homeownership.

From the first column of Table 4.3, we conclude that homeowners have a higher transition rate from unemployment to employment than do renters. That is, owners have, *ceteris paribus*, shorter spells of unemployment, and this

Table 4.3. Estimation results: single risk model

Variables	Unemployment hazard		Selection equation	
	Coeff.	Std. err.	Coeff.	Std. err.
Homeownership	0.3478*	0.0150		
Age 19–24	0.4754*	0.0164	−0.9132*	0.0277
Age 25–29	0.3628*	0.0154	−1.3679*	0.0260
Age 30–39	0.1523*	0.0137	−0.813*	0.0242
Age 50+	−0.4961*	0.0149	0.3122*	0.0280
Female	−0.1101*	0.0117	0.0347	0.0183
Children 0–17 years	0.063*	0.0163	−0.0215	0.0320
Female × children	−0.2993*	0.0199	1.1576*	0.0184
Two adults	0.0327*	0.0108	0.2814*	0.0360
Non-OECD country	−0.8106*	0.0314	−2.4962*	0.0339
Large city	−0.0374*	0.0119	0.6691*	0.0192
Small city	0.0089*	0.0113	1.0426*	0.0184
Basic schooling	−0.2677*	0.0108	−0.3143*	0.0171
High school	0.1249*	0.0173	−0.2645*	0.0274
Higher education	0.1093*	0.0148	−0.382*	0.0243
Non-insured	−0.8212*	0.025	−2.2142*	0.0439
UI replacement rate	−0.333*	0.0285	−0.9939*	0.0514
$U_{e,2}$	1.2816*	0.0139		
$U_{h,1}$	−2.9748*	0.0443		
$U_{h,2}$	2.5764*	0.0444		
$P(U_{e,1}, U_{h,1})$	0.1901*	0.0046		
$P(U_{e,2}, U_{h,1})$	0.1738*	0.0045		
$P(U_{e,1}, U_{h,2})$	0.4440*	0.0058		
$P(U_{e,2}, U_{h,2})$	0.1921*	0.0056		
$Corr(U_e, U_h)$	−0.1754*	0.0128		

*indicates a significant parameter estimate (5% level).
Note: The estimated coefficients of the first column correspond to the parameter vector, β, of the single risk duration model for transitions from unemployment to employment. The estimated coefficients of the third column correspond to the parameter vector, β_h, of the probit model for homeownership status. The standard error for the correlation coefficient has been calculated based on 1,000 drawings from the multivariate normal distribution with mean and covariance matrix set equal to the estimated parameter vector and covariance matrix.

contradicts the positive correlation observed in Oswald's (1996) aggregate data, and in our own regional data, see Section 2.1 above.

With respect to other covariates, it can be noted that age has a negative effect on the hazard rate and women—particularly those with children—also have a lower hazard rate. Education improves the chances of escaping unemployment and the replacement rate of unemployment benefits has a negative effect, which is a standard result.

The unobserved heterogeneity terms in the selection equation, v_h, and in the hazard rate, v_e, are clearly correlated, so it is of importance to correct for selectivity. However, when the model is estimated without correction for selection into homeownership, the coefficient to homeownership in the hazard is still significantly positive, but somewhat surprisingly it is lower. This means that there is a negative correlation between unobserved components in the two equations, such that unobserved characteristics that make the unemployed more likely to be a homeowner also have a negative effect on the transition rate out of unemployment. This finding is to some extent counterintuitive, since one would expect people with more favourable employment prospects to be more likely to acquire housing. The results indicate, however, that this effect is captured by the observed characteristics that we include in the model. The negative correlation is more likely caused by the composition of the pool of unemployed people. In Munch *et al.* (Chapter 9 below), the impact of homeownership on job duration in Denmark is investigated. They find that homeowners are less likely to become unemployed, and this could indicate that people with a higher probability of becoming unemployed are less likely to acquire housing than is the population in general. It is presumably this effect that is captured by the negative correlation. In other words, individuals with more unstable career paths are less likely to buy their own homes and are more often found among the unemployed.

The single risk hazard model offered no support for the Oswald hypothesis, but the main proposed mechanism behind the hypothesis is that homeowners' geographical mobility is expected to be reduced. Therefore, the next step is to estimate the competing risks duration model, where a distinction is made between finding a job by being geographically mobile and finding a job in the local labour market. The first two columns of Table 4.4 show estimated coefficients, β_n, and their standard errors in the hazard rate for finding a job in another region, while columns three and four contain those of the local job hazard rate, β_l. Columns five and six contain parameter estimates of the selection equation.

Before turning to the relationship between homeownership and unemployment duration, we offer some comments on the effects of other covariates. Most variables seem to have a stronger impact on the mobility hazard than on the local job hazard. For example, being 50 or more years of age reduces the local job hazard by 38 per cent ($= exp(-0.48) - 1$) compared to being between 40 and 49 years old, but it reduces the mobility hazard by 68 per cent. Interestingly, some variables have opposite effects on the two destination-specific hazard rates. Unemployed workers living in households with two adults have a higher local job hazard but a lower mobility hazard than do single workers. Living outside the Copenhagen metropolitan area has a strong positive effect on the mobility hazard, while it has a negative effect on the local job hazard. This is probably because of thin market effects, since the Copenhagen metropolitan area is by far the largest local labour market. It should also be noted that the estimated destination-specific hazard rates exhibit negative duration dependence (except for the first couple of months for the mobility hazard), i.e. they decline with unemployment duration, cf. Figure 4.4. Figure 4.4 also reveals that the mobility hazard is much lower than is the local job hazard, reflecting that geographical mobility is a rather rare phenomenon.

Table 4.4. Estimation results: competing risk model

Variables	Mobility hazard		Local job hazard		Selection equation	
	Coeff.	Std. err.	Coeff.	Std. err.	Coeff.	Std. err.
Homeownership	−0.2159*	0.0575	0.3753*	0.0156		
Age 19–24	1.7661*	0.091	0.4306*	0.0167	−0.9127*	0.0277
Age 25–29	1.7013*	0.0914	0.321*	0.0157	−1.3925*	0.026
Age 30–39	0.892*	0.0904	0.139*	0.0138	−0.8333*	0.0243
Age 50+	−1.1524*	0.1452	−0.4831*	0.015	0.3253*	0.0281
Female	−0.1341*	0.0528	−0.117*	0.0119	0.0414*	0.0182
Children 0–17 years	−0.5277*	0.0965	0.0739*	0.0165	−0.0025*	0.0321
Female × children	−0.5401*	0.1151	−0.2744*	0.0201	1.1550*	0.0184
Two adults	−0.2538*	0.0542	0.0476*	0.011	0.261*	0.0361
Non-OECD country	−1.6691*	0.1975	−0.7751*	0.032	−2.4643*	0.034
Large city	1.2285*	0.0696	−0.0801*	0.0121	0.6654*	0.0192
Small city	1.5747*	0.0662	−0.0435*	0.0115	1.0285*	0.0183
Basic schooling	−0.5342*	0.0587	−0.2562*	0.0109	−0.3157*	0.017
High school	0.7122*	0.0725	0.0749*	0.0179	−0.2684*	0.0273
Higher education	0.7414*	0.0723	0.0844*	0.015	−0.3995*	0.0243
Non-insured	0.0588	0.1402	−0.8651*	0.0254	−2.2243*	0.0438
UI replacement rate	0.0493	0.1714	−0.3377*	0.0287	−0.9969*	0.0514
$U_{h,1}$	−2.9766*	0.0444				
$U_{h,2}$	2.5892*	0.0445				
$U_{l,2}$	−1.2876*	0.014				
$U_{m,2}$	3.0594*	0.3161				
$P(U_{m,1}, U_{l,1}, U_{h,1})$	0.1184*	0.0107				
$P(U_{m,2}, U_{l,1}, U_{h,1})$	0.0509*	0.0104				
$P(U_{m,1}, U_{l,2}, U_{h,2})$	0.1585*	0.0101				
$P(U_{m,2}, U_{l,2}, U_{h,1})$	0.0353*	0.0096				
$P(U_{m,1}, U_{l,1}, U_{h,2})$	0.0822*	0.0166				
$P(U_{m,2}, U_{l,1}, U_{h,2})$	0.0985*	0.0165				
$P(U_{m,1}, U_{l,2}, U_{h,2})$	0.3823*	0.0206				
$P(U_{m,2}, U_{l,2}, U_{h,2})$	0.0739	0.0204				
$Corr(U_h, U_l)$	−0.1840*	0.0145				
$Corr(U_h, U_m)$	0.0365	0.0232				
$Corr(U_m, U_l)$	0.2820*	0.0428				

*indicates a significant parameter estimate (5% level).
Note: The estimated coefficients of the first and third columns correspond to the parameter vectors, β_n and β_l, of the competing risks duration model for transitions from unemployment into employment in another region or locally. The estimated coefficients of the fifth column correspond to the parameter vector, β_h, of the probit model for homeownership status. The standard errors for the correlation coefficients have been calculated based on 1,000 drawings from the multivariate normal distribution with mean and covariance matrix set equal to the estimated parameter vector and covariance matrix.

The findings indicate that homeownership has the expected effect, as it indeed lowers the propensity to move for job-related reasons. Hence, there is weak support for the Oswald hypothesis in the sense that ownership reduces the chances of escaping unemployment by being geographically mobile. Also in line with the theoretical search model, homeownership has a positive effect on the probability of finding employment in the local labour market. This positive effect on the much higher local job hazard (see Figure 4.4) overrides the

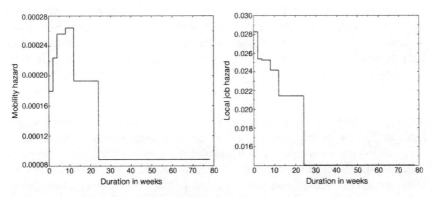

Figure 4.4. Estimated destination-specific hazard rates

negative effect on the mobility hazard, such that there is a positive overall effect of homeownership on the transition rate from unemployment to employment, cf. Table 4.3. Put differently, the *reasoning* behind the Oswald hypothesis is empirically supported, since homeownership reduces the propensity to move for job-related reasons, but because so few workers move to get a job, this mechanism is not important enough to be evident in an overall positive correlation between homeownership and unemployment. Hence, the non-negative correlation found in aggregated regional data would have to come from other sources.

4.5.1. Robustness of the Results

Above, we investigate the association between unemployment and home-ownership through mobility. There is also reason to believe that there is a relationship between homeownership and unemployment that has nothing to do with mobility and likewise a relationship between homeownership and mobility that has nothing to do with unemployment. In terms of the first relationship, it could be argued that a higher housing wealth net of the mortgage debt decreases the escape rate out of unemployment (see e.g. Lentz and Tranaes 2005 for a justification of this relationship in terms of financial wealth), and this relationship is absent for renters. In order to address this issue, we included variables for the market value of the home and the mortgage debt ratio in the home (i.e. they take the value zero for renters). These variables did not have any significant effect on any of the destination-specific hazard rates. Neither did the inclusion of these explanatory variables have any effect on the relationship between homeownership and the cause-specific hazard rates.

In terms of investigating the relationship between homeownership and mobility, we also include a range of explanatory variables that have been found

105

to affect individual mobility. The most prominent are age, level of education, marriage market status, and the presence of children. Since these explanatory variables at the same time are likely to be associated with homeowner status, they should be included in order to justify the empirical test of our theoretical hypothesis. Younger individuals are more likely to be geographically mobile and at the same time less likely to be homeowners, so it could be argued that the negative effect we find between homeownership and geographical mobility in the hazard rate out of unemployment is due to the behaviour of younger individuals. The inclusion of the age dummies confirms that the reported association between homeownership and mobility when returning to employment is not a spurious effect caused by the behaviour of young individuals. Likewise, Greenwood (1997) and Compton and Pollak (2004) have shown that geographical mobility is more pronounced among higher educated individuals, and the results from the homeowner equation reported in Table 4.4 show that more educated people are less likely to own homes. By conditioning on level of education, we purge the results from this confounding effect. Related to this point is the behaviour of married and cohabiting couples. Mincer (1978) argues that families are less likely to be geographically mobile compared to single person households. The reason is that the return to mobility, e.g. through a new job offer for one of the spouses, should be weighted against the combined costs of moving for the household, a comparison that is less likely to favour a move if the spouse is working. In terms of housing decisions, families are more likely to be homeowners. Presumably, they realize they are less likely to move and therefore are more willing to invest in a house, knowing that some of the investment is irreversible as a consequence of the relatively high transaction costs. The latter phenomenon is reinforced by the presence of children. We therefore also condition on marriage status and the presence of children in the empirical model.

To investigate whether the effect of homeownership varies across different types of households, we also included interaction terms between the home-owner variable and a number of other covariates, such as the presence of children and the age group dummies. The interaction term between home-ownership and the presence of children only entered the local job hazard significantly with a positive coefficient. The age group terms also only entered the local job hazard significantly (the effect is biggest for the 40–49-year-olds and smallest for the 25–29-year-olds). However, these household differences are not important enough to change the total effect of homeownership for any of the separate subgroups in any of the hazards.

Another important issue is econometric identification of the homeowner effect. The model could also be identified by including covariates in the home-owner equation that are not included in the unemployment hazard equations. This approach is pursued by Van Leuvensteijn and Koning (Chapter 8 below), who use the regional homeowner rate as an instrumental variable. We also ran regressions using this instrumental variable, but it did not change the results in any significant way.[9]

The robustness of the results was also considered by estimating the model with different specifications of the distribution of unobservables. Specifically, we tried to include more points of support in the destination-specific hazard rates, but this did not change the results. Van den Berg (2001) notes that the methodological and empirical literature provides evidence that discrete distributions are sufficiently flexible to capture 'random effects' unobserved heterogeneity, and our findings seem to support this finding.

Even if the mobility rate in Denmark lies in the intermediate range compared to other European countries (see Section 2), it is of interest to see whether the results still hold in sectors of the economy where mobility is higher. To this end, we estimate the model with a different definition of local labour markets. Instead of using the 51 commuting areas, we use the 275 municipalities. When these smaller municipalities are used, the mobility rate roughly doubles. In addition, we estimate the model for unemployed people below the age of 40, unemployed people with further education and a combination of both (here the mobility rate more than doubles). In all cases, the qualitative results were unchanged; the effect of homeownership is positive on the local job hazard and negative on the mobility hazard.

Finally, the right censoring of transitions from unemployment to states other than employment locally or in a distant labour market could produce biased results if they are endogenous. However, adding extra risks (for non-participation and recall from the last employer) leaves the effects of homeownership almost unchanged.[10]

4.5.2. Discussion

The main result that homeownership overall is negatively associated with the duration of unemployment contrasts the findings for the US by Green and Hendershott (2001b) and for France by Brunet and Lesueur (2003). Apart from different econometric approaches, one particular issue might play an important role in explaining the diverging results. Regional mobility is more important for the functioning of the US labour market, so homeownership has greater potential to do some damage there, cf. the discussion in the introduction and the theoretical section.[11] In Denmark and in many other European countries, regional mobility is lower than in the US. This is also consistent with the model in the sense that transaction costs for sales of houses are typically lower in the US than in Europe. According to Catte *et al.* (2004), the transaction costs for sales of medium-sized houses in the US are around 9 per cent of the sales price, whereas in the European countries (for which they have data), the transaction costs are in all cases above 10 per cent of the sales price (11 per cent in Denmark).

Our theoretical model can thus explain these apparent contradictory results; in countries where culture (linguistic and cultural differences between regions, etc.), geography (landscape size, distance between regions, population spread, etc.), or the spatial distribution of economic activity lead to higher geographical mobility for reasons unrelated to homeownership, it is possible that the effect on the mobility hazard dominates in the overall effect of homeownership on unemployment duration, whereas the opposite may be the case in countries with low 'natural' geographical mobility. That is, the sign of the correlation (in aggregated regional data) between unemployment duration and homeownership depends on the size of the mobility offer arrival rate, α_n, relative to the local job offer arrival rate, α_l.

This line of reasoning illustrates how the macro data correlations found in some of the above-mentioned studies may reflect spurious correlations rather than causal relationships: if 'natural' geographical mobility is high, the proportion of homeowners will be low. At the same time, when mobility is high, geographical mismatches in labour demand and supply are more easily accommodated, and hence unemployment may be low. Conversely, if natural geographical mobility is low, people are more inclined to buy their homes and structural unemployment may be higher. Thus, cross-country/region regressions of the aggregate unemployment rate on the homeownership rate that do not control for the level of natural geographical mobility may erroneously reach the conclusion that homeownership increases unemployment.

Another channel through which the macro data correlations may become spurious is if the causal relationship does not arise through unemployment duration, but rather through job duration. Homeowners may be more likely to become unemployed possibly because they find themselves in 'bad' matches because of their relative reluctance to move for better job opportunities. The latter explanation, however, is rejected by Van Leuvensteijn and Koning (Chapter 8 below) on Dutch data and by Munch *et al.* (2005) on Danish data, since homeowners in these studies have a lower probability of becoming unemployed.

In addition to the geographical or cultural country characteristics discussed above, homeownership also competes with a number of other candidate variables to explain both mobility and unemployment. One candidate variable is relatively easy access to early retirement schemes and disability pensions. In a comparison between Europe and the US, Decressin and Fatas (1995) find that, in Europe, region-specific shocks are absorbed by adjustments in the participation rate, whereas in the US, workers move. For both areas, the unemployment rate plays a minor role as an adjustment mechanism. Also, generous unemployment benefits are available without being conditional on job search in other regions, i.e. monitoring and sanctions in the search process are typically not implemented. The implication is that, first, if an individual becomes unemployed, it may not be necessary to move, even if a job cannot be found in the local labour market. Moreover, reservation wages will be fairly high, and hence, unemployment duration could potentially be quite long. Second, given the relatively generous levels of unemployment benefits, income uncertainty is lowered, and hence, the risk that an individual who loses a job will not be able to pay the mortgage is lower. Therefore, in countries with generous benefit schemes, homeownership may be associated with lower risk than in countries without such a social security net. This would tend to give positive correlations in aggregated regional data between unemployment rates and homeownership, while at the macro level the causal relation would be the opposite. Hence, the apparent conflicting signs of the correlations can easily be explained.

Finally, it should also be mentioned that the markets for rented housing in Denmark are regulated by rent controls, which prolong tenancy durations (although average tenancy duration in the rental sector is still much lower than it is in owner-occupied housing units). We show in a companion paper (see Svarer *et al.* 2005) that this also distorts labour mobility. Thus, the alternative to being a homeowner is being a renter in a regulated market with relatively low mobility.

4.6. Conclusion

This paper has examined the micro data foundation for the positive correlation between homeownership and unemployment as observed by Oswald (1996) and others. Based on a theoretical search model, we first showed that homeowners should have a reduced propensity to move for job reasons, which is the main mechanism proposed behind the hypothesis in the literature. However, in addition, homeowners should also have a lower reservation wage for local jobs because of costs associated with the selling and buying of their homes. The net effect of homeownership on unemployment duration is ambiguous, but if the observed pattern in aggregate data is to be believed, the negative mobility effect should dominate.

Our results support the first two predictions, as owners are less likely to find employment in another region and more likely to find employment locally than are renters, but the net effect of homeownership on unemployment duration is negative, thus contrasting the Oswald hypothesis. Hence, our results do not inform the theoretical prediction stating that homeowners reduce their reservation wage for local jobs, and this effect is quantitatively more important than is the negative mobility effect. This result is found even though the correlation between the unemployment rate and homeownership is positive at the regional level.

We conclude that in a labour market with a low level of mobility, which along with a high homeownership rate can be attributed to other characteristics, such as incentives to leave the labour force, active labour market policies etc., homeownership does not lead to longer unemployment spells on average. It is possible that in countries where geographical mobility is a more important element of the functioning of the labour market (such as in the US), homeownership might have an overall detrimental effect on unemployment. However, this is not likely to be the case in many European countries.

Notes

1. The assumption of zero mobility costs for renters is for simplicity only. It is sufficient for the model's predictions that the costs of moving are larger for homeowners than for those living in rented housing.
2. According to Catte *et al.* (2004), the transaction costs for selling an average-sized house in Denmark are approximately 11 per cent of the sales price. We have no information on the cost of moving out of an apartment. Some contracts state that the rented accommodation should be left in the same condition as it was when it was first occupied. There might therefore be some expenses for painting, etc. It is however very unlikely that these expenses amount to the cost of selling a house.
3. We owe this point to an anonymous referee.
4. Exact moving dates are known for all individuals.
5. Calculations based on the European Community Household Panel show that among all unemployment spells in Denmark that end with employment, 4.1 per cent are also associated with a residential move within the next year (thus not requiring it to be a move to another local labour market). This mobility rate is higher only in Luxembourg and Finland, while it is below 2.5 per cent in Ireland, Italy, Greece, Spain, Portugal, and Austria. In France and the UK, it is 3.2 per cent and 2.8 per cent respectively. Thus, the mobility rate in Denmark is at the high end among European countries.
6. We are grateful to Leif Husted at the Institute for Local Government Studies for providing us with these data.
7. This is discussed further in Sect. 4.5.1.
8. Identification of the homeowner effect is further discussed in Sect. 4.5.1.
9. We estimated the following four different models: (1) only one spell per person and no instrument, (2) one spell and the instrument, (3) multiple spells and no instrument (see Table 4.4), and (4) multiple spells and the instrument. In all cases, there was a significant negative impact of homeownership on the mobility hazard and a significant positive effect on the local job hazard. However, the quantitative impact of ownership changed in the single spell models (compared to the results of Table 4.4, the coefficients to the homeowner variable were 0.1129 and −0.9129 respectively in model 1 and 0.1054 and −1.1656 respectively in model 2). In model 4, the coefficients to the ownership variable were only marginally different from those presented in Table 4.4. All in all, we take this as evidence for the claim that what matters for identification is information about multiple spells.

10. The full set of results reported in this subsection is available upon request.
11. With respect to the study by Brunet and Lesueur (2003), regional mobility is also relatively important for the French labour market as regional migration rates are among the highest in continental Europe; cf. OECD (2000).

References

Andersen, A. K. (2000), *Commuting Areas in Denmark* (Copenhagen: AKF Forlaget).

Brunet, C., and Lesueur, J. Y. (2003), 'Does homeownership lengthen unemployment duration? A French micro-econometric study', mimeo.

Catte, P., Girouard, N., Price, R., and André, C. (2004), 'Housing markets, wealth, and the business cycle', OECD Working Paper 17.

Compton, J., and Pollak, R. (2004), 'Why are power couples increasingly concentrated in large metropolitan areas?', NBER Working Paper 10918.

Coulson, N. E., and Fisher, L. M. (2002), 'Tenure choice and labour market outcomes', *Housing Studies*, 17/1, 35–49.

Danish Economic Council (2002), *Danish Economy* (Copenhagen).

Decressin, J., and Fatas, A. (1995), 'Regional labour market dynamics in Europe', *European Economic Review*, 39, 1627–55.

Flinn, C. J. (2002), 'Labor market structures and inequality: a comparison of Italy and the US', *Review of Economic Studies*, 69, 611–45.

Green, R., and Hendershott, P. (2001*a*), 'Home ownership and the duration of unemployment: a test of the Oswald hypothesis', mimeo.

—— —— (2001*b*), 'Home ownership and unemployment in the US', *Urban Studies*, 38/9, 1501–20.

Greenwood, M. J. (1997), 'Internal migration in developed countries', in M. Rosenzweig and O. Stark (eds.), *Handbook of Population and Family Economics* (Amsterdam: North-Holland), 647–720.

Gregg, P., Machin, S., and Manning, A. (2003), 'Mobility and joblessness', in R. Blundell, D. Card, and R. B. Freeman (eds.), *Seeking a Premier League Economy* (Chicago: University of Chicago Press), 371–410.

Hendershott, P., and White, M. (2000), 'The rise and fall of housing's favored investment status', *Journal of Housing Research*, 11/2, 257–75.

Honoré, B. E. (1993), 'Dentification results for duration models with multiple spells', *Review of Economic Studies*, 60, 241–6.

Kluve, J., and Schmidt, C. M. (2002), 'Can training and employment subsidies combat European unemployment?', *Economic Policy*, 35, 411–48.

Lentz, R., and Tranaes, T. (2005), 'Job search and savings: wealth effects and duration dependence', *Journal of Labor Economics*, 23/3, 467–90.

Lillard, L. A., Brien, M. J., and Waite, L. J. (1995), 'Premarital cohabitation and subsequent marital dissolution: a matter of self-selection?', *Demography*, 32/3, 437–57.

Manning, A. (2003), 'The real thin theory: monopsony in modern labour markets', *Labour Economics*, 10, 105–31.

Mincer, J. (1978), 'Family migration decisions', *Journal of Political Economy*, 86, 749–73.

Munch, J. R., and Svarer, M. (2002), 'Rent control and tenancy duration', *Journal of Urban Economics*, 52, 542–60.

Munch, J.R., Rosholm, M., and Svarer, M. (2005), 'The impact of homeownership on job mobility in Denmark', mimeo.

Nickell, S., and Layard, R. (1999), 'Labour market institutions and economic performance', in O. C. Ashenfelter and D. Card (eds.), *Handbook of Labor Economics*, (Amsterdam: North-Holland), 3029–84.

OECD (2002), *Employment Outlook* (Paris: OECD).

Oswald, A. (1996), 'A conjecture of the explanation for high unemployment in the industrialized nations: part 1', Warwick University Economic Research Paper 475.

Panis, C. (2004), 'Microsimulations in the presence of unobserved heterogeneity', mimeo, RAND Corporation.

—— and Lillard, L. (1994), 'Health inputs and child mortality: Malaysia', *Journal of Health Economics*, 13, 455–89.

Rosholm, M., and Svarer, M. (2004), 'Endogenous wage dispersion and job turnover in a search-matching model', *Labour Economics*, 11, 623–45.

Svarer, M., Rosholm, M., and Munch, J. R. (2005), 'Rent control and unemployment duration', *Journal of Public Economics*, 89, 2165–81.

Upchurch, D. M., Lillard, L., and Panis, C. (2002), 'Nonmarital childbearing: influences of education, marriage, and fertility', *Demography*, 39/2, 311–29.

Van den Berg, G. (1994), 'The effects of changes in the job offer arrival rate on the duration of unemployment', *Journal of Labor Economics*, 12/3, 478–98.

—— (2001), 'Duration models: specification, identification, and multiple durations', in J. J. Heckman and E. Leamer (eds.), *Handbook of Econometrics* (Amsterdam: North-Holland), 3381–460.

5

The Impact of Homeownership on Unemployment in the Netherlands

Aico van Vuuren

5.1. Introduction

The lack of labour mobility is probably one of the main reasons for Europe's long-term unemployment and persistent differences of unemployment figures between different regions (Blanchard and Katz 1992). Oswald (Chapter 2 above) argues that homeownership is one of the key determinants of this lack of mobility. Moreover, he points at five main mechanisms that drive the positive impact on unemployment. The first reason is a direct relationship between mobility and homeownership in the sense that families who own a home face difficulties (and monetary outlays) selling their home. This implies that even though labour demand is more favourable in other areas of the country, workers prefer to stay unemployed. The other four reasons can be described as externalities of homeownership. For example, in the case of an absent renting market, youngsters face difficulties finding the right residence close to the place where jobs are situated.

The concern of economists about the relationship described above is in sharp contrast to the implementation of policies stimulating homeownership. Many European countries, including the Netherlands, have used subsidies for low-income families to reduce the costs of homeownership. In addition, interest payments are tax-deductible in many European countries, while there are quite substantial tax payments for buying a home (Belot and Ederveen 2005). The simultaneous implementation of policies to subsidize homeownership and increasing the costs of buying a home has unambiguous negative effects on mobility, and hence is likely to have a positive effect on unemployment figures.

In a number of studies researchers have focused on the Oswald hypothesis. First, Oswald (Chapter 2 above) investigates the total impact by comparing different countries with different rates in homeownership as well as unemployment rates. He finds a positive relationship between homeownership and the level of unemployment between regions, and this is still among the strongest evidence in favour of the Oswald hypothesis. However, it does not yield any information about the relative impact of the different sources. Many researchers tried to disentangle the total effect of the Oswald hypothesis as outlined in his seminal paper. In this research, the focus is mainly on the direct effect of homeownership on unemployment status, as reported in Oswald (Chapter 2 above) as the first reason to expect a positive relationship between homeownership and regional unemployment rates. At the moment, there are two approaches in which researchers tried to investigate this part of the Oswald hypothesis. First, the approach taken by Van den Berg and Van Vuuren (1998) is indirect in the sense that they investigate the subjective moving costs of the unemployed. The model they use is a model originally developed by Van den Berg and Gorter (1997) in which there are two types of jobs. The first type of job is close to the present residence, and hence an individual does not have to move for that job. The second type of job is too far from the present residence, and hence it is necessary to move. The method adopted by Van den Berg and Van Vuuren is to use subjective answers about the reservation wages of the respondents. When a homeowner faces substantial moving costs, the difference between reservation wages should be larger. They find that homeowners have substantially higher moving costs than non-homeowners, and hence this implies that homeowners are on average longer unemployed. A drawback of their analysis is that they cannot estimate the level of the impact of homeownership on the unemployment rate and can only show that it should be positive.

Another approach is to look at individual unemployment duration data. A drawback of such an approach, however, is that the decision to invest in housing is not exogenous, and hence the estimates of homeownership on the unemployment duration are biased. Green and Hendershott (2001) try to solve this endogeneity problem by using a two-stage estimation method. They find evidence for the positive relationship between unemployment and homeownership supporting the results of Van den Berg and Van Vuuren (1998). Van Leuvensteijn and Koning (Chapter 8 below) use a similar method as Green and Hendershott, but instead of a two-stage estimation process, they use a full information maximum likelihood approach. Munch et al. (Chapter 4 above) apply this method in a model that is similar to the one applied in Van den Berg and Gorter (1997). Van Leuvensteijn and Koning (2004) and Munch et al. (Chapter 4 above) find a negative relationship between the unemployment duration and homeownership. An important question is whether this indicates that the endogeneity problem is not properly dealt with or whether it is due to an omission of the present literature on the Oswald hypothesis.

This paper estimates the model of Munch et al. (Chapter 4 above) using a Dutch dataset. We use a register-based dataset of the Netherlands for the period 1989 to 2001. It contains a random draw from the population of taxpayers in the Netherlands (i.e. everyone who is over 15 and receives income from any possible source). Van Leuvensteijn and Koning (Chapter 8 below) also use this dataset (see also Frijters *et al.* 2000).

The paper is organized as follows. The next section discusses the Dutch housing and labour market for the period of analysis. Section 5.3 describes the data we use for our analysis. In Section 5.4 we set up the empirical analysis, and the results are in Section 5.5. We look at the counterfactual hazard probabilities in Section 5.6. We conclude in Section 5.7.

5.2. The housing and labour market of the Netherlands in the period 1989 to 2000

Our period of analysis concerns a period in the Netherlands that involved many developments over time as well as changes in the system in the housing and labour markets. We review these developments in this section.

The Dutch labour market can be described as a market with a high level of unemployment insurance benefits. The system was changed in two stages in the period of analysis. The original system was subdivided into three systems depending on the duration of unemployment and former work experience (OECD 1997). These systems are called (1) unemployment insurance, (2) unemployment assistance, and (3) social assistance. Individuals who worked at least 26 out of the last 52 weeks were eligible for unemployment insurance for at least 6 months. After this period individuals were eligible for an extended period of unemployment insurance if they worked at least four out of the last five years prior to the start of the unemployment spell. The duration of the extended period of unemployment insurance depends on the number of years in paid employment. Individuals who have only 5–10 years of paid employment experience receive an extended period of 3 months, and individuals with over 10 but less than 15 years receive an extended period of 6 months. For every additional five years of paid employment the duration is extended by 6 months, with a maximum of 4 years. This implies a total maximum duration of 4.5 years for individuals with over 40 years of work experience. The level of unemployment insurance is 70 per cent of gross income before the start of the unemployment spell. After the period of unemployment insurance, individuals may be eligible for unemployment assistance. The eligibility conditions are the same as for the extended period of unemployment insurance. However, unlike the extended period of unemployment insurance, the duration is always equal to one year, with the exception that older workers (i.e. older than 57 years of age at the moment of the start of the unemployment spell) cannot run out of these benefits at all. The level of the unemployment assistance benefit is equal to 70 per cent of the gross minimum wage (e.g. 688 euros in 1995). After the period of unemployment assistance, individuals receive social assistance. The amount is approximately the same as the amount of unemployment assistance, but the eligibility rules are different. For example, individuals who own wealth over a certain amount (4,090 euros in 1993) are not eligible for social assistance. In addition, the own dwelling is disregarded only up to a certain maximum. If the value of the house minus the mortgage exceeds this maximum, the recipient of social assistance should use this money to support his or her own subsistence.

The new system was introduced in 1996. This means that individuals who started their unemployment spell after 1996 were treated by the new rules. The main difference between the new and the old system is that the unemployment assistance system in the Netherlands no longer exists. This means that young individuals (i.e. individuals with less than 5–10 years of paid employment) do not have a long trajectory of non-means-tested unemployment benefits. In addition, unlike in the old system, workers older than 57 years of age at the start of the unemployment spell can run out of non-means-tested benefits. In order to compensate for this, workers with more than 40 years of work experience at the start of the unemployment spell receive 5 years instead of 4.5 years of unemployment benefits in the new system.

Dutch unemployment figures varied a lot in the period of analysis. The unemployment rate was 7.6 per cent in 1989 and then decreased to 6.5 per cent in 1991. Thereafter it increased to 8.5 per cent in 1994. Since that period there has been a sharp decrease in all years of our analysis, and it went down as low as 3.4 per cent at the end of 2000.

The period of analysis is a period in which house prices increased without any interruption. Figure 5.1 shows the development of house prices over this period. At the end of the Eighties the average price of a house was around 70,000 euros, while it was 190,000 euros in the year 2000. Measured in 1990 euros, we find that house prices roughly doubled over the period of analysis. At the same time, homeownership increased from around 44 per cent in the early Nineties to 54 per cent in 2002 (Belot and Ederveen 2005). Individuals who buy a house face a number of taxes and fees that need to be paid. The largest part of this is due to the property transfer tax which equals 6 per cent over our sample period.[1] In addition to this there are notary and mortgage fees. Note that some of these fees are tax-deductible, and hence the real costs can differ from the monetary outlays. Belot and Ederveen (2005) calculate the total costs to be equal to 9 per cent of the purchase of the house, which is average for the OECD countries they consider.

5.3. The Data

I use a Dutch dataset known as the Income Panel Register Database. This database is gathered from the registers of the tax office and stored at Statistics Netherlands for statistical research. Virtually any question asked of individuals

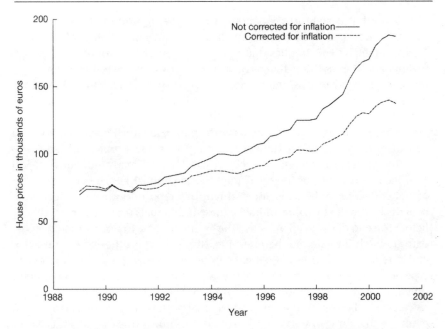

Figure 5.1. The development of house prices over the period 1989–2000. The corrected series are measured in 1990 euros

who are in the payroll tax system is included in the dataset. In addition, some information not filled in by the respondents but known by the tax authorities is also in the dataset. The period that is available extends from 1 January 1989 to 31 December 2000.

For my analysis I use only a part of the total dataset. It is set up as follows: from the total dataset Statistics Netherlands draws a sample of registration numbers. The size of the sample is around 75,000, and this is approximately equal to 1 per cent of the Dutch labour force. Together with the individuals drawn directly from this dataset, Statistics Netherlands adds those individuals who are in the same household. Hence, individuals in large households are oversampled. The total size of the dataset is approximately 270,000 individuals for each year.

Individuals have to fill in their income and the source of income they earned as well as the start and end of the period in which they earned this type of income. In this setup, individuals who earned a particular type of income the whole year have a start date of 1 January and an end date of 31 December. I match the different years in order to derive the employment and unemployment spells. It is important to realize that unemployment is not a source

117

of income but a state in the labour market, being unimportant to the tax office. Hence, there is more than one income source that matches the state of unemployment. This implies that individuals report transitions even though for our analysis nothing happens. In those cases, we take this as an ongoing spell. Related to this, many individuals report very small breaks in their unemployment benefits collection, after which they continue receiving these benefits. This is particularly the case at the start and end of every calendar year. I take these spells as ongoing whenever the period in which no unemployment benefits were collected is no longer than 3 weeks. A final problem with the construction of the unemployment spells is that relatively many individuals report 1 January as the start of their collection period and 31 December as their last day of collection of benefits, after which they report no further collection of benefits in the next year. Most likely, these individuals found their job already before the end of the year, but since they were not able to reconstruct the exact date at which they started their new job, they just report the end of the year as end date of the collection of benefits. In order to show the importance of this type of non-perfect information of the tax registers, I illustrate the constructed unemployment spells ignoring this problem. These are illustrated in Figure 5.2. As can easily be seen, there are relatively many individuals with exactly 1 year of unemployment benefits collection, and the same is true for 2, 3, and 4 years. When I exclude the individuals who report the end of the collection period as being 31 December (and who did not receive any benefits at the start of the next year), then I obtain the picture as found in Figure 5.3. This picture looks more like a normal histogram of unemployment spells. I take the problem of non-perfect information into account in my empirical analysis to be discussed in Section 5.4.

I use the first ten unemployment spells of individuals over the period 1989 to 2000. I exclude the spells of individuals who were reported to be a child of or raised by the head of the household at the start of the unemployment spell. These individuals are usually in a different situation from the population of individuals that we tend to describe by the model. The number of unemployment spells are reported in Table 5.1. In total we have around 20,000 individuals with at least one unemployment spell, and as can be seen from the table, there are a substantial number of recidivists in our dataset. The average age of the sample is around 38 years, and it increases when we look at individuals who have multiple spells. The percentage of females is somewhat over 40 per cent for the first unemployment duration and drops for the later unemployment durations. Almost half of the observations in the first unemployment spell are from individuals who are head of the household. It increases for the later unemployment spells. There is no clear pattern for the other two types of positions within the household. The variables for employment type (i.e. civil servant, employed in the business sector, and self-employed)

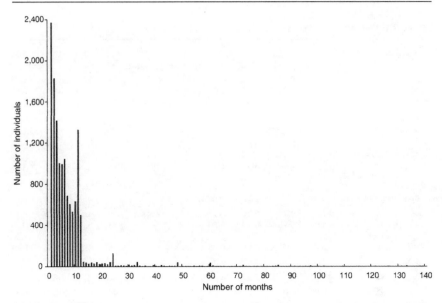

Figure 5.2. Histogram of the unemployment spells, including spells that terminate at the end of December

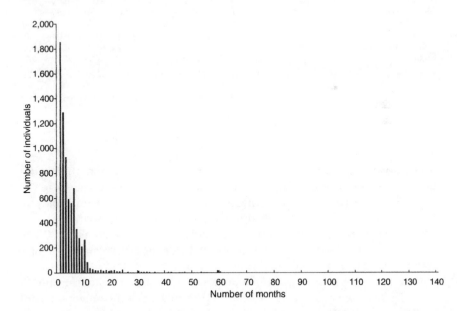

Figure 5.3. Histogram of the unemployment spells after exclusion of spells that terminate at the end of December

Table 5.1. Descriptive statistics for the unemployment spells

Employment spell	1	2	3	4	5	6	7	8	9	10
Age	38.33	39.93	42.15	44.47	46.49	47.29	46.44	45.77	45.18	46.73
Female	0.42	0.43	0.43	0.42	0.38	0.34	0.32	0.31	0.28	0.32
Children	0.36	0.45	0.45	0.43	0.40	0.40	0.46	0.48	0.51	0.43
Position in the household										
Single	0.08	0.07	0.07	0.06	0.07	0.07	0.05	0.03	0.04	0.04
Head of household	0.48	0.51	0.52	0.55	0.59	0.63	0.65	0.69	0.70	0.68
Partner	0.28	0.31	0.33	0.33	0.30	0.26	0.27	0.25	0.22	0.26
Type of employment										
Civil servant	0.11	0.12	0.12	0.13	0.14	0.14	0.15	0.17	0.17	0.16
Employed in business sector	0.17	0.18	0.19	0.20	0.21	0.22	0.23	0.23	0.24	0.24
Self-employed	0.04	0.04	0.05	0.05	0.05	0.06	0.06	0.06	0.08	0.08
Regions										
Groningen	0.04	0.04	0.04	0.05	0.04	0.05	0.05	0.06	0.08	0.07
Friesland	0.04	0.05	0.05	0.06	0.06	0.07	0.09	0.11	0.14	0.16
Drenthe	0.01	0.03	0.03	0.03	0.03	0.04	0.04	0.06	0.07	0.04
Overijssel	0.07	0.07	0.08	0.08	0.08	0.08	0.10	0.11	0.10	0.13
Flevoland	0.02	0.02	0.02	0.02	0.02	0.02	0.02	0.02	0.01	0.00
Gelderland	0.12	0.13	0.12	0.12	0.12	0.12	0.12	0.09	0.08	0.09
Utrecht	0.06	0.06	0.05	0.05	0.04	0.03	0.02	0.03	0.01	0.02
Noord-Holland	0.16	0.14	0.14	0.13	0.12	0.12	0.10	0.10	0.08	0.10
Zuid-Holland	0.21	0.19	0.17	0.17	0.16	0.15	0.13	0.11	0.12	0.10
Zeeland	0.02	0.03	0.03	0.03	0.03	0.04	0.03	0.02	0.03	0.05
Noord-Brabant	0.17	0.17	0.19	0.19	0.20	0.21	0.21	0.19	0.18	0.14
Limburg	0.08	0.08	0.08	0.08	0.09	0.09	0.09	0.09	0.10	0.10
Number of observations	19,869	10,972	6,817	4,290	2,672	1,572	825	448	250	135

indicate whether individuals were ever employed in this sector. This definition is convenient since it abstracts from the problem that individuals in the registers do not have any employment type whenever they are unemployed. I distinguish between the twelve different regions in the Netherlands.

I define a transition to the local labour market when it is within the COROP area in the Netherlands. These are areas that divide the Netherlands into forty different regions that are economically related.

Table 5.2 lists the unemployment durations as well as the number of individuals with at least one unemployment spell. In general the unemployment spell decreases with the number of unemployment spells that someone has already experienced. Although there are some exceptions, the unemployment spells are shorter for the individuals who are homeowners.

Table 5.2. Numbers and average unemployment durations for the total dataset, homeowners and non-homeowners

	Total		Homeowner		Non-homeowner	
	number	duration	number	duration	number	duration
1	48,831	26.06	18,200	14.63	36,631	32.86
2	22,897	20.71	9,328	15.64	13,569	24.19
3	12,911	19.01	5,551	17.22	7,360	20.37
4	7,731	19.25	3,487	17.65	4,244	20.57
5	4,610	18.60	2,103	16.96	2,507	20.18
6	2,760	17.29	1,276	15.86	1,484	18.52
7	1,497	16.25	743	14.80	754	14.08
8	852	15.45	434	13.80	418	17.17
9	486	14.80	269	15.01	217	14.54

5.4. Empirical implementation

The analysis is based on the joint distribution of homeownership versus renting and the distribution of unemployment spells. We denote by H the status at the housing market. In addition we use $T = \min(T_L, T_N)$ for the unemployment duration, where T_L is the unemployment duration that terminates due to a transition to the local labour market, and T_N is an unemployment duration that terminates due to a transition to the non-local labour market. The vector x is used for the set of characteristics that have an impact on the decision to become a homeowner, whereas x_1 is used for the set of characteristics that have an impact on the unemployment duration (excluding homeownership). The set of variables included in x_1 is a subset of the variables included in x. The variable V contains the unobserved time-independent characteristics related to the outcome vector (H, T). The dimension of this variable is equal to 3, and we denote V_i; $i = 0, 1, 2$ for the scalars of unobserved heterogeneity related to (1) the housing decision, (2) the duration of an unemployment spell that terminates in a transition to the local labour market, (3) the duration of an unemployment spell that terminates in a transition to the non-local labour market. The distribution of V is denoted by G.

I model the housing decision as a probit model. This implies that the time-dependent individual characteristics that influence the housing decision are assumed to be drawn from a standard normal distribution that is independent of V. I denote by H^* the nuisance parameter, with $H = 1$ if $H^* > 0$, and zero otherwise. I specify this parameter as $H^* = x\beta_0 + v_0 + u$ with $u \sim N(0, 1)$. The unemployment duration T is modelled as a competing risks model (Lancaster 1990). I denote the hazard rates out of unemployment to employment in the local and non-local labour market by θ_L and θ_N. I use the following mixed proportional hazards specification for the local labour market

$$\theta_L(H, x_1, t, v_1) = \exp(\xi(H, x_1, \gamma_1) + x_1\beta_1)\psi_L(t, H)v_1$$

where β_1 is a vector of coefficients that corresponds to the set of characteristics x_1. The vector γ_1 measures the impact of homeownership on the outflow out of unemployment to the local labour market. The function ξ represents the interdependence between x_1 and H. In particular we allow the relationship between unemployment duration and homeownership to be dependent on regional characteristics. The function ψ_L is the baseline hazard. I allow homeowners to have different baseline hazards. The main reason for this more flexible specification is related to the difference in unemployment benefits collection of the homeowners as discussed in the previous sections. I use a piecewise constant baseline hazard function for our analysis. A similar representation for the non-local labour market is assumed:

$$\theta_N(x_1, t, v_2) = \exp(\xi(H, x_1, \gamma_2) + x_1\beta_2)\psi_N(t, H)v_2$$

where β_2 is a vector of coefficients, and the function ψ_N is the baseline hazard for this market. For individuals who had no terminating unemployment spells at the end of December, the conditional likelihood contributions equal

$$
\begin{aligned}
L_i(x_i, x_{1,i}, v) = {} & \Phi(x_i\beta_0 + v_0)^{H_i}(1 - \Phi(x_i\beta_0 + v_0))^{(1-H_i)} \\
& \times \left\{\theta_L(H, x_{1,i}, s, v_1)\right\}^{d_{2,i}(1-d_{3,i})(1-d_{4,i})} \\
& \times \exp\left(-\int_0^{t_i} \theta_L(H, x_{1,i}, s, v_1)ds\right) \\
& \times \left\{\theta_N(H, x_{1,i}, s, v_2)\right\}^{(1-d_{2,i})(1-d_{3,i})(1-d_{4,i})} \\
& \times \exp\left(-\int_0^{t_i} \theta_N(H, x_{1,i}, s, v_2)ds\right)
\end{aligned}
$$

where d_2 is equal to 1 if the individual transits to a job in the local labour market and zero if the transit is to the non-local labour market. The variable d_3 indicates right censoring.

As stated in the data section there are relatively many individuals with unemployment spells that terminate at the end of the year. It is unlikely that these individuals really found a job in that period. Instead of taking the reported unemployment spell and using the conditional likelihood contributions as described above, I assume that these individuals ended their spells at some stage over the year. I correct the likelihood contributions for these individuals accordingly.

For the parameterization of the model, we use a two-point distribution for the unobserved heterogeneity terms (as in Munch et al., Chapter 4 above).

Hence, the joint distribution of V has eight mass points (not necessarily with positive probability). For the identification of the model I do not include a constant in x and x_1, and I restrict the baseline hazards to equal 1 in the first period. These restrictions are sufficient for identification and hence the estimates for the unobserved heterogeneity distribution. This implies that the mean of the unobserved heterogeneity distribution can be interpreted in the same way as the constant term in regression analysis.

In order to avoid problems with left censoring, I ignore unemployment spells that are ongoing at the moment individuals first enter the panel. Although these spells have a likelihood contribution that can be calculated from the analysis of Ridder (1984) (see also Lancaster 1990), the assumptions underlying these calculations are restrictive.

Some individuals leave unemployment through non-participation instead of through employment. We assume that these individuals are right-censored. This is a valid assumption when the unobserved characteristics that determine the hazard of a transition to non-participation are independent of the unobserved characteristics that determine the other hazards. This assumption is not always valid, as discussed in, for example, Frijters and Van der Klaauw (2006).

Including multiple spells has the advantage that some of the identifying assumptions related to a simple single spell duration model no longer hold. Especially, the restriction that x_1 and t need to be proportional is no longer necessary (see Honore 1993 and Van den Berg 2001). Define $L^U_{ij_u}$ as the likelihood contribution of individual i for unemployment spell j_u. This contribution is the same as L_i as defined in the previous subsection. In addition, $L^E_{ij_u}$ is defined as the likelihood contribution of individual i for employment spell j_e. The total likelihood contribution of individual i equals:

$$L_i = \int \prod_{j_u=1}^{M_u} L^U_{ij_u}(v_0, v_1, v_2)$$

with M_u the number of unemployment spells. In another paper, I discuss the additional assumptions necessary for the estimation of the parameters (see Van Vuuren 2007).

5.5. Results

I estimate our reduced form model for the first ten unemployment spells as described in the previous section. We do not estimate the hazard of leaving unemployment to non-participation. Table 5.3 lists the results of this exercise. The figures are measured in terms of the monthly hazard rates. We find a strong and significant impact of the fraction of homeownership on the likelihood that someone is a homeowner. The presence of children has a positive impact on the likelihood of owning a home, being female slightly decreases this likelihood. Individuals who received a scholarship for higher education in the period of analysis have a higher likelihood of owning a home. In addition, we find that age does not have an important impact on the decision as to whether an individual owns a home. The single exception is the youngest age group, which has a much smaller probability of owning a house. Single individuals as well as heads of households are less likely to own a home. In addition, individuals who were ever working in the private sector or were self-employed have a high likelihood of owning a house. Note that the baseline here contains individuals who were managers and individuals who never stated that they were self-employed or working in either the private or public sector. There are some differences between regions, but it is not related to urbanization in these different regions.

I find that homeowners have higher hazard rates out of unemployment to a job in the local labour market. The impact is significant but not very large. The presence of children in the household has a negative impact, and being female has a negative impact on the hazard rate for a job in the local labour market as well. Whether an individual received a scholarship for higher education has virtually no impact on the hazard rate in the local labour market. This hazard rate decreases with the age of an individual. Singles and heads of households have a lower hazard to leave unemployment for the local labour market, while individuals who ever worked in the private sector have a higher hazard rate. Again, there are some differences between the regions.

Homeownership has a negative but insignificant impact on the hazard of leaving unemployment for the non-local labour market. Note that although the point estimate is about the same in absolute values compared to the point estimate we found for the local labour market, the comparison between these two estimates is somewhat difficult. This is related to the fact that the levels of unobserved heterogeneity components also differ (as can be seen from the last row of Table 5.3). Both the presence of children and being female have a positive impact on the hazard of leaving unemployment for the non-local labour market. Both results are somewhat surprising, and not in line with the results of Van den Berg and Van Vuuren (1998), who find that females face higher non-monetary costs of moving to a new residence. Older individuals have lower hazard rates for leaving unemployment for the non-local labour market. In addition, spouses of heads of households have a lower hazard rate for leaving unemployment for the non-local labour market. This is in line with the results of Van den Berg and Van Vuuren (1998). Individuals who stated that they worked in the private sector have a low hazard of leaving unemployment for the non-local labour market. To a smaller extend this is also true for civil servants and the self-employed.

The baseline hazards out of unemployment into the local and non-local labour markets have the same shape. They both increase in the first year and

Table 5.3. Results of the reduced form duration model

	Homeowner	θ_L	θ_N
Fraction of homeowners	7.564	.	.
	(0.138)		
Homeowner	.	0.050	−0.134
		(0.023)	(0.083)
Personal characteristics			
Presence of children	0.448	−0.054	−0.259
	(0.050)	(0.015)	(0.060)
Female	−0.068	−0.295	0.658
	(0.055)	(0.018)	(0.066)
Higher education	0.164	−0.009	−0.663
	(0.041)	(0.014)	(0.069)
Age groups (base: below 30)			
Between 30 and 40	1.603	−0.198	−0.409
	(0.052)	(0.016)	(0.059)
Between 40 and 55	1.673	−0.420	−1.380
	(0.063)	(0.020)	(0.090)
55 and over	1.687	−1.118	−2.259
	(0.071)	(0.025)	(0.125)
Position in household (base: spouse of head)			
Single	−2.824	−0.258	0.757
	(0.066)	(0.026)	(0.091)
Head of household	−0.884	−0.147	0.629
	(0.050)	(0.018)	(0.067)
Occupation (base: manager and other)			
Private sector	0.181	0.053	−0.519
	(0.046)	(0.016)	(0.077)
Civil servant	0.102	0.018	−0.448
	(0.056)	(0.019)	(0.089)
Self-employed	0.379	−0.020	−0.326
	(0.078)	(0.028)	(0.113)
Regions (base: Groningen)			
Friesland	0.249	0.020	−0.323
	(0.100)	(0.041)	(0.173)
Drenthe	0.562	−0.033	0.186
	(0.112)	(0.047)	(0.167)
Overijssel	0.232	0.086	−0.003
	(0.099)	(0.038)	(0.147)
Flevoland	0.217	0.001	0.442
	(0.186)	(0.060)	(0.188)
Gelderland	0.313	0.067	−0.091
	(0.089)	(0.036)	(0.140)
Utrecht	0.057	0.038	−0.117
	(0.115)	(0.041)	(0.160)
Noord-Holland	0.491	0.004	0.047
	(0.088)	(0.035)	(0.134)
Zuid-Holland	0.532	−0.005	−0.164
	(0.085)	(0.034)	(0.132)
Zeeland	0.455	0.039	−0.166
	(0.158)	(0.049)	(0.195)

(Cont.)

Table 5.3. *(Continued)*

	Homeowner	θ_L	θ_N
Noord-Brabant	0.390	0.077	−0.102
	(0.086)	(0.035)	(0.134)
Limburg	0.224	0.012	−0.353
	(0.104)	(0.038)	(0.154)
Baseline hazard			
Homeowners			
3–6 months	.	1.996	2.207
		(0.033)	(0.226)
6–9 months	.	1.914	3.109
		(0.048)	(0.431)
9–12 months	.	4.317	10.058
		(0.125)	(1.456)
12–15 months	.	2.911	6.431
		(0.131)	(2.072)
15–18 months	.	0.311	1.946
		(0.020)	(0.472)
Renters			
3–6 months	.	1.762	1.844
		(0.031)	(0.167)
6–9 months	.	2.081	4.029
		(0.050)	(0.416)
9–12 months	.	3.950	6.105
		(0.111)	(0.896)
12–15 months	.	2.091	1.825
		(0.100)	(0.817)
15–18 months	.	0.336	1.159
		(0.018)	(0.251)
Mass points			
$v_{.,0}$	−8.656	0.393	0.011
	(0.125)	(0.015)	(0.002)
$v_{.,1}$	−2.336	1.123	0.093
	(0.100)	(0.043)	(0.013)
Probabilities			
$P(V_0 = v_{00}, V_1 = v_{10}, V_2 = v_{20})$	0.088	.	.
	(0.007)		
$P(V_0 = v_{00}, V_1 = v_{11}, V_2 = v_{21})$	0.139	.	.
	(0.010)		
$P(V_0 = v_{01}, V_1 = v_{10}, V_2 = v_{20})$	0.465	.	.
	(0.011)		
$P(V_0 = v_{01}, V_1 = v_{11}, V_2 = v_{21})$	0.307	.	.
	(0.011)		
Wald Tests for joint significance			
All variables	6,447	3,461	137

then decrease in later quarters. Remember that this is the period in which for most of the individuals the unemployment insurance benefits are terminated. After this period, individuals receive social assistance. The increase is higher for the non-local labour market which suggests that unemployed workers start looking for a job primarily in the local labour market for the first months of the unemployment spells. Thereafter the focus on the non-local labour market increases gradually. The baseline hazard fluctuates much more over time for homeowners than for renters. This may be due to the fact that individuals who are homeowners usually receive lower benefits from social assistance and hence become less selective with respect to the offered jobs.

I estimated a second model specification in order to check the robustness of the results. In the second specification, I estimate the impact of homeownership on the hazard rate of leaving unemployment, taking account of the different regions in the Netherlands. The results of this specification are not radically different from the previous exercise and are summarized in Table 5.4. However, I find some differences between the different regions. The impact of homeownership on the hazard rate of leaving unemployment for the local labour market is positive for almost all of the regions. It is significant for six out of the twelve regions. I find very mixed results for the non-local labour market. There are many regions in which there is a surprisingly positive impact, but this impact is never significant. The impact is negative for five regions, and it is significant for the largest region of Zuid-Holland.

5.6. Estimation of counterfactual hazard rates

In order to increase the insight into our results, I calculate the counterfactual probabilities of leaving unemployment for the two states. Denote $\tilde{h}$ as the (counterfactual) tenure state of an individual. This variable is equal to 1 if we consider the individual to be a homeowner and zero otherwise. The probability that an individual observed and considered to be a homeowner has to wait t periods for an acceptable job offer from the local labour market equals

$$P(T_L \leq t|x; H = 1; \tilde{h} = 1) = \sum_{v_0,v_1,v_2} P(T_L \leq t|x; \tilde{h} = 1; V_0 = v_0; V_1 = v_1; V_2 = v_2)$$
$$\times \frac{P(H = 1|V_0 = v_0)P(V_0 = v_0; V_1 = v_1; V_2 = v_2)}{P(H = 1)}$$

The counterfactual distribution of receiving an acceptable job offer from the local labour market of someone being observed to be a homeowner when he would no longer own a house equals

$$P(T_L \leq t|x; H = 1; \tilde{h} = 0) = \sum_{v_0,v_1,v_2} P(T_L \leq t|x; \tilde{h} = 0; V_0 = v_0; V_1 = v_1; V_2 = v_2)$$
$$\times \frac{P(H = 1|V_0 = v_0)P(V_0 = v_0; V_1 = v_1; V_2 = v_2))}{P(H = 1)}$$

Table 5.4. Results of the reduced form duration model

	Homeowner	θ_L	θ_N
Fraction of homeowners	7.570	.	.
	(0.138)		
Homeownership			
Groningen	.	0.032	−0.127
		(0.081)	(0.305)
Friesland	.	0.057	0.204
		(0.052)	(0.250)
Drenthe	.	0.048	0.203
		(0.070)	(0.242)
Overijssel	.	0.166	0.166
		(0.044)	(0.178)
Flevoland	.	−0.059	0.086
		(0.102)	(0.300)
Gelderland	.	0.071	−0.015
		(0.036)	(0.151)
Utrecht	.	0.132	0.211
		(0.055)	(0.215)
Noord-Holland	.	0.088	−0.012
		(0.035)	(0.129)
Zuid-Holland	.	0.076	−0.397
		(0.030)	(0.137)
Zeeland	.	0.079	0.368
		(0.075)	(0.305)
Noord-Brabant	.	0.136	0.008
		(0.032)	(0.126)
Limburg	.	0.111	−0.207
		(0.043)	(0.196)
Personal characteristics			
Presence of children	1.602	−0.198	−0.406
	(0.050)	(0.015)	(0.060)
Female	1.671	−0.418	−1.361
	(0.055)	(0.018)	(0.067)
Higher education	0.447	−0.055	−0.264
	(0.041)	(0.014)	(0.069)
Age groups (base: below 30)			
Between 30 and 40	−0.068	−0.293	0.656
	(0.053)	(0.016)	(0.059)
Between 40 and 55	0.164	−0.009	−0.661
	(0.063)	(0.020)	(0.091)
55 and over	1.664	−1.117	−2.250
	(0.071)	(0.025)	(0.125)
Position in household (base: spouse of head)			
Single	−2.824	−0.257	0.755
	(0.066)	(0.026)	(0.091)
Head of household	−0.883	−0.146	0.625
	(0.050)	(0.018)	(0.067)
Occupation (base: manager and other)			
Private sector	0.180	0.053	−0.515
	(0.046)	(0.015)	(0.078)
Civil servant	0.102	0.018	−0.453
	(0.056)	(0.019)	(0.089)
Self-employed	0.379	−0.020	−0.319
	(0.078)	(0.028)	(0.113)

(Cont.)

Table 5.4. *(Continued)*

	Homeowner	θ_L	θ_N
Regions (base: Groningen)			
Friesland	0.251	0.020	−0.529
	(0.100)	(0.060)	(0.256)
Drenthe	0.563	−0.029	−0.021
	(0.112)	(0.069)	(0.242)
Overijssel	0.234	0.027	−0.178
	(0.099)	(0.055)	(0.198)
Flevoland	0.220	0.071	0.299
	(0.186)	(0.092)	(0.286)
Gelderland	0.313	0.057	−0.173
	(0.089)	(0.054)	(0.190)
Utrecht	0.059	−0.002	−0.304
	(0.115)	(0.059)	(0.217)
Noord-Holland	0.493	−0.015	−0.040
	(0.088)	(0.052)	(0.177)
Zuid-Holland	0.534	−0.020	−0.127
	(0.086)	(0.051)	(0.173)
Zeeland	0.454	0.027	−0.472
	(0.160)	(0.075)	(0.289)
Noord-Brabant	0.392	0.032	−0.205
	(0.086)	(0.052)	(0.182)
Limburg	0.228	−0.018	−0.351
	(0.104)	(0.056)	(0.206)
Baseline hazard			
Homeowners			
3–6 months	.	2.042	1.428
		(0.157)	(0.772)
6–9 months	.	1.572	2.145
		(0.187)	(1.369)
9–12 months	.	5.183	6.306
		(0.652)	(6.369)
12–15 months	.	1.747	4.957
		(0.493)	(33.148)
15–18 months	.	0.271	4.939
		(0.074)	(2.527)
Renters			
3–6 months	.	1.869	1.995
		(0.023)	(0.137)
6–9 months	.	2.010	3.709
		(0.037)	(0.320)
9–12 months	.	4.099	7.610
		(0.090)	(0.836)
12–15 months	.	2.459	3.422
		(0.084)	(0.913)
15–18 months	.	0.330	1.330
		(0.014)	(0.232)
Mass points			
$v_{\cdot,0}$	−8.659	0.393	0.012
	(0.125)	(0.020)	(0.002)
$v_{\cdot,1}$	−2.339	1.118	0.096
	(0.100)	(0.058)	(0.016)

(Cont.)

Table 5.4. (Continued)

	Homeowner	θ_L	θ_N
Probabilities			
$P(V_0 = v_{00}, V_1 = v_{10}, V_2 = v_{20})$	0.083	.	.
	(0.007)		
$P(V_0 = v_{00}, V_1 = v_{11}, V_2 = v_{21})$	0.213	.	.
	(0.010)		
$P(V_0 = v_{01}, V_1 = v_{10}, V_2 = v_{20})$	0.474	.	.
	(0.010)		
$P(V_0 = v_{01}, V_1 = v_{11}, V_2 = v_{21})$	0.231	.	.
	(0.011)		
Wald Tests for joint significance			
All variables	6,434	3,459	137
Homeownership variables	.	39	15

Hence, the difference between the two equations is the net effect of owning a house on the arrival rate of acceptable job offers from the local labour market. Using these techniques it is also possible to find the same difference for the non-local labour market. The actual and counterfactual distributions can also be calculated using exactly the same method, but changing $H = 1$ into $H = 0$ in the equations above. Finally, the probability of receiving an acceptable offer can be calculated using

$$P(T \leq t|x;, H = 1; \tilde{h} = 1) = 1 - \left(1 - P(T_L \leq t|x;, H = 1; \tilde{h} = 1)\right)$$
$$\times \left(1 - P(T_N \leq t|x;, H = 1; \tilde{h} = 1)\right)$$

The results of these simulations are shown in Figures 5.4–5.7. I find that homeowners reduce their probability of receiving a job offer from the local labour market for any month of unemployment duration when they would become renters. On the contrary, the probability of receiving a job offer from the non-local labour market increases for low levels of the unemployment duration. This probability is reduced for higher levels of unemployment duration. The pictures for the renters are not much different from the mirror image of those of the homeowners.

From these figures it is also possible to calculate the likelihood that a worker finds a job in the non-local labour market. This likelihood equals 7.4 per cent for a homeowner, while it is 8.8 per cent for a renter. About 0.5 per cent of this difference can be attributed to differences in characteristics between buyers and sellers.

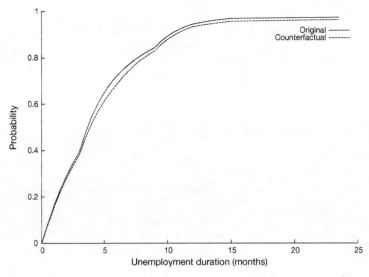

Figure 5.4. Actual and counterfactual probability of receiving an acceptable job offer from the local labour market for homeowners

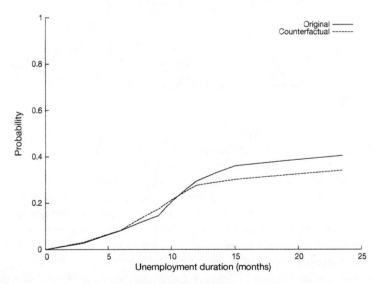

Figure 5.5. Actual and counterfactual probability of receiving an acceptable job offer from the non-local labour market for homeowners

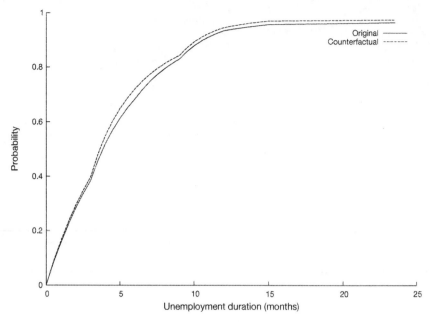

Figure 5.6. Actual and counterfactual probability of receiving an acceptable job offer from the local labour market for renters

5.7. Conclusions

In this paper I estimated the model of Munch *et al.* (Chapter 4 above) using a Dutch dataset. I used a register-based dataset of the Netherlands for the period 1989 to 2001. It contains a random draw from the population of taxpayers in the Netherlands (i.e. everyone who is over 15 and receives income from any possible source). I found very similar results for the Netherlands as were found earlier for Denmark by Munch *et al.* (Chapter 4 above). Homeowners are in general more likely to find a job in the local labour market, but have a smaller likelihood of finding a job in the non-local labour market. The overall impact of homeownership on the hazard rate of leaving unemployment is positive, and this is in contrast to the well-known Oswald hypothesis. I find an inverted U-shape for the duration dependence of unemployment: in the first couple of months the likelihood of finding a job increases, but it decreases after an individual has been unemployed for more than a year. The differences are larger for homeowners than for renters.

My conclusion is that the Oswald hypothesis is not correct when we look at European data. However, it is still an open question why this is the case. In my working paper I claim that this may be due to an endogeneity problem.

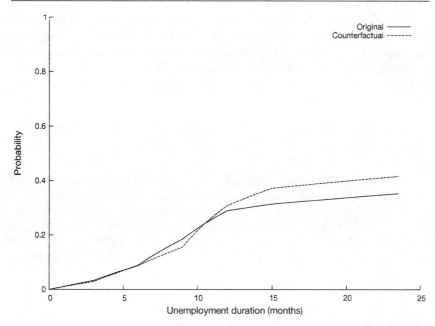

Figure 5.7. Actual and counterfactual probability of receiving an acceptable job offer from the non-local labour market for renters

Individuals make decisions about their tenure status while taking account of their labour market perspectives, and this can result in a selective sample of homeowners. This endogeneity problem is not that easy to solve in general. I show that the use of multiple spells can be helpful, but without further information about the reasons why people change tenure status there is no guarantee that the endogeneity bias is absent when multiple unemployment durations are used. In addition, there is a possibility that the original Oswald hypothesis did not take into account all important aspects for the differences in tenure status and the labour market. For example, homeowners may face liquidity constraints when they become long-term unemployed.

The results do not claim that the taxes that increase the transaction costs for buying a house are a very disturbing factor in the labour market. Even though I find that homeowners are not very likely to accept a job very far from their present home, renters are not very likely to accept such a job either. I found that homeowners have a 7.4 per cent probability of accepting a job in the non-local labour market, while it is 8.8 per cent for renters. This is in line with the findings of Van den Berg and Van Vuuren (1998), who find that the non-monetary costs of moving to another house are relatively high in comparison to the monetary costs.

My results may be influenced by the high level of regulation of the Dutch rental market. This price regulation is a cause for the existence of a shortage of supply of rental houses, and this may make renters less mobile as well. As a consequence, these renters may also be less willing to accept jobs for which they have to move. The strict interpretation of the Oswald hypothesis assumed an unregulated rental market.

Note

1. The property transfer tax is officially 5 per cent in the Netherlands, but a temporary supplement was charged from 1979 onwards. This temporary supplement was originally charged to help the government solve the budgetary problems just after the oil crisis, but at present the supplement can be interpreted as permanent. I assume in my empirical analysis that individuals never anticipated an end to this temporary increase in the property transfer tax. This seems a valid assumption in that the temporary period was already 10 years at the start of our sample period.

References

Belot, M., and Ederveen, S. (2005), 'Indicators of cultural and institutional barriers in OECD countries', CPB research memorandum (The Hague).

Blanchard, O. J., and Katz, L. R. (1992), 'Regional evolutions', Brookings Papers on Economic Activity, 1–75.

Frijters, P., and Van der Klaauw, B. (2006), 'Job search and non participation', *Economic Journal*, 116, 895–936.

——Lindeboom, M., and Van den Berg, G. J. (2000), 'Persistencies in the labour market', Working Paper (Amsterdam).

Green, R., and Hendershott, P. (2001), 'Home ownership and the duration of unemployment: a test of the Oswald hypothesis', Working Paper, Aberdeen University.

Honoré, B. (1993), 'Identification results for duration models with multiple spells', *Review of Economic Studies*, 60, 241–6.

Lancaster T. (1990), *The Econometric Analysis of Transition Data* (Cambridge: Cambridge University Press).

OECD (1997), *Making Work Pay* (Paris: OECD).

Oswald, A. J. (1999), 'The housing market and Europe's unemployment: a non-technical paper', Warwick University. Reproduced as Ch. 2 above.

Ridder, G. (1984), 'The distribution of single-spell duration data', in G. R. Neuman and N. C. Westergard-Nielsen (eds.), *Studies in Labour Market Dynamics* (Berlin: Springer-Verlag), 45–74.

Van den Berg, G. J. (2001), 'Duration models: specifications, identification and multiple durations', in J. J. Heckman and E. Leamer (eds.), *Handbook of Econometrics* (Amsterdam: North-Holland), 3381–460.

____ and Gorter, C. (1997), 'Job search and commuting time', *Journal of Business and Economic Statistics*, 15, 269–81.

____ and Van Vuuren A. P. (1998), 'Job search and the non-monetary costs with moving to a new residence', Working Paper, Free University, Amsterdam.

Van Vuuren, A. P. (2007), 'The relationship between expectations of labor market status, homeownership and the duration of unemployment', Working Paper, Amsterdam.

6

Do Homeowners Stay Unemployed Longer? Evidence Based on French Data[*]

Carole Brunet and Jean-Yves Lesueur

6.1. Introduction

Differences in structure relating to residential tenure status (respective share of homeowners and renters) have recently been proposed as an explanation of international or interregional differences in unemployment rates, especially in Europe and the United States.

Along these lines, Oswald (1996, 1997, 1998) obtained many results from macroeconomic data on countries belonging to the Organization for Economic Cooperation and Development (OECD): the correlation between unemployment levels or growth rates and homeowners' share is 0.2, both between and within countries. These results are based on a simple evaluation of the statistical relationship between the two variables or, alternatively, on estimations introducing countries or regions fixed-effects in order to control for unobserved heterogeneity. Nickell and Layard (1999) arrive at a similar result when studying twenty OECD countries: a 10 per cent change in the share of homeowners is associated with a variation of 1–1.5 per cent of the unemployment rate.

Although the hypothesis of a positive relationship between homeownership rate and unemployment rate, which is sometimes referred to as Oswald's hypothesis, is based on macroeconomic evidence, its theoretical foundations are mainly microeconomic. They relate to the idea that individual efficiency

[*] We would like to thank Professor Claude Montmarquette for his remarks and suggestions. The use of data from the TDE-MLT survey was made possible by the Research Directorate of the Ministry of Employment (DARES) and the General Planning Commission (CGP). The authors also thank François Dubujet (INSEE) and Muriel Chavret from the Paris Chamber of Solicitors for access to data on housing transactions.

in job search depends positively on individual spatial mobility. As homeowners are less mobile than renters because of higher mobility costs due to property ownership, they experience both higher unemployment rates and longer unemployment periods than renters. Other things being equal, an increase in the number of homeowners implies a decrease in the number of matches between job seekers and vacancies, which translates into a higher unemployment rate. This direct microeconomic mechanism is amplified by macroeconomic effects (changes in housing prices) and indirect effects (negative externalities due to traffic and congestion costs).

However, because of aggregation and selection bias, macroeconomic evidence can hardly be used as a proper test of microeconomic mechanisms underlying Oswald's hypothesis. Two major questions arise when microeconomic behaviour is to be inferred from aggregated data (Green and Hendershott 2001a, 2001b). The first question relates to restrictive aggregation conditions that have to be met for macroeconomic results to reflect individual behaviour. The second one concerns the choice process of individuals with respect to their residential tenure status: it is necessary to control for non-randomness of individuals' self-selection in order to obtain consistent estimates. Only microeconomic data can reveal individual heterogeneity and then allow proper treatment of the problem.

Green and Hendershott (2001a, 2001b) present a micro-econometric study that uses US data to evaluate the effect of housing tenure status on the length of individual unemployment spells. Their results are qualitatively in line with Oswald's hypothesis although the effect of homeownership on unemployment duration amounts to only one-eighth of that found with aggregated data. However, other micro-econometric studies have shown better outcomes in the labour market for homeowners: namely, lower unemployment probability and shorter unemployment spells (Van Leuvensteijn and Koning, Chapter 8 below) on the one hand, and a negative effect of homeowning on residential mobility (Van Ommeren 1996) on the other. In a recent contribution to this debate, Coulson and Fisher (2002) reject Oswald's hypothesis on the basis of econometric estimations successively based on US individual data from the Current Population Survey (CPS) (March 2000) and from the Panel Study of Income Dynamics (PSID) (1993). The results obtained with data from the CPS show that, whatever the specification used, the probability of unemployment is negatively correlated with homeownership. Moreover, the estimation of a wage equation reveals that homeowners receive, *ceteris paribus*, higher wages. Finally, the estimation of a Weibull duration model using data from the PSID confirms that unemployment spells are shorter for homeowners than for renters. However, these results should be considered with caution, as neither the endogenous nature of the residential tenure status nor unobservable heterogeneity is dealt with in the different estimations. In addition, sample building and a small number of observations (204),

138

75 per cent of which are censored, cast doubt on the consistency of the results. Thus, whereas Oswald's hypothesis seems overall consistent with stylized facts obtained from macroeconomic evidence, micro-econometric results fail to reveal the mechanisms that are supposed to be at play, or display ambiguous features.

This paradox calls for an analysis of interdependencies between housing tenure status and labour market behaviour. The matter is of special importance as the last decades have been characterized, in France as in most European countries, by a massive increase both in the share of homeowners and in the unemployment rate. Taking France as an example, the unemployment rate amounted to less than 5 per cent of the working population in the Fifties, against more than 10 per cent in the Nineties. Although the number of people becoming homeowners has been stationary during this last decade (Dubujet and Le Blanc 2000), the share of primary homes occupied by their owners increased from 30 per cent in 1955 to 55 per cent in 1996 (Louvot-Runavot 2001).

Part of this tendency is due to public policies aimed at facilitating home-ownership (preferential rate loans, subsidized loans, zero-interest-rate loans). This trend is also rooted in profound changes as regards the links between housing and labour markets, especially the expansion of suburbanization and daily commuting.

Since the late Sixties, many developments have taken place in the analysis of housing and real estate markets in order to take account of specific features of homes (durability, consumption and investment aspects, spatial fixity, heterogeneity, sensitivity to public interventions), which led to amending standard microeconomics in several ways (Smith *et al.* 1988; Goffette-Nagot 1994). Two main conclusions emerge once specific aspects associated with housing are acknowledged. First, homeowning means higher mobility costs relative to renting, and thus constitutes an impediment to mobility. As the choice of a particular residential status is by nature an inter-temporal one, people who decide to become homeowners may have, *ceteris paribus*, lower expectations about mobility or more optimistic views about their ability to deal with high costs should mobility be required. Secondly, the more or less constrained choice of a residential status is also a choice for a distance to different social locations, among which the workplace.

In the face of the diversity of factors involved in an analysis of links between residential tenure status and unemployment duration, we are left without a unique theoretical background in this regard. The objective of this study is thus to provide an analysis of the influence of the residential tenure status (owning or renting) of unemployed individuals on their probability of finding a job by using developments from search theory (Mortensen 1986) and its micro-econometric applications (Lancaster 1990). Such an orientation, which aims at including the spatial dimension in job search models, embraces the more

139

general framework of the spatial mismatch analysis (Holzer *et al.* 1994; Rogers 1997; Van den Berg and Gorter 1997; Bouabdallah *et al.* 2002; and Wasmer and Zenou 2002 and 2006). Taking account of housing and its specific features (heterogeneity, spatial fixity, durability) leads to an examination of mobility constraints on individuals according to their residential status and the effects on the duration of unemployment.

The outline of this paper is as follows. The first section reviews problems that arise when testing Oswald's hypothesis and suggests a procedure of estimation using duration models. The second section describes the sample's main features and offers a first non-parametric analysis of distinctive effects of residential status on the hazard rate of leaving unemployment. The third section presents estimation results from parametric duration models that control both for the endogenous selection rule underlying the choice of a residential status and for unobserved heterogeneity. The last section concludes by offering research perspectives in the light of the results obtained.

6.2. Estimation of an unemployment duration model with endogenous residential tenure status

The effect of residential tenure status on unemployment duration has received little attention in empirical studies, for two main reasons. First, interactions between housing and labour markets have become a research subject only recently, due to increased homeownership, expansion of both suburbanization and daily commuting. Secondly, their measurement encounters econometric problems resulting from the combination of a duration analysis and a simultaneous underlying decision-making process. We will first give an overview of econometric problems that arise in such an analysis and then present our estimation procedure.

6.2.1. *Empirical studies on the effect of homeownership on labour market outcomes*

Three main approaches have been taken in the applied literature about the effect of homeownership on labour market outcomes. The first one ignores the endogeneity issue of the residential status and directly examines its impact on wages or unemployment duration, as in Coulson and Fisher (2002). As mentioned in the introduction, there are good reasons to cast doubt on results obtained without taking into account individual self-selection in a particular housing arrangement.

In contrast to Coulson and Fisher (2002), the treatment of residential status endogeneity is central to the Green and Hendershott (2001*b*) study of US data. They estimate a two-regime duration model where the endogeneity of the choice of residential status is controlled for by introducing the appropriate inverse of Mill's ratio in each equation. Results confirm the endogeneity of the residential tenure status variable, which displays a negative but small effect on the hazard rate of leaving unemployment: unemployment spells of homeowners last on average 0.2 months longer than those of renters.

However, the introduction of Mill's ratio in a duration equation in order to account for individual self-selection implies a particular model specification (i.e. an accelerated failure time model) and residuals in order to follow the normal distribution. Besides, estimations conducted by Green and Hendershott do not account for censoring of the duration data, although it amounts to up to 20 per cent of the sample: censored observations are treated as completed or are simply deleted, which then causes another attrition bias. More generally, taking account of individual selection through a two-regime duration model makes the likelihood function quite hard to express. In referring to the specification adopted in Heckman and Borjas (1980) in the case of complete durations, the authors circumvent this difficulty by choosing a log-linear specification for duration, conditional on a Weibull distribution.

Lastly, Van Leuvensteijn and Koning (Chapter 8 below) and Munch, Rosholm, and Svarer (Chapter 4 above) use competing risks and discrete duration models to analyse employment and unemployment spells, while the choice of homeownership is simultaneously estimated using a logit equation. Endogeneity is accounted for by assuming that unobserved components of each equation follow a joint distribution summarized by a number of correlated mass points following Heckman and Singer (1984). This specification allows a full information procedure, with treatment of censoring and selection in homeownership.

However, this methodology proves hard to apply when the choice of a residential status is not binary, as the number of mass points to be estimated increases with the number of equations.

In the face of these restrictions, we adopt a more flexible estimation procedure that allows us to control both for censoring and for the endogeneity of a multiple residential status variable and to measure the effect of this multiple residential status on the length of an unemployment spell. The econometric method is based on the procedure suggested by Heckman and Robb (1985) to deal with self-selection.

6.2.2. Econometric specification

As we shall see in the descriptive statistics of the sample, the individuals in our sample are distributed between three types of residential tenure status: homeowner ($j = 1$), renter ($j = 2$), and housed free of charge ($j = 3$), which mainly concerns young workers living in their parents' home (30 per cent of the sample). So, residential tenure status results from a multinomial logit selection equation that conditions its choice (latent variable M_{ij}^*) to individual characteristics Z_i.

M_{ij}^* represents the utility differential that an individual i experiences when comparing utility level alternatively associated with residential status j, denoted by U_{ij}, or $m, j \neq m$, denoted by U_{im}.

We have:

$$M_{ij}^* = U_{ij} - U_{im} = \alpha' Z_i + \mu_{ij}, \quad \forall j \neq m, \ j = 1, 2, 3$$

And we observe:

$$M_{ij} = 1 \Leftrightarrow \mathrm{Prob}(U_{ij} > U_{im}) \Leftrightarrow \mathrm{Prob}(Y = j) = \frac{\exp^{\beta_j' Z_i}}{1 + \sum\limits_{m=1}^{J-1} \exp^{\beta_m' Z_i}}, \quad \forall j \neq m$$

The discrete selection variable is instrumented by variables Z_i that control for, besides individual features, perceived constraints to homeowning access and features of the local housing market. The estimated probabilities $\hat{M}_{ij}$ are then introduced for final estimation in a log-normal parametric duration model.[1] Besides observable characteristics, the presence of unobservable heterogeneity terms, v_i, is tested, adopting a Gamma distribution[2] for the v_i effects (Greene 1997, pp. 946–7). On these hypotheses, the following duration model is estimated:

$$DU_i = \left[1 + \frac{1}{k} \lambda_i \right]^{1-k} \lambda_i^{-1} \tag{6.1}$$

where DU_i is the duration of unemployment for individual i, $\frac{1}{k}$ is the Gamma variance of the unobserved component, and λ_i is the log-normal hazard rate defined as:

$$\lambda_i = \frac{1}{\sigma t_i} \frac{\varphi(w_i)}{1 - \phi(w_i)} \tag{6.2}$$

and:

$$w_i = \frac{\log t_i - \beta' X_i - \sum\limits_{k=1}^{3} \gamma_k \hat{M}_{ij}}{\sigma} \tag{6.3}$$

where X_i is a vector that represents variables of interest regarding labour market outcomes. Parametric estimation of the duration model under this specification makes it possible to obtain unbiased estimators for β and γ.

The flexibility of this method has several benefits, especially in our duration models framework: the procedure does not require a specific hypothesis on the distribution of residuals and allows non-linear transformations. Moreover, the procedure is simple to apply (having good instruments is still crucial, as in any instrumentation strategy) and offers a nice economic interpretation, as the instrumented variable that reflects individuals' choices is, in its own right, a variable of the econometric model.

The first criticism that can be levelled at this procedure is that it does not proceed to a rigorous statistical correction of the selection bias, as the estimated probability cannot represent the inverse of Mill's ratio. The extent to which the estimated probability corrects the bias is thus unknown.

The second criticism relates to uncertainties about the uniformity of the effect of the endogenous variable to be instrumented. Indeed, we implicitly assumed that once the bias due to non-randomness of the choice of a residential status is controlled for, the residential status has a similar effect on each subgroup. This allows an estimation of the average effect of the residential status on the whole sample. However, it is possible that individuals with different residential statuses experience different average effects. This heterogeneity seems all the more plausible if we model the decision to choose a particular residential status as a beneficial one. In this kind of heterogeneous model, the instrumental variable estimator can identify the average effect of the residential status only under a strong hypothesis, and the model should be specified differently in order to disentangle several parameters of interest. In the homogeneous model, these parameters are equivalent and reduce to the average effect on the whole population (Heckman 1990; Blundell and Costa Dias 2002).

Heckman (1990) provides some elements of response to each of these queries about the Heckman and Robb method. On the one hand, this method has proved efficient for the analysis of unions' influence on wages by producing results similar to those obtained from sophisticated procedures. On the other hand, variations of unobservable characteristics between the two subgroups in the main equation seem to contribute only slightly to the endogeneity of the variable whose effect is to be measured.

6.3. Sample description and non-parametric results

The data used in the econometric estimations come from three sources. Individual data have been taken from the survey *Trajectoires des demandeurs d'emploi-Marchés Locaux du Travail* (TDE-MLT) carried out by the Research Directorate of the Ministry of Employment (DARES) on a cohort of individuals who became unemployed between April and June 1995 and were followed for thirty-three months. Information about housing costs has been taken from a database built by the *Institut National de la Statistique et des Études Economiques* (INSEE) and the Paris Chamber of Solicitors. This is supplemented by data from the population census of 1999 and from the town censuses of 1988 and 1998, both held by INSEE.

The sample includes 3,965 individuals and is free of left-censoring regarding unemployment duration, as the initialization of the database matches the registration by individuals with the national employment agency.

The main descriptive statistics of the sample are presented before we proceed to a non-parametric estimation of the effect of residential status on unemployment duration.

6.3.1. *Sample descriptive statistics*

The average duration of an unemployment spell is between ten and eleven months (see Table 6.1 for a listing of the variables). Although 74 per cent of the individuals had returned to employment after unemployment spells, the average duration of which was about seven months, 26 per cent were still unemployed by the end of the survey, the average duration of the unemployment spell being twenty months. Some 58 per cent of the individuals in the sample receive unemployment benefits.

Educational attainment amounts to a technical qualification in the case of nearly half the individuals; 18 per cent have a university degree. The most frequent positions are those of workman, 44 per cent, and of employee, 39 per cent. Executives and liberal professionals account for only 5 per cent of the sample.

Unemployment was due to dismissal in 36 per cent of the cases and to contract termination in 46 per cent.

Over 63 per cent state that they spend less than ten hours per week job seeking, while almost 16 per cent spend more than twenty hours per week looking for a job.

Regarding residential tenure status, 24 per cent of the surveyed people are or are becoming homeowners.[3] Their residential duration is about 10 years, and 16 per cent have a financial burden arising from their main dwelling. Renters represent 52 per cent of the sample. They have lived in their dwelling for less than 5 years on average, and 46 per cent of them receive rent subsidy. Some 24 per cent do not incur any costs for their accommodation, 95 per cent of whom are young people living in their parents' home.

The people surveyed are spread over eight employment areas, which are defined based on the commuting distance: Cergy-Pontoise, Mantes, and Poissy-les-Mureaux (Île-de-France region), Roubaix and Lens (Nord region), Aix-en-Provence, Etang-de-Berre, and Marseille (Provence-Alpes-Côte d'Azur— PACA region). Nearly two-thirds live in suburbs, and more than three quarters have a driving licence.

Table 6.1. List of variables (number of observations, 3,965)

Variable	Mean
Dichotomous variables:	
Home: homeowner	0.24
Rent: renter	0.52
Free: free of charge	0.24
Age when entering the dwelling:	
Agent 1 [0; 16]	0.22
Agent 2 [16; 24]	0.24
Agent 3 [24; 34]	0.34
Agent 4 [34; 50]	0.18
Agent 5 [50 and over]	0.012
Couple: living as couple	0.56
Celib: being single	0.37
Autres (divorced or widowed)	0.08
Monop: mono parental household	0.11
Femar: married women	0.26
CPPLP: father is executive or professional	0.08
PIITP: father has intermediary profession	0.13
EMPYP: father is employee	0.11
INACP: father is non-participant	0.01
OUVRP: father is workman	0.54
Distance from home to employment area:	
Centre 1: near [0; 15 km]	0.46
Centre 2: remote [15; 45 km]	0.43
Centre 3: very remote [45 km and plus]	0.11
Type of the township:	
Banlieue: suburb	0.63
Rural: rural	0.03
Vilis: isolated town	0.04
Vilc: main town	0.30
Censu: uncensored duration of unemployment	0.74
Enfpro: homeowner's child in his parents' home	0.16
CF: financial constraints related to housing	0.16
SPEC: home acquisition from 1987 to 1991	0.23
SPECIDF: home acquisition, in IDF from 1987 to 1991	0.09
ALLOCLOG: housing subsidy	0.46
INDEMCHO: unemployment benefits	0.58
PERMIS: driving license	0.77
Age: CLASSE 1: [16; 25]	0.29
CLASSE 2: [25; 34]	0.33
CLASSE 3: [34; 50]	0.33
CLASSE 4: [50 and over]	0.05
Franc: French	0.88
Europ: European	0.03
Femme: female	0.46
Search intensity (hours/week):	
PEURECHE, MOYRECH 1: [0; 10]	0.63
MOYRECH 2: [10; 20]	0.22
BCQRECH: [20 and over]	0.16
Educational attainment:	
NDIPL: no diploma	0.32
DIPLTEC: technical diploma	0.49
ENSUP: college degree	0.18

(Cont.)

Table 6.1. (*Continued*)

Variable	Mean
Type of previous occupation:	
CPPL: executive or professional	0.05
PIIT: intermediary profession	0.12
EMPY: employee	0.39
OUVR: workman	0.41
Reason for leaving previous occupation:	
PRECA: end of contract	0.46
DEMIS: resignation	0.13
LICEN: dismissal	0.36
Other	0.04
Employment area:	
ROUBAIX	0.17
LENS	0.16
CERGY	0.12
MANTES	0.10
POISSY	0.12
MARSEILLE	0.17
AIX	0.09
ETANG	0.07
Continuous variables	
HOMEest: homeowner (estimated probability)	0.24
RENTest: renter (estimated probability)	0.53
FREEest: free of charge (estimated probability)	0.23
CHOMDUR: unemployment duration in months	10.41
DEPDUR: length of residence in the department by time of entrance into the dwelling	23
PROINDEX: dwellings sale price index	290
PROIDF: dwellings sale price index in IDF	106
LOCINDEX: renting cost	2,436
D: distance to the most visited township	4
POPINDEX: population index	223
VACRES: vacant dwellings rate	6.28
PROPRO: share of homeowners in the population	56
NBMEN: number of household members	3.59

More than 62 per cent are younger than 35, 54 per cent are men, 56 per cent live with someone, and 37 per cent are single. The individuals surveyed are heads of household in 44 per cent of cases, their spouses in 25 per cent of cases, and their children in 28 per cent of cases.

Combining several criteria makes it possible to gain first insights into the discriminating effects of residential tenure status on unemployment duration as well as the individual characteristics that seem to be associated with it. Unemployment among homeowners thus seems to last longer than that among renters (almost a year for homeowners, whereas renters stay unemployed for less than eleven months). Those who are housed free of charge are unemployed for shorter spells, lasting eight months on average. Similarly, analysing the sample by age group and socio-professional category reveals strong differences relating to residential status. Some 50 per cent of executives and liberal professionals are homeowners, this share declining to 34 per cent of those in intermediary professions, 20 per cent of workmen, and 26 per cent of employees. Age group structure relative to residential status is also greatly differentiated, as practically no one under the age of 25 owns a house, 14 per cent of individuals aged between 25 and 34 are homeowners, and this share reaches 42 per cent and 52 per cent respectively between the age of 34 and 50 and then after the age of 50.

This simple descriptive analysis shows that socio-demographic features that may affect labour market performance are also factors influencing residential tenure status. We will now proceed to a non-parametric estimation of individuals' unemployment duration in order to obtain a preliminary measure of the influence of residential tenure status on unemployment exit rates.

6.3.2. Non-parametric analysis

In order to complete the descriptive analysis, we estimated survival rates in unemployment using the Kaplan–Meier non-parametric estimator. This allows an examination of survival time in unemployment without taking into account observable heterogeneity between individuals by measuring the instantaneous probability of finding employment (hazard rate) and the survival rate in unemployment. The hazard rate corresponds to the share of individuals who find a job at time t, knowing these individuals have been unemployed until time t. Survival and integrated hazard functions evaluated on the basis of stratified samples show discriminating effects of residential tenure status on unemployment duration. We thus observe that on average, the survival time in unemployment is, *ceteris paribus*, longer for homeowners (Figure 6.1) than for those with a different residential tenure status. This gap is increased by the presence of individuals who are housed free of charge (30 per cent of the sample) and whose survival time in unemployment is always shorter than that of renters (Figure 6.2).

Figures 6.1 and 6.2 show the differential effects of residential tenure status and reinforce observed statistical features of average unemployment duration of the three above-mentioned strata. These estimations are made, however, on the basis of a strong hypothesis of population homogeneity within each stratum. They should be enriched by an analysis of unemployment duration that takes into account inter-individual heterogeneity. With respect to the developments mentioned in Section 6.2, we thus proceed to a parametric estimation of a duration model that controls for the endogeneity of the residential tenure status choice.

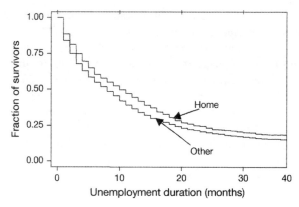

Figure 6.1. Survival function by homeowning

Note: Home: Homeowners
Other: Other

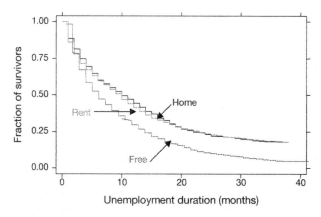

Figure 6.2. Survival function, by residential status

Note: Home: Homeowners
Rent: Renters
Free: Free of charge

6.4. Estimation results

6.4.1. *Multinomial logit estimation of the residential status choice*

In order to control for the endogeneity of the residential tenure status choice, we apply, as a first step, the residential status indicator to a set of variables that account for both environmental factors and individual features.[4]

Environmental variables represent local features of the housing market and residence area that influence the choice of the residential status. First, the cost of owning relative to renting is represented by several elements. An index of the average sale price of property at town level is introduced. It is computed by taking the mean of sale prices of different types of property (old and new houses, old and new flats) from 1994 to 1996. To take account of the specific features of the housing market in the Île-de-France region, a dummy variable that takes value 1 for towns located in this area is coupled with the price index and introduced into the regression. Finally, an index for the cost of renting has been obtained by computing the average town rent on the basis of the rents reported by the individuals surveyed. Although this index does not represent the true cost of renting, it is used as a *proxy* for lack of other available information, as the variations between towns indicate inter-communal differences on the renting market. These price indexes reflect dwellings' intrinsic features, which are not recorded in the survey, as well as spatial characteristics whose influence can be controlled for. We thus introduce distance to the most visited town, distance to jobs, and the type of towns where the individuals live (rural, suburb, main town, or isolated town) as explanatory variables for the decision to be a homeowner. Indicators for housing market tightness are also introduced through a town population index, the incidence of vacant dwellings, and the share of homeowners in the population at *Département* level. In considering the distribution of purchases of dwellings over time, we control for the effect of the speculative bubble that affected the property market from 1987 to 1991, especially in the Île-de-France region. Indeed, during that time, a favourable economic climate and measures aimed at relaxing legal regulations on the property market (Méhaignerie law of 1986) encouraged the development of the speculative bubble that translated into abnormal price dynamics (Renard 1996). In the estimation we therefore use a binary variable that takes the value 1 for all homeowners who acquired their dwelling during the speculation phase. A specific variable for acquisition in the Île-de-France region in that same period is also introduced.

Among the personal characteristics that affect the choice of a residential status, age when moving into the dwelling is introduced to reflect attitudinal variations among individuals during their life cycle with respect to residential status. We also take into account individuals' marital status (living as a couple, or single), household structure (number of household members, one-parent family), socio-professional category, and gender. We use the socio-professional category of the individuals' father as a *proxy* for permanent income because of positive externalities on children from their parents' level of income and human capital.

Variables reflecting French or European nationality take into account possible differences in residential status preferences as well as potential discrimination towards foreigners. Length of stay in the *Département* when moving into the dwelling is introduced to reflect a preference for immobility.

149

Estimations are processed using the White correction, so that unbiased student tests can be obtained in case of heteroskedasticity. Estimation results can be found in Table 6.2. The model is overall significant, with a pseudo-R^2 that equals 0.48. Contingency tables indicate that the average of good predictions is 82 per cent, 66 per cent being 'success' event predictions.

We are especially interested in describing homeowners' behaviour, and not all variables that we introduced exert a statistically significant marginal effect on individual probabilities of belonging to the three subgroups. Explanatory variables determine as predicted the probability of being a homeowner, and most associated coefficients are significant at usual threshold levels. Nonetheless, we cannot find a significant effect of the variable representing age when moving into a dwelling, although this is different in the case of the other two subgroups, where it has significant conventional effects. In addition, two variables—namely, the socio-professional category of the individuals' father, except if he does not participate in the labour market, and the distance to the most visited town—have non-significant coefficients for the three types of residential status.

The index of original housing costs has a regular negative influence on the probability of homeownership once we control for the effects of the speculative bubble, except in the Île-de-France region, where the effect is positive. Features of the property market can explain this unusual price effect in the Paris area, where housing prices are highly correlated with housing attributes that we cannot control for although they are crucial in the acquisition of housing (proximity to schools, public facilities, means of transport, infrastructure). This is also apparent in the marginal effects exerted by these variables on the probability of renting. Finally, the cost of renting has a positive effect on the probability of becoming a homeowner, while the effect is the opposite as regards the probability of renting.

Spatial variables have expected effects: an increase in the distance to jobs reduces the probability of homeowning, while it has no effect on the two other subgroups. Living in a suburban area, as compared to other locations, increases the probability of being a homeowner, which is in line with stylized facts about French urban growth in the last decade (Bessy-Pietri 2000). This variable does not affect the probability of being a renter or of being housed free of charge.

Variables that represent housing market features also have predicted effects: the more populated the town, the less (respectively the more) individuals will be homeowners (respectively renters); the incidence of vacant dwellings has a positive (negative) influence on the probability of being a homeowner (renter), whereas the share of homeowners in the population has the opposite effect.

Note that no environmental variables (but one) have any effect on the probability of being housed free of charge.

Table 6.2. Multinomial logit logit analysis of residential status choice

Independent variables	Home (Home-owning)		Rent (Renting)		Free (Free of charge)	
	Marginal effect	Student statistic	Marginal effect	Student statistic	Marginal effect	Student statistic
PROINDEX: dwellings sale price index	−0.0002	−1.70*	0.0002	1.51 ns	0.000	0.04 ns
PROIDF: dwellings sale price index in IDF	0.0004	2.88***	−0.0003	−2.08**	−0.000	−0.90 ns
LOCINDEX: renting cost	0.0001	2.77***	−0.0000	−2.87***	0.000	0.74 ns
SPEC: dwelling acquisition from 1987 to 1991	0.04	1.78*	−0.0196	−0.81 ns	−0.021	−1.73*
SPECIDF: dwelling acquisition in IDF from 1987 to 1991	0.103	2.36**	−0.143	−3.22***	0.041	1.21 ns
D: distance to the most visited township	−0.003	−1.54 ns	0.003	1.341 ns	0.000	0.12 ns
Distance from home to workplace:						
Centre 1: near [0; 15 km] = base						
Centre 2: remote [15; 45 km]	−0.284	−6.88***	0.282	6.37***	0.002	0.08 ns
Centre 3: very remote [45 km and over]	−0.217	−9.49***	0.233	7.16***	−0.017	−0.65 ns
Type of the township:						
Banlieue: suburb	0.038	1.76*	−0.022	−0.92 ns	−0.016	−1.01 ns
Autres: rural, main town, isolated town = base						
IPOP: population index	−0.004	−8.27***	0.004	8.40***	−0.000	−1.26 ns
VACRES: vacant dwellings rate	0.126	6.37***	−0.136	−6.37***	0.011	0.83 ns
PROPRO: share of homeowners	−0.016	−2.14**	0.009	1.14 ns	0.007	1.45 ns
Age when entering the dwelling:						
Agent 1 [0; 16] = base						
Agent 2 [16; 24]	−1.158	−2.75***	0.303	5.18***	−0.146	−6.53***
Agent 3 [24; 34]	−0.034	−0.53 ns	0.355	5.12***	−0.321	−6.76***
Agent 4 [34 and over]	−0.050	−0.78 ns	0.249	3.68***	−0.199	−7.73***
Couple: living as couple	0.132	4.37***	0.270	5.37***	−0.401	−6.93***
Celib: single	−0.147	−4.44***	0.012	0.29 ns	0.135	3.71***
Autres (divorced or widowed) = base						
Monop: mono-parental household	−0.113	−3.56***	0.066	1.86**	0.047	1.95**
FEM: female	0.088	4.72***	−0.025	−1.23 ns	−0.063	−4.86***

(Cont.)

151

Table 6.2. (Continued)

Independent variables	Home (Home-owning)		Rent (Renting)		Free (Free of charge)	
	Marginal effect	Student statistic	Marginal effect	Student statistic	Marginal effect	Student statistic
NBMEN: number of household's members	0.017	2.90**	-0.070	-9.32***	0.053	10.28***
Franc: French	0.127	5.22***	-0.176	-6.74***	0.049	4.04***
Europ: European	0.225	2.70***	-0.353	-5.37***	0.128	1.32 ns
DEPDUR: length of residence in the department when entering the dwelling	0.006	8.71***	-0.005	-7.07***	-0.001	-1.50 ns
CPPLP: father is executive or professional	0.055	1.59 ns	-0.037	-1.08 ns	-0.019	-1.07 ns
PIITP: father is intermediary profession	-0.008	-0.33 ns	0.026	1.08 ns	-0.018	-1.41 ns
INACP: father is non-participant	-0.144	-2.50**	0.202	3.46***	-0.058	-5.64***
EMPYP: father is employee	0.032	1.15 ns	-0.037	-1.27 ns	0.005	0.27 ns
OUVP: father is workman = base						
CPPL: executive or professional	0.174	3.55***	-1.166	-3.48***	-0.008	-0.21 ns
PIIT: intermediary profession	0.074	2.59***	-0.033	-1.14 ns	-0.041	-3.31***
OUV: workman	-0.051	-2.52**	0.064	2.92***	-0.013	-0.99 ns
EMPY: employee = base						
% of correct predictions.	80.58		69		95	
% of correct 'success' predictions.	40		73		86	
Pseudo-R^2	0.48					
Log-likelihood	-2085.74					
Number of observations	3965					

***: significant at 1%
**: significant at 5%
*: significant at 10%; ns: not significant

Living as a couple has a positive influence on the probability of being a homeowner as well as a renter, whereas being single or having a one-parent household produces the opposite effect. The probability of being a homeowner is higher for women, French, or European individuals, and increases with the number of household members and length of residence in the *Département*.

Social origin variables (socio-professional category of the father) indicate that children of workmen or of those not participating in the labour market are less likely to be homeowners than are children of employees. With regard to individual socio-professional categories, executives and people in intermediary professions have a higher probability of being homeowners.

The model's overall significance indicates potential endogeneity of the residential status variable. We use the estimated probabilities for individuals of having a particular residential status to evaluate the effect of homeownership on the duration of individual unemployment spells.

6.4.2. Estimation of the unemployment duration model: the effect of homeownership

The model presented in the second section is estimated by introducing the estimated probabilities of being a homeowner or renter respectively, denoted by variables 'HOMEest' and 'RENTest', whereas the variable 'FREEest', representing people who are housed free of charge, is our base category. In addition, covariates are introduced that account for other local and individual features of the housing market, personal characteristics, job search strategies, and unemployment benefits.

Specific account is taken of public subsidies for housing, as they are often blamed as a source of immobility. Another variable represents the effects of financial constraints resulting from the main residence.

The personal features that we introduce are individuals' age, sex, nationality, marital status, educational attainment, last position, socio-professional category, reasons for unemployment, and possession of a driving licence. The effects of job search strategies are identified through a series of variables that indicate job search intensity. Public labour market policies are represented by a variable that takes value 1 if the individual receives unemployment benefit. Lastly, the employment area to which an individual belongs is introduced in the estimation to account for local labour market specificities.

Parameters are estimated through maximization of the following log-likelihood:

$$\ln L = \sum_{j=1}^{n} \left[\theta^{-1} \ln \left\{ 1 - \theta \ln S_j(t_{0j}) \right\} - \left(\theta^{-1} + d_j \right) \ln \left\{ 1 - \theta \ln S_j(t_j) \right\} + d_j \ln h_j(t_j) \right]$$

Results are presented in Table 6.3.

Table 6.3. Estimation results of the lognormal duration model with Gamma correction

Variable	Coefficients	Student statistic
HOMEest: homeownership (estimated prob.)	0.369	1.96**
RENTest: rental	0.056	0.58 ns
FREEest: free of charge housed = base		
CF: main home financial constraints	−0.074	−1.14 ns
ALLOCLOG: housing subsidy	0.222	4.64***
INDEMCHO: unemployment benefits	0.583	10.48***
PERMIS: driving licence	−0.401	−6.34***
Age: Classe 1: [16; 25] = base		
Classe 2: [25; 34]	0.259	4.24***
Classe 3: [34; 50]	0.561	7.46***
Classe 4: [50 and over]	1.054	7.22***
Franc: French	−0.371	−3.76***
Europ: European	−0.240	−1.64 ns
Female	0.072	1.29 ns
Couple	−0.250	−3.27***
Search intensity (hours/week):		
PEURECHE, MOYRECH 1: [0; 10] = base		
MOYRECH 2: [10; 20]	−0.157	2.95***
BCQRECH: [20 and over]	−0.141	−2.33**
Educational attainment:		
NDIPL: no diploma = base		
DIPLTEC: technical diploma	−0.168	−3.50***
ENSUP: university degree	−0.245	−3.78***
Socio-professional category of last position:		
CPPL: executive or professional	0.106	0.92 ns
PIIT: intermediary profession	0.055	0.76 ns
EMPY: employee	0.250	4.25***
OUVR: workman = base		
Reason for leaving last position:		
PRECA: end of contract	−0.148	−1.21 ns
DEMIS: resignation	0.098	0.75 ns
LICEN: dismissal	0.274	2.20**
Other = base		
Employment area:		
ROUBAIX	−0.432	−6.32***
LENS	−0.233	−3.23***
CERGY	−0.421	−6.09***
MANTES	−0.311	−3.78***
POISSY	−0.394	−5.48***
MARSEILLE/AIX/ETANG = base		
CONSTANTE	2.199	12.42***
Ln(σ)	0.176	12.77***
Ln(θ)	−22.45	−48.37***
σ	1.19	
θ	1.77×10^{-10}	
Log-likelihood	−4554.10	
Number of observations	3280	
Wald χ^2	729.36	

***: significant at 1%
**: significant at 5%
*: significant at 10%
ns: not significant

The effect of the estimated probability of homeownership on the duration of unemployment is positive and statistically significant at a 5 per cent threshold. Thus, our results based on French data do not reject Oswald's hypothesis. This is similar to the outcome of the Green and Hendershott (2001*a*) study, though they apply a different method of estimation, using US data. Moreover, we do not find any statistically significant difference in duration of unemployment between renters and people housed free of charge. So, mobility costs associated with homeownership seem to have, *ceteris paribus*, a negative effect on the hazard rate of leaving unemployment. Note the divergence between on the one hand the descriptive statistics and the Kaplan–Meier estimation in Section 6.3 and on the other hand the results obtained by estimating a parametric duration model taking into account endogenous residential status, censoring, and unobservable heterogeneity.

Housing subsidy recipients are unemployed for longer periods, as are unemployment benefit recipients. People holding a driving licence are unemployed for significantly shorter periods of time.

Demographic variables exert conventional effects: living as a couple reduces the length of unemployment, age has a positive and increasing effect on the duration of unemployment, whereas French or European individuals are unemployed for shorter periods, the effect of having French nationality being stronger.

Job search intensity reduces the duration of unemployment, although coefficients indicate that the marginal productivity of search efforts is decreasing. If the reason for leaving the last position was dismissal, individuals experience longer unemployment spells.

Those who have a technical diploma or university degree spend less time unemployed than those without a diploma, the effect of a university degree being larger. Moreover, those who held an employee position are unemployed for significantly longer periods than workmen.

Finally, people in Paris or in the northern regions spend less time unemployed than those living in the PACA region.

6.5. Concluding remarks

Macroeconomic stylized facts revealing a correlation between homeownership and unemployment rates led us to examine the relationships between housing and labour markets at the microeconomic level. The objective was to isolate the influence of homeownership on the duration of individual unemployment spells.

As we had to take into account individuals' self-selection regarding their residential tenure status and wished to use flexible estimation procedures with respect to unemployment duration data, we applied an instrumental variables method that was first proposed by Heckman and Robb (1985).

Estimation of a multinomial logit model for the choice of residential tenure status revealed the influence of several individual features and was enriched by the introduction of variables reflecting spatial characteristics as well as housing costs.

Having corrected for unobserved heterogeneity, the examination of the influence of residential tenure status using different duration models does not reject Oswald's hypothesis. However, the extent to which underlying mechanisms have an effect through individual search efforts and/or reservation wages is still an open question.

Future research should thus take greater account of individual search behaviour—especially with respect to spatial constraints during job search—in order to explore links between residential location, mobility costs due to tenure status, and labour market transitions. A structural parameters estimation of a job search model including these elements would be an even more robust test of Oswald's hypothesis.

Notes

1. We first estimated different parametric and semi-parametric models in order to evaluate alternative hypotheses regarding the shape of the hazard rate. The comparison between different specifications (Gamma, Weibull, exponential, and log-normal) with regards to Akaike information criterion and Cox–Snell residuals shows that the log-normal distribution suits the data the best. The hazard rate of leaving unemployment is thus non-monotonous, first increasing until a peak between the eleventh and twelfth month, and then decreasing. In addition, the Cox proportional hazard model is not supported by the data.
2. v terms are distributed as a Gamma function with mean 1 and variance $\frac{1}{k}$, then $g(v) = \frac{k^k}{\Gamma(k)} e^{-kv} v^{k-1}$, where Γ is the gamma distribution.
3. The discrepancy between sample and national figures regarding homeowners' share lies in the fact that 62 per cent of individuals in the sample are less than 35 years old. Moreover, as Van Leuvensteijn and Koning, for example, demonstrate in Chapter 8, homeowners face a lower risk of unemployment than individuals with alternative residential tenure status.
4. The Hausman Test does not reject the assumption of independence of irrelevant alternatives.

References

Bessy-Pietri, P. (2000), 'Les formes récentes de la croissance urbaine', *Economie et Statistique*, 336/6, 35–52.

Blundell, R., and Costa Dias, M. (2002), 'Alternative approaches to evaluation in empirical microeconomics', Working Paper, University College London, Institute for Fiscal Studies.

Bouabdallah, K., Cavaco, S., and Lesueur, J. Y. (2002), 'Recherche d'emploi, contraintes spatiales et durée de chômage: une analyse micro-économétrique', *Revue d'Economie Politique*, 112/1, 137–56.

Coulson, N. E., and Fisher, L. M. (2002), 'Tenure choice and labour market outcomes', *Housing Studies*, 17, 35–49.

Dubujet, F., and Le Blanc, D. (2000), 'Accession à la propriété: le régime de croisière?', *INSEE Première*, 718.

Goffette-Nagot, F. (1994), 'Analyse micro-économique de la péri urbanisation: un modèle de localisation résidentielle', Thèse, Document de recherche 43, INRA.

Green, R. K., and Hendershott, P. H. (2001a), 'Homeownership and unemployment in the US', *Urban Studies*, 38/9, 1509–20.

―――― (2001b), 'Homeownership and the duration of unemployment: a test of the Oswald hypothesis', NBER Working Paper.

Greene, W. H. (1997), *Econometric Analysis* (Englewood Cliffs, NJ: Prentice-Hall).

Heckman, J. J. (1990), 'Varieties of selection bias', *American Economic Review (Papers and Proceedings)*, 80/2, 313–18.

―――― and Borjas, G. (1980), 'Does unemployment cause future unemployment? Definitions, questions and answers from a continuous time model of heterogeneity and state dependence', *Economica*, 47/187, 247–83.

―――― and Robb, R. (1985), 'Alternative methods for evaluating the impact of interventions: an overview', *Journal of Econometrics*, 30, 239–67.

―――― and Singer, B. (1984), 'A method for minimizing the impact of distributional assumptions in econometric models for duration data', *Econometrica*, 52/2, 271–320.

Holzer, H. J., Ihlandfeld, K. R., and Sjoquist, D. L. (1994), 'Work, search and travel among white and black youth', *Journal of Urban Economics*, 35, 320–45.

Lancaster, T. (1990), *The Economic Analysis of Transition Data* (Cambridge: Cambridge University Press).

Louvot-Runavot, C. (2001), 'Le logement dans l'union européenne: la propriété prend le pas sur la location', *Economie et Statistique*, 343/3, 29–50.

Mortensen, D. T. (1986), 'Job search and labour market analysis', in O. Ashenfelter and R. Layard (eds.), *Handbook of Labour Economics*, ii (Amsterdam: North-Holland), ch. 15.

Nickell, S., and Layard, R. (1999), 'Labor market institutions and economic performance', in O. Ashenfelter and D. Card (eds.), *Handbook of Labour Economics*, iii (Amsterdam: North-Holland), 3029–84.

Oswald, A. J. (1996), 'A conjecture on the explanation for high unemployment in the industrialised nations: part I', University of Warwick Economic Research Paper 475.

―――― (1997), 'Thoughts on NAIRU', correspondence to *Journal of Economic Perspectives*, 11, 227–8.

Oswald, A. J. (1998), 'The missing piece of the unemployment puzzle', CEPR/ESRC, Workshop on Unemployment Dynamics, London, 4 November.

Renard, V. (1996), 'Quelques caractéristiques des marchés fonciers et immobiliers', *Economie et Statistique*, 294–5/4,5, 89–97.

Rogers, C. L. (1997), 'Job search and unemployment duration: implications for the spatial mismatch hypothesis', *Journal of Urban Economics*, 42, 109–32.

Smith, L. B., Rosen, K. T., and Fallis, G. (1988), 'Recent developments in economic models of housing markets', *Journal of Economic Literature*, 26, 29–64.

Van den Berg, G., and Gorter, C. (1997), 'Job search and commuting time', *Journal of Business and Economics Statistics*, 15/2, 269–81.

Van Ommeren, J. N. (1996), 'Commuting and relocation of jobs and residences', Ph.D. thesis, Tinbergen Institute Research Series.

Wasmer, E., and Zenou, Y. (2002), 'Does city structure affect job search and welfare?', *Journal of Urban Economics*, 51, 515–41.

———— (2006), 'Equilibrium search unemployment with explicit spatial frictions', *Labour Economics*, 13/2, 143–65.

Part III

Country Studies: Job Mobility and Homeownership

7

Housing Tenure, Job Mobility, and Unemployment in the UK[*]

Harminder Battu, Ada Ma, and Euan Phimister

7.1. Introduction

The nature of housing tenure has long been blamed for discouraging spatial mobility and thereby having an impact upon labour market outcomes. In the early 1980s in the UK the main culprit was deemed to be local authority housing (McCormick 1983). Hughes and McCormick (1981, 1987) examined the longer-distance migration rates of those in local authority housing and found that they were lower than those of both owner-occupiers and those in private rented accommodation. Although, the latest research suggests that these effects may have lessened (Hughes and McCormick 2000), the relative immobility of public renters may stem from public housing rents being below market rates, the restricted transferability within public housing, long waiting lists, and security of tenure. Public renters are then 'locked in' and face higher costs if they accept a job that involves a long-distance move.

More recently, the blame has been pinned on private homeownership. Oswald (1996 and Chapter 2 above) in a series of papers, using macro time series and cross-section data for OECD countries, and regions within a number of those countries, has argued that homeownership causes unemployment. One explanation revolves around the reduced mobility of homeowners relative to private renters owing to the costs of buying and selling homes. Subsequent and arguably more sophisticated micro-econometric tests have placed doubt upon the alleged relationship. Coulson and Fisher (2002) for the US find that unemployment duration is shorter for homeowners relative to renters, though neither unobserved heterogeneity nor the endogenous nature of housing tenure is accounted for. Van Leuvensteijn and Koning (Chapter 8 below)

[*] This article was published in *The Economic Journal*, 118, 311–28; Blackwell Publishing, 2008; copyright Royal Economic Society, 2008.

do account for the endogeneity of homeownership and find using Dutch data that employed homeowners are less likely to become unemployed relative to employed renters. More recently, Munch *et al.* (Chapter 4 above) using Danish data find shorter unemployment spells amongst homeowners compared to renters, after controlling for the endogeneity of homeownership.

This paper assesses the impact of housing tenure on individual unemployment and job mobility in the UK and makes two key contributions to the literature. First, we examine the effects of both homeownership and public renting relative to private renting and ascertain whether the old culprit of public housing is still having an effect, given the decline in public renting and the evidence of rising migration rates of public tenants (Hughes and McCormick 2000). Recent papers do not examine the impact of public renting (Van Leuvensteijn and Koning, Chapter 8 below; Munch *et al.*, Chapters 4 above and 9 below).[1] Second, by considering job mobility as well as unemployment, we are able to explore the potential differential impacts of housing tenure across socio-economic class. This further links this paper to the previous literature which showed large differences in the UK in the migration patterns of manual and non-manual workers (Hughes and McCormick 1994; McCormick 1997). We use an approach similar to that of Munch *et al.* (Chapter 4 above) and make a distinction between local and non-local jobs, with the latter involving a residential move. The basic argument here is that homeowners and public tenants have a lower reservation wage in local areas compared to other regions and are more likely to accept a local job and less likely to take employment in distant areas (Barcelo 2001). Though this distinction has been made in the UK (Hughes and McCormick 2000) the empirical research in the UK has made no explicit allowance for this.

In order to explore the impact of housing tenure on unemployment and job mobility, we estimate competing risk duration models for exits from unemployment (and the current job) to a new job to two destinations: to a job which occurs with a residential move across a local authority district (LAD) boundary; to a job which does not occur with such a 'long distance' move. In this framework, the Oswald hypothesis may be interpreted as the implication that the impact of homeownership (relative to private renting) on the overall hazard rate across both destinations for transitions out of unemployment is negative. We expect that being a public tenant would have similar effects relative to being a private renter.

In the empirical model we control for the endogeneity of housing tenure types, and allow for correlated unobserved heterogeneity effects. To identify the model we follow Munch *et al.* (Chapter 4 above), where identification of the tenure status on job and unemployment duration is achieved by having multiple spells on individuals and having a subset of individuals going through different housing tenures within the sample (Abbring and Van den Berg 2003; Van den Berg 2001).

The paper has the following structure. In the next section we provide an overview of the dataset we utilize. In Section 7.3 we set out very briefly the essence of the econometric model that we estimate. Section 7.4 provides our results, and the final section concludes.

7.2. Data

The dataset employed is the British Household Panel Survey (BHPS). This is a nationally representative longitudinal dataset with 10,000 individuals in 5,500 households per year, and commenced in 1991. This dataset is rich and includes a wide range of information about individual and household demographics, labour force status, employment, and housing tenure. The data on job duration and unemployment spells are drawn from waves 1–13 (1991 to 2003). Only participants aged 16 to 65 are included in the sample. Participants are interviewed annually, with the first wave of the survey conducted in 1991. At each interview, respondents are asked detailed information on employment since the last interview.

From this data we construct a complete sequence of labour market spells recorded to the nearest calendar month for a balanced panel of individuals. A 'spell' is either a job, a period of unemployment, or a period out of the labour market, or a period of self-employment. Jobs are defined by the 'present position' of employees and so include job changes within existing employers. Inconsistencies in this data arise primarily from differences between what individuals recall about their employment status at the previous interview and what was actually recorded at the previous interview. Following Upward (1999) these problems are reconciled by applying the principle that information recorded closest to any particular event is the most reliable. The information on personal and household characteristics, as well as job-related characteristics, are recorded annually. This information could vary within a job or unemployment spell if its length spans two or more interviews. On the other hand, a worker may go through multiple job spells in a year, and because the job characteristics of job spells that began and ended between interviews were not collected, these shorter jobs spells have to be dropped from all estimations if we incorporate job and employer characteristics into the model. Spells where data were missing on any of the variables used in the analysis were also dropped from the sample. Finally, our sample contains only spells which started after September 1990, the date at which full information on new unemployment/jobs spells from the first interview is available; i.e. spells that were ongoing at that point are excluded. A number of these sample restrictions require comment. Including ongoing spells would over-represent long duration spells and be non-random (Lancaster 1990). As a result, the econometrics would have to adjust for the sample selectivity induced. Selectivity issues are also a concern with respect to the loss of short spells and are associated with the balanced panel of individuals. However, these criteria are required to satisfy the conditions for a flow sample required for model estimation, to ensure that we can correctly match employment status changes with residential changes and have full information on the covariates.[2]

In order to examine the impact of housing tenure on mobility, we use both the unemployment and employment spells created and (in both cases) consider two types of exit: an exit from unemployment (a job) to a new job without a residential move and an exit from unemployment (a job) with a residential move. The BHPS allows us to identify different types of moves from information recorded on whether individuals have changed address in the last twelve months and their local authority district (LAD) of residence and we define a move as one where the individual changed LAD.[3] Whilst LADs may be an imperfect measure of local labour markets (see McCulloch 2003), they have been widely used within the BHPS to capture moves (Böheim and Taylor 2002, 2007; Rabe 2006) and there is also some evidence to indicate that they do capture job-related moves. For example, Buck (2000) examines the reasons for moving across three types of moves (within a LAD, moves out of a LAD but within a region, and moves that cross regional boundaries) and finds that job-related moves tend to be over longer distances with significantly fewer job-related moves within LADs compared to the other two types of moves. The differences between the other two types of moves are small in terms of reason for moving, indicating that the key distinction is between intra-LAD and inter-LAD moves. Defining moves across eleven regional boundaries in the UK is also not wholly satisfactory, since some intra-regional but long-distance moves are excluded, and this also results in too few moves (the interregional migration rate is substantially lower). In addition, for those in public rented housing the use of LADs may be appropriate, since there are particular barriers to moves across local authority boundaries because of the operation of allocation systems.[4]

Exits without a move include all residential moves where the local authority district has not changed.[5] Exits from unemployment (or an existing job) into a new job with a residential move are defined as exits where the individual moved across a LAD boundary in the twelve months preceding or the twelve months following unemployment (job) exit. This time window of twenty-four months around the exits allows the timing of labour market transitions and residential changes to differ slightly, so that changes in residence can proceed or occur after the specific month of the employment change.

As reported in Table 7.1, using these definitions provides a basic sample of 9,237 employment spells (based on 2,773 individuals) and 1,940 unemployment spells (based on 1,170 individuals), of which 790 of the former and 177 of the latter end with a non-local move. A succinct way of summarizing spell data is to consider the Kaplan–Meier estimate of the survivor functions for

Table 7.1. Summary statistics for job and unemployment spells

Exit to	Count	Job percentage	Count	Unemployment percentage
(New) Job without a non-local move	4,314	46.7 (84.5)	1,143	58.9 (86.3)
(New) Job with a non-local move	790	8.6 (15.5)	177	9.1 (13.7)
Other exits and censored observations	4,133	44.7	620	32.0
Number of spells	9,237	100	1,940	100
Individuals	2,773		1,170	
Duration in months	**Mean**	**SD**	**Mean**	**SD**
Job without a non-local move	21.87	22.17	6.54	8.50
Job with a non-local move	22.88	23.91	5.27	6.53
Other exits and censored observations	33.47	34.53	12.64	16.11
Summary statistics	**Mean**	**SD**	**Mean**	**SD**
Homeownership	0.793	0.405	0.618	0.486
Public renter	0.114	0.318	0.263	0.440
Private renter	0.091	0.287	0.119	0.323
Age 16–24	0.077	0.267	0.174	0.379
Age 25–34	0.304	0.460	0.275	0.446
Age 35–44	0.309	0.462	0.221	0.415
Age 45 or above	0.310	0.463	0.331	0.471
Female	0.566	0.496	0.471	0.499
Children 0–15 years	0.465	0.499	0.374	0.484
No qualifications	0.167	0.373	0.292	0.455
O-levels or equivalent	0.183	0.387	0.197	0.398
A-levels or equivalent	0.121	0.326	0.127	0.333
Nursing and other qualifications	0.303	0.460	0.240	0.427
First degree or above (including teaching)	0.214	0.410	0.134	0.341
Spouse works	0.620	0.485	0.434	0.496
Married	0.755	0.430	0.622	0.485
Ln (monthly pay)	6.928	0.842		

Calculated by Spell. See appendix for detailed definition of characteristics.

job and unemployment spells. These are illustrated in Figures 7.1 and 7.2 by house tenure type. Figure 7.1 does suggest that there are overall differences in job mobility between tenure types with homeowners (with or without a mortgage) having longer job durations. For unemployment, Figure 7.2 indicates (before allowing for individual characteristics and mobility) that there are differences in unemployment exits, with those in public housing having longer unemployment spells. Both these observations are supported by the statistical evidence, with the equality of the survivor functions rejected at 1 per cent significance in both cases using the log rank test.

Table 7.1 also provides information on the structure of job and unemployment spell exits and reports sample means for certain key characteristics associated with the spells. Of the uncensored job spells 15.5 per cent end with employment outside the local area with the remainder (84.5 per cent) ending with a new job locally. In terms of typical characteristics, Table 7.1 reveals

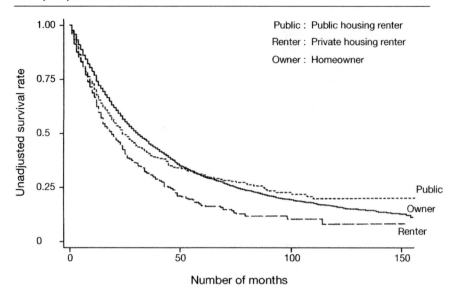

Figure 7.1. Kaplan–Meier estimates of the job tenure survival function by house tenure

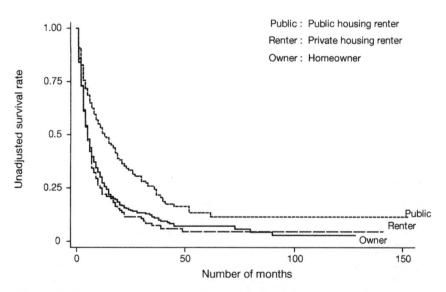

Figure 7.2. Kaplan–Meier estimates of the unemployment survival function by house tenure

that 79.3 per cent of the job spells are associated with homeowners (either owned outright or with a mortgage). This is significantly higher than a previous estimate of 69 per cent as reported in a European-wide study (Norris and Shiels 2004), a figure generated by the Office of National Statistics using the General Household Survey 2003[6] and higher than a range of European countries including the Netherlands (54 per cent), Denmark (51 per cent), and France (56 per cent) (Norris and Shiels 2004). A number of factors contribute to the high percentage of homeowners in our job duration sample. First, in spells where the housing tenure stays unchanged, the average spell length of homeowners is almost a year longer than those of tenants (27.9 months as against 18.5 months). Second, the sample is restricted to cover only employed individuals, and employed individuals are more likely to own a home. Finally, restricting the sample to a balanced panel also increases the homeownership share by around 3 percentage points. In terms of other characteristics, around half of the job spells are taken up by people who are educated to post-secondary level. The mean natural log of monthly earnings is 6.928, which is equal to a value of £1020.45 at 2005 prices. The majority of the workers in the sample are from dual-earning households, with 62 per cent of the job spells associated with workers whose spouses are also working. An even larger percentage (75.5 per cent) of the job spells are associated with workers who are married.

Turning briefly to the unemployment spells, we see that somewhat more than 10 per cent end with a job outside the local area, but as with job mobility, the vast majority (86 per cent) end with employment locally. In this sample, unsurprisingly, around 62 per cent are homeowners, significantly lower than the job duration sample. The unemployed sample also tends to be largely male, more likely to be unmarried, and with a significant number (30 per cent) possessing no qualifications. Less than half (43 per cent) have a spouse in employment (compared to 62 per cent of those in employment).

7.3. Empirical specification

The empirical approach employed builds on that used by Munch *et al.* (Chapter 4 above). For both the job and unemployment duration models to capture the impact of housing tenure, we need to distinguish between two types of transition: into a new local job and into a new job with a non-local residential move. Hence the basic specification is an underlying competing risks model with these two exit types. It is particularly important to account for unobserved differences, or heterogeneity; otherwise any estimates of the effects of duration or duration dependence are likely to be biased (Heckman 1981). In our model unobserved heterogeneity is incorporated in the model by using the mass-point approach introduced by Heckman and Singer (1984) assuming a mixed proportional hazard model (Lancaster 1990). Finally, housing tenure is potentially endogenous. For example, an individual may only make the decision (or have access to a mortgage) to become a homeowner when they are in stable employment, so that the observed correlation between ownership and unemployment might be negative. Here we allow for this possibility by simultaneously modelling the probability of being a homeowner or a public or private renter using a multinomial logit with mass points which are allowed to be correlated with the unobserved heterogeneity in the two exit types.

7.3.1. Model

In both unemployment and job models each person is assumed to exit to one of two states $r = 1$ or 2. For any period t, define the hazard to state r, $h_r(t)$. The influence of observed covariates and unobserved heterogeneity are captured by modelling each exit type using a mixed proportional hazard model, i.e.

$$h_r(t|z_{1t}, z_{2t}, \boldsymbol{x}', v_r) = h_{r0}(t) \exp\left(z_{1t}\lambda_{1r} + z_{2t}\lambda_{2r} + \boldsymbol{x}'\beta_r + v_r\right) \qquad (7.1)$$

where $h_{r0}(t)$ is the baseline transition intensity or hazard for the exit type, v_r is a random variable capturing unobserved heterogeneity, z_{1t}, z_{2t} dummy variables capturing whether the individual is a homeowner or public renter respectively, and $\boldsymbol{x}$ is the vector of other covariates assumed to influence the exit hazard. Specifically, the vector of covariates $\boldsymbol{x}$ included age, gender, children under 16, marital status, whether there is a working partner present, plus a set of regional and time dummies. In addition, for the job duration model, the vector of covariates contains a set of dummies to control for occupational status and industry plus regional and time dummy variables.

The probability of each housing tenure type is a multinomial logit model with unobserved effects, i.e.

$$
\begin{aligned}
P_k\left(\boldsymbol{x}_m, u_1, u_2\right) &= \Pr(y_t = k|\boldsymbol{x}, u_1, u_2) \\
&= \frac{\exp\left(\boldsymbol{x}'\delta_k + u_k\right)}{1 + \exp\left(\boldsymbol{x}'\delta_1 + u_1\right) + \exp\left(\boldsymbol{x}'\delta_2 + u_2\right)}
\end{aligned} \qquad (7.2)
$$

$k = 1, 2$, where $y_t = 3 - 2z_{1t} - z_{2t}$.

7.3.2. Estimation

The estimation framework assumes that the observed data are continuous and does not explicitly allow for the grouped nature of the observed data. When time aggregation is relatively low (the employment spells case), the evidence suggests that the performance of the continuous model is at least as good as models explicitly accounting for the discrete nature of the data (Bergstrom and Edin 1992; ter Hofstede and Wedel 1998). However, at higher levels of time aggregation (the unemployment spells case) ignoring grouping in the data may induce biases. To ensure robustness of the results, we estimated a discrete model accounting for the grouped nature of the data for the unemployment spells which showed that the results were not sensitive to the use of the continuous time model (Keifer 1990).[7]

In principle, the unemployment and employment spells could have been estimated simultaneously in a multi-state duration model. However, this would have meant the estimation of a basic model with a very large number of mass points, significantly increasing computational complexity and severely limiting the extent to which the sensitivity and robustness of the model could be explored. Nevertheless, the results should be interpreted with the caveat that potential correlations in unobserved heterogeneity between unemployment and employment spells have been ignored.

A key issue in the literature is how one deals with the endogeneity of homeownership. There are two basic approaches in the literature. The traditional approach is to use instruments or exclusion restrictions, i.e. in this case variables that influence housing tenure but not labour market outcomes. Van Leuvensteijn and Koning (Chapter 8 below) use the regional share of homeowners as an instrument for homeownership; Flatau *et al.* (2003) use individual's age; and Munch *et al.* (Chapter 4 above) use homeownership of parents in 1980 and the proportion of homeowners in the municipality where the individual was born.

The second approach is to use multiple spells where at least within some spells the treatment effect varies within the spell. Here we have multiple unemployment (job) spells available for a specific individual, and for some their housing tenure status also varies across these spells. Abbring and Van den Berg (2003) and Van der Berg (2001) show that under these conditions, the treatment effect is identified without the need to find any instrument, and this approach has been used in a number of recent papers (Panis and Lillard 2004; Munch *et al.*, Chapters 4 above and 9 below) and is used here. We have also checked the robustness of our results using an instrument/exclusion restriction approach using information from the BHPS on family background, e.g. father's occupation. The results were qualitatively similar to those found using the multiple spells approach.

The contribution of an individual to the likelihood function can be written as

$$
L = \prod_{m=1}^{M} \left\{ \begin{aligned} & \iiint \int P_1\,(x_m, u_1, u_2)^{z_{1tm}}\,P_2\,(x_m, u_1, u_2)^{z_{2tm}} \\ & \times (1 - P_1\,(x_m, u_1, u_2) - P_2\,(x_m, u_1, u_2))^{1-z_{1tm}-z_{2tm}} \\ & \times h_l\,(t|z_{1tm}, z_{2tm}, x_m, v_l)^{d_{lm}}\,h_n(t|z_{1tm}, z_{2tm}, x_m, v_n)^{d_{nm}} \\ & \times \exp\left(-\int_0^t h_l\,(s|z_{1sm}, z_{2sm}, x_m, v_l)\,ds \right. \\ & \left. \qquad -\int_0^t h_n\,(s|z_{1sm}, z_{2sm}, x_m, v_n)\,ds\right) \end{aligned} \right\} \, dG\,(u_1, u_2, v_l, v_n)
$$

where d_{lm}, d_{nm} are indicator variables associated with exits to new jobs without and with across LAD residential moves respectively. Right-censored spells $d_{im} = 0$, $d_{nm} = 0$, i.e. spells with any other exit type, contribute via the survivor function term. M is the number of spells for each individual, and $G(u_1, u_2, v_l, v_n)$ is the joint CDF of the unobserved heterogeneity variables. The simplest specification for this joint distribution is taken allowing for two points for each unobservable, giving a possible combination of sixteen possible points.[8] Finally, a non-parametric baseline hazard function is used with the baseline hazards for each exit type varying across six different intervals.

Clearly the key to the effectiveness of this estimation strategy is the number of multiple spells per individual. In the job duration sample there are 2,773 individuals. The average number of job spells experienced by individuals in the sample is 3.33, with 80 per cent of individuals having more than one spell. In the unemployment duration sample there are 1,169 individuals, who experienced 1,940 unemployment spells. The average number of unemployment spells experienced by individuals in the sample is 1.66, with 47 per cent of individuals having more than one spell. This is comparable with Munch *et al.* (Chapters 4 and 9) who identify their models with 2.75 unemployment spells per individual and 1.73 employment spells per individual. Finally, in 2.94 per cent of the unemployment spells the individual has experienced more than one type of housing tenure during the spell. The corresponding figure for job spells is 9.24 per cent.

7.4. Results

Tables 7.2, 7.3, and 7.4 present the results of the models for unemployment and job mobility respectively. In Tables 7.2 and 7.3 we also report estimates for a simpler competing risks duration model for exits to a new job with and without a move (columns 4 and 6). These provide a basic comparator to allow us to evaluate the impact of ignoring unobserved heterogeneity and the endogeneity of housing tenure. Further evidence on whether unobserved heterogeneity should be accounted for is provided by the non-linear Wald Test result for the hypothesis that all correlations between the unobserved heterogeneity components are zero. This is reported in the second panel of all the tables. Finally, Table 7.4 reports the competing risk model results disaggregated by socio-economic class.

7.4.1. *Unemployment duration*

The unemployment duration model results are shown in Table 7.2. Coefficients and standard errors are presented, and figures in bold are statistically significant at the 5 per cent level. As stated earlier, the Oswald hypothesis may be interpreted as the implication that the impact of homeownership (relative

Table 7.2. Housing tenure and unemployment spells results

	Homeownership		Public renting		Exit to new job with move				Exit to new job without move			
	(1)		(2)		(3)		(4)		(5)		(6)	
Control for correlated unobserved heterogeneity	Yes		Yes		Yes		No		Yes		No	
Control for tenure endogeneity	n/a		n/a		Yes		No		Yes		No	
	Coeff.	SE	Coeff.	SE	Coeff.	SE	Coeff.	SE	Coeff.	SE	Coeff.	SE
Homeowner					−0.112	0.326	**−1.094**	**0.182**	0.095	0.229	**0.290**	**0.103**
Public renting					**−1.168**	**0.506**	**−1.612**	**0.279**	−0.076	0.238	−0.070	0.118
Age 25–34	0.240	0.380	0.389	0.437	−0.694	0.357	−0.406	0.219	−0.181	0.132	−0.155	0.098
Age 35–44	0.617	0.477	**1.689**	**0.519**	**−1.279**	**0.408**	**−0.962**	**0.266**	−0.203	0.142	−0.194	0.104
Age 45 or above	**1.806**	**0.415**	**1.501**	**0.503**	**−2.864**	**0.514**	**−2.101**	**0.307**	**−0.644**	**0.148**	**−0.535**	**0.105**
Female	−0.167	0.283	**−0.750**	**0.328**	−0.188	0.271	**−0.428**	**0.165**	0.083	0.081	0.091	0.063
Children under 16	**0.844**	**0.313**	**2.325**	**0.357**	**−0.738**	**0.286**	**−0.481**	**0.192**	−0.106	0.089	−0.067	0.068
O-levels	0.201	0.407	**−0.941**	**0.461**	0.371	0.419	0.446	0.270	0.060	0.119	0.029	0.092
A-levels	**1.691**	**0.486**	**−1.545**	**0.579**	0.729	0.400	**0.838**	**0.286**	**0.363**	**0.137**	**0.355**	**0.104**
Nursing or equivalent	**1.007**	**0.392**	**−0.969**	**0.447**	0.000	0.426	0.319	0.267	**0.327**	**0.109**	**0.360**	**0.087**
First degree or above	0.773	0.444	**−2.921**	**0.534**	**0.972**	**0.421**	**1.117**	**0.263**	0.233	0.147	**0.218**	**0.107**
Working partner	**0.808**	**0.404**	**−1.693**	**0.438**	0.329	0.381	0.230	0.234	**0.603**	**0.106**	**0.519**	**0.089**
Married	0.099	0.386	0.013	0.415	**0.839**	**0.349**	**0.823**	**0.254**	−0.117	0.118	−0.086	0.095
Log-likelihood*			−5,652.5				−804.2				−3,887.0	
H0 Unobserved heterogeneity correlations zero (χ^2_6)	14.67** (P < 0.023)											

Figures in bold are statistically significant at 5%.

* Log-likelihood for the joint estimation consistent with the equation on page 169. This specification allowed for unobserved heterogeneity with two mass points for each tenure and exit type, generating sixteen possible combinations, with probability of being in each tenure type modelled as multinomial logit.

**Wald Test of the joint hypothesis that all correlations between unobserved heterogeneity components are zero.

Dummies for standard regions, industries, standard occupations, and time periods are included in all estimations, but results are not reported (see appendix for definitions).

All competing risk models estimated use a non-parametric baseline hazard function with the baseline hazard varying across six different intervals.

to private renting) on the overall hazard rate for transitions out of unemployment is negative. The results set out in Table 7.2 indicate that under the simple competing risks estimation (columns 4 and 6) unemployed homeowners are more likely to obtain jobs locally (without a move) and are less likely to obtain employment non-locally (with a move). The negative effect of private ownership on job attainment via spatial mobility suggests partial support at the micro level for the Oswald hypothesis. Given that the second effect dominates, there is also support for the Oswald hypothesis in aggregate terms.

However, the results from the estimation of the full competing risk model suggest that accounting for unobserved heterogeneity and the tenure endogeneity is important. The hypothesis that the correlations between unobserved components are zero is rejected, while in the full model estimation results the observed private ownership effect dissipates (columns 3 and 5), providing no support for the Oswald hypothesis in overall terms or in terms of the specific job mobility hazard. As such, these results are in line with most of the micro-econometric studies for the USA (Goss and Phillips 1997; Coulson and Fisher 2002) and Australia (Flatau *et al.* 2003). Our results are weaker, though, than the comparable Danish study by Munch *et al.* (Chapter 4 above). They find a positive effect on the local job hazard alongside a negative effect on the mobility hazard even after controlling for unobserved heterogeneity and the endogeneity of tenure. The former dominates, so they also reject the Oswald hypothesis in aggregate terms. The weakness of our results *vis-à-vis* the Danish study may reflect our smaller sample (with no attrition in Danish administrative data) and also institutional differences across the countries (e.g. the UK has a much higher ownership rate and a relatively small and unregulated private rented sector, and there are differences in the nature of social housing). Our results can also be contrasted with two other studies which offer broad support for the Oswald hypothesis. Brunet and Lesueur (Chapter 6 above), using French data, find that homeownership has a positive effect on unemployment duration, though some concerns have been raised about how they deal with selection bias (Munch *et al.*, Chapter 4 above). Green and Hendershott (2001*a*) have found using US data that homeownership raises the duration of unemployment although the effects are very small.

We find that, in contrast to homeowners, unemployed public renters are spatially constrained, since they are less likely to enter employment with a move, compared to private renters, and this holds regardless of whether we control for unobserved heterogeneity and tenure endogeneity. No positive effect is found in terms of the transition into a local job for public renters. In overall terms, unemployed public renters are more likely to stay unemployed, and this result accords with the older UK literature on public housing (Hughes and McCormick 1981, 1987) and indicates that, despite the rises in migration rates documented by Hughes and McCormick (2000) during the 1990s, public tenants still face difficulties in the labour market. One caveat to this result is that in estimations using a six-month window for residential moves before and after a job change this negative public housing effect was not observed. We can speculate that this six-month window may be too short to capture the effects of the bureaucratic procedures involved in arranging moves within the public housing sector across local authority districts, or the possibility of residential moves by the unemployed to seek work.

Let us turn our attention to the other variables. Age has a positive effect on homeownership and has a negative effect on both the transition into employment locally or with a move (older workers find it harder to find a job whilst unemployed). One obvious argument might be that older unemployed individuals are perhaps less willing or capable of acquiring new skills, and this reduces their attractiveness in the labour market and their ability to gain employment. On top of this there is evidence of a negative spatial effect whereby older unemployed individuals find it even more difficult to gain employment outside their own region. It may be that older individuals have accumulated more wealth and have become more attached to a particular geographical area, and so find it more difficult to relocate to a new area for a job compared to the young (aged below 25).

Individuals with higher educational qualifications show a greater probability of being homeowners and are less likely to be in public sector accommodation. Education could act as proxy for wealth and lifetime earnings, making it easier to obtain a mortgage to purchase a property. Educational qualifications also raise the likelihood of gaining employment, be it locally or otherwise, though the effects for the latter are stronger (the educated are more willing to move, possibly because they tend to find higher-paying jobs). Having a working partner has a differential effect across the two types of job entry. Though there is a positive effect on the likelihood of gaining local employment, there is no such effect on the chances of gaining employment with a move. This is suggestive of a spatial constraint for dual-earner couples in which one of the earners has to make a compromise in the labour market.

7.4.2. Job duration

The job duration model results are shown in Table 7.3. Let us start our discussion by focusing on our housing tenure variables. With respect to homeownership, we find a significant negative effect with respect to the transition into non-local employment in our simplest empirical estimation (column 4). In particular, we find that for employed homeowners their transition rate into employment with a move is 68 per cent $(1-\exp[-1.131] = 0.677)$ lower than that for private renters. No such effect is evident for local moves. The negative effect becomes smaller in the case of the transition to non-local employment where the selection equation for tenure is modelled simultaneously with job durations and where we control for unobserved heterogeneity

Table 7.3. Housing tenure and job spells results

	Homeownership		Public renting		Exit to new job with move				Exit to new job without move			
	(1)		(2)		(3)		(4)		(5)		(6)	
Control for correlated unobserved heterogeneity	Yes		Yes		Yes		No		Yes		No	
Control for tenure endogeneity	n/a		n/a		Yes		No		Yes		No	
	Coeff.	SE	Coeff.	SE	Coeff.	SE	Coeff.	SE	Coeff.	SE	Coeff.	SE
Homeowner					**−0.665**	**0.124**	**−1.131**	**0.090**	−0.109	0.090	−0.016	0.060
Public renting					−0.260	0.205	**−0.954**	**0.160**	0.140	0.121	**0.191**	**0.075**
Age 25–34	0.138	0.128	**0.583**	**0.195**	**−0.529**	**0.146**	−0.216	0.125	**−0.593**	**0.077**	**−0.239**	**0.062**
Age 35–44	**0.748**	**0.167**	**0.775**	**0.250**	**−1.313**	**0.176**	**−0.923**	**0.146**	**−0.901**	**0.084**	**−0.283**	**0.066**
Age 45 or above	**1.136**	**0.164**	**0.632**	**0.254**	**−2.179**	**0.198**	**−1.754**	**0.162**	**−1.427**	**0.086**	**−0.629**	**0.067**
Female	−0.118	0.115	**−0.720**	**0.182**	0.067	0.114	0.048	0.083	0.066	0.047	0.007	0.038
Children under 16	**0.463**	**0.100**	**1.102**	**0.150**	−0.073	0.100	**−0.299**	**0.085**	**0.091**	**0.039**	**0.072**	**0.034**
O-levels	0.245	0.161	**−1.152**	**0.206**	0.327	0.180	**0.370**	**0.152**	0.086	0.058	**0.124**	**0.053**
A-levels	**0.664**	**0.173**	**−1.518**	**0.250**	0.220	0.207	0.313	0.167	0.114	0.069	**0.235**	**0.060**
Nursing or equivalent	0.247	0.132	**−1.233**	**0.176**	0.135	0.185	**0.353**	**0.146**	−0.090	0.055	**0.204**	**0.051**
First degree or above	0.265	0.155	**−3.373**	**0.315**	0.341	0.212	**0.616**	**0.159**	**0.227**	**0.068**	**0.478**	**0.061**
Working partner	**0.514**	**0.126**	−0.353	0.178	**−0.247**	**0.113**	**−0.385**	**0.093**	**0.200**	**0.046**	**0.113**	**0.043**
Ln (pay)	**0.208**	**0.080**	**−0.467**	**0.106**	**0.462**	**0.090**	**0.338**	**0.073**	**0.289**	**0.033**	**0.110**	**0.027**
Married	**0.564**	**0.110**	−0.291	0.152	−0.065	0.126	**0.208**	**0.101**	**−0.166**	**0.050**	**−0.154**	**0.048**
Log-likelihood*			−30,607.2				−48,950.4				−214,930.5	
H0: Unobserved heterogeneity correlations zero. (χ^2_6)	65.12** (P < 0.001)											

Figures in bold are statistically significant at 5%.

*Log-likelihood for the joint estimation consistent with the equation on page 169. This specification allowed for unobserved heterogeneity with two mass points for each tenure and exit type, generating sixteen possible combinations, with probability of being in each tenure type modelled as multinomial logit.

**Wald Test of the joint hypothesis that all correlations between unobserved heterogeneity components are zero.

Dummies for standard regions, industries, standard occupations, and time periods are included in all estimations, but results are not reported (see appendix for definitions).

All competing risk models estimated use a non-parametric baseline hazard function with the baseline hazard varying across six different intervals.

(column 3). The negative transition to non-local employment effect is still strong and significant, though: homeowners are less likely to leave their job for a job with a residential move (their non-local job transition rate is 49 per cent lower compared to private renters). Our results are consistent with the view that transaction costs encourage homeowners to set higher reservation wages for more distant jobs compared to private renters. Only two other studies examine the relationship between tenure and job duration. Van Leuvensteijn and Koning (Chapter 8 below) find using Dutch data that employed homeowners are less likely to become unemployed compared to employed renters. Their study does not account for spatial moves so is not strictly comparable with ours. The study by Munch *et al.* (Chapter 9 below) for Denmark does account for moves and also finds a strong and negative effect on job changes to non-local jobs, though the effects are smaller than our findings. For public renters, spatial constraints are also evident, with public renters more (less) likely to obtain a local (non-local) job. However, these effects dissipate once we control for tenure selection and unobserved heterogeneity (columns 3 and 5).

In general, the likelihood of being a homeowner rises with age, consistent with the suggestion that when individuals have accumulated enough wealth they switch to homeownership. For those who are in employment, age reduces the hazard rate into both types of employment, though the coefficients for non-local jobs (with moves) are larger. Older individuals have more stable jobs, and the older they get, the less likely they are to move to gain employment. The absolute size of the coefficients for the age group dummies becomes larger when we control for unobserved heterogeneity.

Being more highly educated increases the chance of being a homeowner and reduces the probability of being a public renter. Having more education also raises the likelihood of entering another job, though the effect is more significant for local employment. The highly paid are more (less) likely to be homeowners (public renters), and they are also more likely to cut the current job short and take on a new one, especially one involving a move. The two family-related variables (being married and having a working partner) increase homeownership and reduce public renting. Married couples may desire greater stability and want to 'settle down', resulting in lower mobility. Reduced mobility may lead to lower annual-equivalent transaction costs in house purchases and enhance the likelihood of homeownership. Being married also allows for the possibility of pooling income and wealth and ameliorating any wealth constraint on ownership. Having a spouse who is working again loosens the wealth constraint that single earners face when considering purchasing a home.

As per the unemployment duration estimations, the influence of these variables on employment exits is mixed. Being married has a strong negative effect on the hazard to local employment, with no effect for non-local employment. A negative dual-earner effect is suggested when we examine the results for having a working partner. Having a working spouse reduces the transition into distant employment, but has a positive effect on local employ-ment (columns 3 and 5). This suggests that dual-earner household's mobility for jobs is reduced. Usually this is couched in gender terms with female spa-tial immobility reflected in what is labelled the 'tied mover hypothesis'. Here females in dual-career households are more likely to be the trailing spouse. They move at the behest of their partner, and in doing so experience a labour market loss. Mincer (1978) argued that families maximize total family income. Where the husband's gain outweighs the loss to the wife, the family moves. With husbands typically being the primary earner, married women are charac-terized as tied movers, in that they move for the benefit of the family, and in doing so experience a loss. A significant body of research broadly con-firms this hypothesis and the deleterious impact on labour market outcomes (McGoldrick and Robst 1996; Büchel and Battu 2003; Nivalainen 2004).

7.4.3. Job duration by socio-economic class

Hughes and McCormick (1994) show that the migration decisions of workers vary considerably across socio-economic classes. Table 7.4 explores whether these types of effect also manifest themselves in the current empirical frame-work. For the unskilled/partly skilled group we have only seventy-four non-local job exits. Therefore, the results here convey little information, with few variables being statistically significant, and the null hypothesis that the unob-served heterogeneity components are important is not rejected. In contrast, the estimation results for the professional/managerial and skilled manual/non-manual classes are more informative. In both estimations, the hypothesis that all the correlations between unobserved components are zero is rejected, with most estimated coefficients as expected (if not always statistically significant at 5 per cent). Most interesting, there is some evidence of a differential effect of homeownership on exits with a residential move across LADs, with the neg-ative impact relative to private renting greater for skilled manual/non-manual classes compared to the professional/managerial class. From a simple job search perspective any negative homeownership effect is a function of the job offer arrival rate and the difference in the probabilities of receiving a job offer above the reservation wage when a tenant and relative to when an individual is a homeowner. From this perspective, the difference in the negative homeown-ership effect across groups may reflect differences in job arrival rates and/or the differences in the probabilities of acceptable offers.

7.5. Conclusions

This paper examines the effects of housing tenure on individual job mobility in the UK using the British Household Panel Survey. As such, our analysis represents the first explicit micro study of the Oswald hypothesis using UK

Table 7.4. Job spells results by socio-economic class

| | Professional/managerial (SEC1) | | | | Skilled manual/non-manual (SEC2) | | | | Unskilled/partly skilled (SEC3) | | | |
| | Exit to new job with move | | Exit to new job without move | | Exit to new job with move | | Exit to new job without move | | Exit to new job with move | | Exit to new job without move | |
	Coeff.	SE	Coeff.	SE	Coeff.	SE	Coeff.	SE	Coeff.	SE	Coeff.	SE
Homeowner	**-0.605**	**0.226**	-0.122	0.183	**-0.819**	**0.239**	-0.265	0.154	0.106	1.163	-0.261	0.286
Public renting	0.420	0.793	**0.855**	**0.326**	-0.543	0.493	-0.048	0.193	-1.881	1.608	-0.185	0.282
Age 25–34	**-0.923**	**0.342**	**-0.691**	**0.160**	-0.319	0.284	**-0.600**	**0.111**	0.045	0.995	-0.325	0.244
Age 35–44	**-2.069**	**0.368**	**-1.072**	**0.165**	**-0.959**	**0.347**	**-0.796**	**0.126**	-1.312	1.084	**-0.581**	**0.256**
Age 45 or above	**-2.651**	**0.389**	**-1.508**	**0.169**	**-2.237**	**0.375**	**-1.312**	**0.127**	**-3.083**	**1.291**	**-1.180**	**0.266**
Female	0.140	0.173	0.114	0.071	0.257	0.276	0.038	0.081	-0.591	0.729	0.163	0.136
Children under 16	0.043	0.171	0.095	0.066	-0.403	0.224	0.108	0.062	0.013	0.690	0.154	0.126
O-levels	**1.466**	**0.524**	0.052	0.158	0.235	0.331	0.132	0.082	-1.257	0.936	-0.008	0.140
A-levels	0.617	0.593	0.176	0.159	0.364	0.334	0.149	0.097	-0.665	1.020	0.185	0.184
Nursing or equivalent	0.868	0.511	0.085	0.139	-0.002	0.325	-0.152	0.085	-0.709	1.025	-0.162	0.130
First degree or above	0.824	0.514	**0.346**	**0.144**	0.531	0.399	0.215	0.114	-0.986	1.868	0.287	0.247
Working partner	-0.178	0.173	**0.183**	**0.078**	-0.335	0.252	**0.214**	**0.075**	-0.850	0.758	0.076	0.149
Ln (pay)	**0.804**	**0.183**	**0.265**	**0.061**	**0.375**	**0.188**	**0.291**	**0.053**	-0.318	0.484	**0.295**	**0.082**
Married	-0.041	0.207	**-0.213**	**0.096**	-0.174	0.230	**-0.173**	**0.079**	0.382	1.025	0.107	0.159
Log-likelihood*	-12,178.9				-13,273.5				-4,962.8			
H0: Unobserved heterogeneity correlations zero. (χ_6^2)	28.93** (P < 0.001)				27.19** (P < 0.001)				4.63** (P < 0.591)			
Number of exits	423		1,657		285		1,929		74		709	

Figures in bold are statistically significant at 5%.
* All estimations are for the specification which allows for unobserved heterogeneity with two mass points for each tenure and exit type, generating sixteen possible combinations, with probability of being in each tenure type modelled as multinomial logit.
** Wald Test of the joint hypothesis that all correlations between unobserved heterogeneity components are zero.
Dummies for standard regions, industries, standard occupations, and time periods are included in all estimations, but results are not reported (see appendix for definitions).
All competing risk models estimated use a non-parametric baseline hazard function with the baseline hazard varying across six different intervals.

data. Beyond this, our analysis is distinctive in two ways. We examine the effects of public rented as well as private homeownership, and we control for unobserved heterogeneity and endogeneity of housing tenure. We also take explicit account of spatial mobility by distinguishing between local and non-local jobs.

Despite the limitations of this study, e.g. the approximate way in which local labour markets can be captured and the difficulties in dealing with incomplete job history information, our results indicate that spatial mobility and distance matter. However, there are differential effects across tenure types, and it matters whether we start with the employed or the unemployed. In general our results indicate that homeownership is a constraint for the employed, and public renting is more of a constraint for the unemployed. Employed homeowners have a lower probability of gaining employment in more distant labour markets relative to private renters, and these negative effects appear larger for the skilled manual/non-manual relative to the professional/managerial socio-economic class. For the unemployed, public renting seems to be the more powerful constraint; unemployed public renters appear much less likely to enter a distant job than private renters. There is no support for the Oswald hypothesis that private homeownership raises unemployment duration.

In rejecting the basic Oswald hypothesis our results are consistent with the vast bulk of previous microeconomic studies from other countries (Munch *et al.*, Chapter 4 above; Van Leuvensteijn and Koning, Chapter 8 below; Coulson and Fisher 2002). In contrast, our results with some caveats suggest that the impact of public renting on mobility remains a constraint for the unemployed, and that homeownership negatively impacts on overall job mobility, which may induce negative aggregate losses at the macro level.

Further research needs to distinguish between those who own outright and those who own with a mortgage, with the latter exhibiting varying degrees of debt. Those with weak equity (highly leveraged) may be much keener to obtain re-employment in order to maintain mortgage payments. Furthermore, our analysis says nothing about match quality across space. If there is no change in residence (no regional move) do individuals enter a lower level job that does not match their qualifications? This is a focus for future research.

VARIABLE DEFINITIONS

1. Homeowner. Dummy variable equals 1 if the home is owned (with or without mortgage) by the individual or other family member(s) in the household, zero otherwise.
2. Public renter. Dummy variable equals 1 if the home is rented from a local authority or housing association by the employee or other family member(s) in the household. Private renter is the reference group.
3. Age categories with the following bands: 25–34, 35–44, and 45 plus. These are dummy variables, equal to 1 if the age falls within the category. The reference age group is 16–24.
4. Female. This equals 1 if the employee is female.
5. Children under 16. This is a dummy variable which equals 1 if there are one or more children in the household who are aged below 16.
6. Married. This equals 1 if the employee is married or cohabiting.
7. Working partner. This equals 1 if the employee is married and the spouse/partner is working, where working is defined as being employed or self-employed. It equals zero in all other cases, including those who are unmarried.
8. Four indicators for highest educational qualifications in the UK. These are O-levels or equivalent; A-levels or equivalent; nursing or other higher qualifications; first degree or above (university degree, teaching qualification, or higher). The reference group is having no qualifications.
9. Ln (pay). This is monthly pay defined as the natural log of usual gross monthly pay.
10. Seven industry indicators created using the Standard Industrial Classification (SIC) 1980 identifiers. The reference group is an amalgamation of four groups: SIC 0 (agriculture, forestry, and fishing), SIC 1 (energy and water supplies), SIC 2 (extraction of minerals and ores other than fuels, etc.), and SIC 9 (other services). The industry dummies represent the six remaining industries: SIC 3 (metal goods, engineering, and vehicles industries), SIC 4 (other manufacturing industries), SIC 5 (construction), SIC 6 (distribution, hotels, and catering), SIC 7 (transport and communication), and SIC 8 (banking, finance, insurance, business services, and leasing).
11. Nine occupational categories created using the 1990 Standard Occupational Classification (SOC): SOC 1—managers and administrators; SOC 2—professional occupations; SOC 3—associate professional and technical; SOC 4—clerical and secretarial; SOC 5—craft and related occupations; SOC 6—personal and protective service occupations; SOC 7—sales occupations; SOC 8—plant and machine operatives and the reference group; SOC 9—other occupations.

12. Seven regional dummies defined as South-West, East Anglia, Midlands, North-West, Yorkshire and the North-East, Scotland, and Wales. The South-East is the reference group.

13. Socio-economic class of current job in BHPS is defined from three-digit standard occupational code and employment status variables: SEC 1 (professional, managerial, and technical occupations); SEC 2 (skilled manual, skilled non-manual); SEC 3 (partly skilled and unskilled occupations).

Notes

1. In non-UK studies, a focus on public renting is less warranted. For example, in the case of Denmark an emphasis on rent controls is more meaningful. Svarer *et al.* (2005) examine the effects of Danish rent controls on unemployment duration and find that the net effect of rent controls is to raise unemployment duration.
2. There are 857 job spells dropped from the sample because of the lack of between-interview information. Eliminating ongoing spells drops 2,412 job spells and 126 unemployment spells. Restricting the sample to spells for individuals present in all waves eliminates 3,665 job spells and increases the overall average duration of a job spell by around two months on average. Similarly, 1,152 unemployment spells are dropped, increasing the overall unemployment duration by around half a month.
3. There are 278 LADs in Britain, with a population ranging between 60 and 300,000 (Böheim and Taylor 2007).
4. The boundary definitions for LADs follow those that were in use for the Census of 1991.
5. Those that do not move may instead widen their search space, and so commuting may represent a substitute for migration. Benito and Oswald (1999) find that commuting times are higher amongst homeowners and Murphy *et al.* (2006) show that strong housing market conditions can inhibit migration and make commuting a more attractive alternative to moving.
6. This estimate covers only the household reference person, i.e. the head of the household.
7. The full set of discrete results are available on request from the authors.
8. Exploratory estimations with three points of support for each unobservable were also conducted. It was not generally possible to identify these extra mass points.

References

Abbring J. H., and Van den Berg, G. J. (2003), 'The non-parametric identification of treatment effects in duration models', *Econometrica*, 51/5, 1491–517.

Barcelo, C. (2001), 'Modelling housing tenure and labour mobility: an empirical investigation', mimeo, Banco de Espana.

Benito, A., and Oswald, A. (1999), 'Commuting in Great Britain in the 1990s', unpublished draft, Department of Economics, University of Warwick.

Bergstrom, R., and Edin, P. (1992), 'Time aggregation and the distributional shape of unemployment duration', *Journal of Applied Econometrics*, 7/1, 5–30.

Böheim, R., and Taylor, M. P. (2002), 'Tied down or room to move? Investigating the relationships between housing tenure, employment status and residential mobility in Britain', *Scottish Journal of Political Economy*, 49/4, 369–92.

———— (2007), 'From the dark end of the street to the bright side of the road? The wage returns to migration in Britain', *Labour Economics*, 14/1, 99–117.

Buck, N. (2000), 'Using panel surveys to study migration and residential mobility', in D. Rose (ed.), *Researching Social and Economic Change* (London: Routledge), 250–72.

Büchel, F., and Battu, H. (2003), 'The theory of differential overqualification: does it work?', *Scottish Journal of Political Economy*, 50/1, 1–16.

Coulson, E. N., and Fisher, L. M. (2002), 'Labor market outcomes of homeownership', *Housing Studies*, 17, 35–50.

Flatau, P., Forbes, M., Hendershott, P., and Wood, G. (2003), 'Homeownership and unemployment: the roles of leverage and public housing', NBER Working Paper no. 10021.

Goss, E. P., and Phillips, J. M. (1997), 'The impact of homeownership on the duration of unemployment', *Review of Regional Studies*, 27/1, 9–27.

Green, R. K., and Hendershott, P. H. (2001a), 'Homeownership and unemployment in the US', *Urban Studies*, 38/9, 1509–20.

——— (2001b), 'Homeownership and the duration of unemployment: a test of the Oswald hypothesis', mimeo, NBER Working Paper.

Heckman, J. J. (1981), 'Heterogeneity and state dependence', in S. Rosen (ed.), *Studies in Labour Markets* (Chicago: University of Chicago Press), 91–139.

——— and Singer, B. (1984), 'A method for minimizing the impact if distributional assumptions in econometric models for duration data', *Econometrica*, 52, 271–320.

Hughes, G., and McCormick, B. (1981), 'Do council housing policies reduce migration between regions?', *Economic Journal*, 91, 919–37.

——— (1987), 'Housing markets, unemployment and labour market flexibility in the UK', *European Economic Review*, 31/3, 615–41.

——— (1994), 'Did migration in the 1980s narrow the North–South divide?', *Economica*, 61/244, 509–27.

——— (2000), *Housing Policy and Labour Market Performance*, London: Department of the Environment, Transport and the Regions.

Keifer, N. (1990), 'Econometric methods for grouped duration data', in J. Hartog *et al.* (eds.), *Panel Data and Labor Market Studies* (Amsterdam: North-Holland), 97–117.

Lancaster, T. (1990), *The Econometric Analysis of Transition Data* (Cambridge: Cambridge University Press).

McCormick, B. (1983), 'Housing and unemployment in Great Britain', *Oxford Economic Papers*, 35, 283–305.

——— (1997), 'Regional unemployment and labour mobility in the UK', *European Economic Review*, 41, 581–9.

McCulloch, A. (2003), 'Local labour markets and individual transitions into and out of poverty: evidence from the British Household Panel Study waves 1 to 8', *Environment and Planning A*, 35/3, 551–68.

McGoldrick, K. M., and Robst, J. (1996), 'Gender differences in overeducation: a test of the theory of differential overqualification', *American Economic Review*, 86, 280–4.

Mincer, J. (1978), 'Family migration decisions', *Journal of Political Economy*, 86, 749–73.

Murphy, A., Muellbauer, J., and Cameron, G. (2006), 'Housing market dynamics and regional migration in Britain', Nuffield College, UK.

Nivalainen, S. (2004), 'Determinants of family migration: short moves vs. long moves', *Journal of Population Economics*, 17/1, 157–75.

Norris, M., and Shiels, P. (2004), 'Housing developments in European countries', Department of the Environment, Heritage, and Local Government, Ireland.

Oswald, A. (1996), 'A conjecture of the explanation for high unemployment in the industrialized nations: part I', Warwick University Economic Research Paper 475.

Panis, C., and Lillard, L. (2004), 'Health inputs and child mortality: Malaysia', *Journal of Health Economics*, 13, 455–89.

Rabe, B. (2006), 'Dual-earner migration in Britain: earnings gains, employment, and self-selection', ISER Working Paper 2006-1, University of Essex, Colchester.

Svarer, M., Rosholm, M., and Munch, J. (2005), 'Rent control and unemployment duration', *Journal of Public Economics*, 89, 2165–81.

ter Hofstede, F., and Wedel, M. (1998), 'A Monte Carlo study of time aggregation in continuous-time and discrete-time parametric hazard models', *Economics Letters*, 58/2, 149–56.

Upward, R. (1999), 'Constructing data on unemployment spells from the PSID and the BHPS', Centre for Research on Globalization and Labour Markets, School of Economic Studies, Nottingham.

Van den Berg, G. J. (2001), 'Duration models: specification, identification and multiple durations', in J. J. Heckman and E. Leamer (eds.), *Handbook of Econometrics* (Amsterdam: North-Holland), 3381–460.

8

The Effect of Homeownership on Labour Mobility in the Netherlands[*]

Michiel van Leuvensteijn and Pierre Koning

8.1. Introduction

The European labour market is often characterized by its low mobility, both within as well as between countries. Since the introduction of EMU, this problem has become more prominent, as the mobility of labour is one of the few short-term adjustment mechanisms still left. One reason for the low labour mobility in Europe is that there are cultural and linguistic barriers. This, however, does not explain the differences in interregional mobility within a country, or changes in labour mobility through time. One of the explanations for this may be that homeownership diminishes labour mobility and increases unemployment. The idea is that homeowners will not move to other regions when faced with an economic downturn, as they are more attached to their homes. Also, they may be faced with decreases in housing prices. Thus, the probability of unemployment would be higher for homeowners.

Although the idea that homeownership has a positive effect on unemployment is based on microeconomic assumptions, most studies addressing the effect of homeownership on labour mobility and unemployment use macro- or meso-economic data. With aggregated data for the US, Green and Hendershott (2001) show that homeownership indeed constrains labour mobility, and thus increases unemployment for middle-aged classes, due to high transaction and moving costs involved. Using data of the OECD countries, Nickell (1998) finds similar results. However, these studies do not reveal the underlying

[*] The authors would like to thank Rob Alessie, Casper van Ewijk, Bas van der Klaauw, Jos van Ommeren, Gusta Renes, and two anonymous referees for valuable comments. Statistics Netherlands is gratefully acknowledged for providing access to the IPR data. Of course, the usual disclaimer applies.

This article was published in *Journal of Urban Economics*, 55, 580–96; copyright Elsevier 2004.

behaviour of individuals. For example, it may well be that lower job mobility of homeowners results from higher job commitment, also reducing the risk of unemployment. Obviously, this cannot be measured in meso or macro studies.

Instead of using macro- or meso-economic data, we will use longitudinal data of individual employees. This helps us to correct for spurious relationships and identify effects of homeownership on labour mobility, and the reverse. Movements on both the housing market and the labour market are used to estimate the impact of homeownership on job mobility as well as the probability of becoming unemployed. We use longitudinal data collected by the Dutch tax department (Income Panel Research data (IPR), for 1989–98). In the IPR, about 75,000 individuals are followed over time. These individuals can move between jobs, between unemployment and employment, between homes, and between regions. In modelling these transitions, several variables in the IPR may be useful: age, income, the number of children, gender, homeownership, job tenure, and housing duration.

Our analysis contributes to the literature on labour and housing market mobility in a number of respects. First, the IPR provides us with a rather unique panel allowing us to link individual labour and housing market histories of a large sample of employees. The IPR data are comparable with the British Household Panel Survey, which also combines both types of information (see e.g. Böheim and Taylor 2000). Second, and in contrast to many other empirical studies on job mobility, we also explicitly model the probability of homeownership, so as to correct for endogeneity bias. To minimize the biasing impact of distributional assumptions, this is done in a non-parametric fashion. Third, we analyse the impact of homeownership not only on job-to-job mobility, but also (and simultaneously) on the risk of becoming unemployed or non-participant. This means we estimate a job duration model with multiple ('competing') risks.

The further structure of the paper is as follows. Section 8.2 describes the literature on the relationship between the housing market and labour mobility. Section 8.3 presents the empirical model, whereas the data are described in Section 8.4. In Sections 8.5 and 8.6, the estimation results and conclusions are presented.

8.2. Theory and review

There are two strands of literature that describe the relationship between the housing market and the labour market, depending on the macro- or micro-economic focus. Contributions in the first strand mostly try to explain labour migration. Here, the starting point is the Harris–Todaro model. In Harris and

Todaro (1970), a neoclassical model is developed in which (international) migration is caused by geographical differences in the supply and demand for labour. Regions with a limited supply of labour will have a relatively high expected wage, which is the product of the complement of the unemployment rate and the wage if employed. High expected wages will attract a large inflow of labour from low-wage regions. This inflow of labour is mirrored by an outflow of capital.

Green and Hendershott (2001) add to this the role of homeownership to explain high unemployment and low labour migration. There are a number of ways in which homeownership influences labour migration. First, in regions with an economic downturn homeowners are faced with a drop in house prices, making homes highly illiquid assets. Moving to another region to find a job may therefore be costly for homeowners. Second, high interest rates in times of recession may also result in a lock-in to below-market mortgages, with similar consequences for labour mobility. Third, high transaction costs may cause a decrease in labour mobility.

Various macro studies address the relationship between homeownership and unemployment empirically. For example, Nickell (1998) analyses the relationship between homeownership and unemployment, using a panel of twenty OECD countries, from 1989 to 1994. With these data, Nickell shows that unemployment is (seemingly) positively correlated with homeownership, with an elasticity of 0.13. This means that a rise of homeownership of 10 percentage points results in an increase in unemployment of 1.3 percentage points. Green and Hendershott (2001) estimate an elasticity of 0.18, using aggregated data for the different states of the United States for the period 1970–90. This estimate is close to the estimate of Oswald (Chapter 2 above), with an elasticity equal to 0.2. He analyses the relationship between homeownership and unemployment, using panel time series data for nineteen OECD countries, from 1960 to 1990. This relationship is found not only between countries, but also between the regions of France, Italy, Sweden, Switzerland, the USA, and the UK.

For the Netherlands, Hassink and Kurvers (1999) show that regions with high homeownership rates do not have high unemployment rates when tested at a meso-economic level. They estimate the relationship between unemployment rate and homeownership for 348 regions for the period 1990–8, and find homeownership to have a negative impact on unemployment. This suggests a simultaneity problem: workers in regions with high economic growth and low unemployment will have higher incomes, and therefore be more likely to buy a house. Apparently this is what is picked up in the estimation of the model.

Next to this, the relationship between labour mobility and the housing market is also studied on in a microeconomic context. Van Ommeren (1996) develops a theoretical search model in which the acceptance of a job offer depends not only on the direct gain in wage utility, but also on the once-only costs associated with moving residence and search costs. These on-the-job search costs are modest for most professions, compared to the once-only costs associated with moving residence. The once-only costs associated with moving to another residence depend strongly on housing status (see e.g. Van den Berg 1992).

Recently, various empirical studies have addressed the relationship between the housing market and labour mobility, making use of individual, longitudinal data. With the British Household Panel Survey, Henley (1998) finds for the United Kingdom that unemployed are less likely to move than employed workers. Using the same data, Böheim and Taylor (2000) come to a similar result. Using Probit models with pooled data for the United Kingdom, they find that regions with high unemployment show less home mobility. Also, they find that homeowners change jobs less than tenants. For the Netherlands, Van Ommeren *et al.* (2000) estimate a search model for job movers with (retrospective) panel data from the beginning of the Nineties. He finds homeowners to be less likely to move to another home than tenants are. Also, he finds no evidence that job and residential moves are mutually related. Van der Vlist (2001) concludes that homeowners are less likely to move to another home and to change jobs.

To sum up, the two strands of literature portray different, but not necessarily contradictory, pictures. Macro studies, using variation between countries or regions over time, suggest that high homeownership rates may lead to higher unemployment, in particular in periods of economic downturn. Micro studies, using (longitudinal) data of individuals or households, find homeownership to be associated with lower residential mobility and lower job-to-job mobility. This suggests that homeowners have more job commitment, and thus may also have a lower risk of unemployment. However, little is known on the exact causality of these effects. The question remains, to what extent homeownership is driven by job commitment, and to what extent the reverse holds.

8.3. The empirical model

Our empirical model consists of two parts: the job duration model and the housing model. In the job duration model, we explain the individual labour market histories of a flow sample of employees. With this information, we identify the impact of various explanatory variables, including housing state, on labour mobility. Also, since individuals are followed over time, we control for unobserved heterogeneity. Within the context of duration models, this means that we assume a (non-parametric) distribution of random effects. The same principle holds for the housing model. Here, we explain a sequence of housing states, measured on a yearly basis. These data allow us to estimate a random effects logit model.

Initially, the job duration and the housing model are treated separately, and without the inclusion of random effects. As a result, the estimated impact of housing state on job mobility may be biased. Next, we estimate a simultaneous model, where the job duration and the housing model are linked by the possible correlation of their random effects.

8.3.1. The job duration model

In this paper we use hazard rate or—stated differently—duration models to examine the impact of homeownership on job spells. The hazard rate is defined as the rate at which an event takes place over a short period of time, given that this event has not occurred so far. The hazard rate, θ, measures the probability of leaving a job or over a specific (small) time interval $(T, \ T + dt)$, given that one occupies this job up to T:

$$\theta = \Pr(T < t < T + dt | t \geq T) \tag{8.1}$$

In the job duration model, the time interval dt is normalized to one month. Three types of transitions may take place: into another job, into becoming unemployed, or into becoming non-participant. Therefore, the hazard rate out of employment is modelled into three possible competing risks. The impact of several exogenous variables, like age, sex, or income, may vary with respect to these risks.

The competing risks have a *proportional* (or *loglinear*) structure (see e.g. Lancaster 1990). b denotes the index of a particular risk ($b = 1, 2 \ldots B$). Thus, the risk into b at time t can be described as:

$$\theta_b(t|y_t, X_t) = \exp\left[\alpha_b y_t + \beta_b X_t + \Psi(t)\right] \tag{8.2}$$

with $b = 1, 2, 3$, in which y_t equals 1 if the individual is a homeowner at time t (and zero if one rents a home), and X_t is a matrix representing individual covariates that may change over time t. Some of these characteristics do not vary over time, but are defined at the beginning of the duration spell. Obviously, the most relevant variable—that of the housing state y—is time-dependent. Ψ denotes the impact of duration dependence. In the estimation of the model, we use a (non-parametric) step function for Ψ. Further, notice that the variables that change over time do so only on a calendar-year base. So residential transitions may coincide with job movements within a calendar year, whereas the exact sequence of events is unknown.

8.3.2. The housing model

We assume the housing state y to follow a logit specification:

$$\Pr(y_t = 1|X_t, h_t) = \frac{\exp\left[\gamma X_t + \Phi(t) + \delta h_t\right]}{1 + \exp\left[\gamma X_t + \Phi(t) + \delta h_t\right]}$$

$$\Pr(y_t = 0|X_t, h_t) = 1 - \Pr(y_t = 1)$$

(8.3)

As becomes apparent from (8.3), we assume the housing probability to be driven by the same time-varying covariates as the job duration model, X_t. In addition to this, we use the regional homeownership rate h_t as an instrumental variable, affecting only the housing status. In our data, we have 538 regions. Also, since h_t pertains to average group behaviour, it should be noted at this point that the assumptions for identification here are stronger than in models where instruments are measured on an individual basis (see Manski 1993). We will discuss these assumptions in detail in Section 8.5, when we come to the estimation results. Further, similar to (8.2), $\Phi(t)$ denotes a step function describing the impact of job tenure.

8.3.3. Unobserved heterogeneity

The IPR data we use provide us with a limited amount of registered individual information. Obviously, more characteristics may be relevant in explaining the differences in e.g. the risk of unemployment or that of moving to another home. In particular, job commitment—which is approximated by the job tenure variable—may be measured imperfectly. The more important the impact of such unobserved heterogeneity, the larger the potential biasing impact of endogeneity effects. Endogeneity may arise if the choice of buying or renting a home is correlated with the risk of job transitions, becoming unemployed, or non-participant.

Within the context of duration models, several methods have been developed to allow for unobserved heterogeneity. To minimize the impact of distributional assumptions, we adopt a non-parametric method which has been introduced by Heckman and Singer (1984). They assume that a sample consists of two (or more) (unobserved) sub-samples with different levels of time-invariant unobservable effects. Then, for all sub-samples the corresponding weights are estimated, as well as the impact of unobserved differences on the hazard. This mass-point methodology is also used for the housing model. The unobserved differences in both models can then be linked, so as to allow for cross-correlation.

To allow for the presence of unobserved heterogeneity, we specify the risks (with index b) as a so called mixed proportional hazard (MPH) structure.

The mixing is with respect to v, which can be interpreted as a time-invariant random effect:

$$\theta_b(t|y_t, X_t, v_b) = \exp\left[\alpha_b y_t + \beta_b X_t + \Psi(t) + v_b\right] \qquad (8.4)$$

where $b = 1, 2, 3$.

We also extend the housing model with random effects, u:

$$\Pr(y_t = 1|Z_t, u) = \frac{\exp\left[\gamma X_t + \Phi(t) + \delta h_t + u\right]}{1 + \exp\left[\gamma X_t + \Phi(t) + \delta h_t + u\right]} \qquad (8.5)$$

$$\Pr(y_t = 0|Z_t, u) = 1 - \Pr(y_t = 1)$$

To correct for endogeneity bias, we allow v_1, v_2, v_3, and u to be correlated. Like Heckman and Singer (1984), we do this by modelling K combinations of mass points for $\{v_1, v_2, v_3, u\}$, with probability weights P_1, $P_2 \ldots 1 - P_1 - \ldots - P_{k-1}$, respectively. Thus, the unknown distribution of $\{v_1, v_2, v_3, u\}$ is represented by a non-parametric distribution with a finite number of points of support. The first point of support is normalized to $\{0, 0, 0, 0\}$. Thus, in this specification one has to estimate the parameters $\{\alpha, \beta, \gamma, P_1, P_2 \ldots P_{K-1}\}$ as well as $K - 1$ combinations of $\{v_1, v_2, v_3, u\}$. We do this by using maximum likelihood estimation. We start by estimating the model without unobserved heterogeneity ($K = 1$, where there is only one point of support and $P_1 = 1$). Subsequently, we increase the number of points of support K iteratively, so as to improve the fit of the model. We perform a likelihood ratio test to determine the optimal K: that is, the number of points of support where the inclusion of an additional point of support, $\{v_1, v_2, v_3, u\}$, together with an additional weight, improves the likelihood significantly.

Correlation between the v's and u is not explicitly specified in the model, but follows from the combination of mass points. In principle, 4^{K-1} points of support allow for all possible forms of correlation between the four random effects. However, this makes the empirical model computationally very burdensome. Therefore, with increasing K, we add a fixed point of support for $\{v_1, v_2, v_3, u\}$. For $K = 2$, this means that we allow only the random effects of the v's and u to be fully correlated. For $K > 2$, however, the model becomes more flexible.

The mass-point methodology we use resembles that of Abbring (1997) and Holm (2002), who both estimate a bivariate model with limited dependent or duration data. Abbring (1997) studies the impact of punitive sanctions on the job-finding rate of unemployed employees. Both the job-finding process and the risk of being sanctioned are influenced by random effects that may be correlated. Analogously, Holm (2002) studies the effect of training on search durations. He also uses a random effect approach, both in the training allocation model as well as in the hazard rate model of finding a job.

8.3.4. *The likelihood*

As stated before, if we do not allow for time-invariant (unobserved) heterogeneity, the likelihood function of the model consists of two model parts that can be estimated separately. For ease of exposition, we first derive these two likelihood contributions, conditional on the unobserved components $\{v_1, v_2, v_3, u\}$. Next, we integrate with respect to the unobserved mass points, so as to obtain the joint likelihood of the model.

Basically, our model explains two types of information:

ELAPSED JOB DURATIONS

- T = the elapsed job duration, starting from the moment of inflow in the IPR sample.
- d = a censoring indicator, which equals 1 if the job duration is right censored, and zero otherwise.
- b = the destination that follows the job duration spell. This destination can be another job ($v = 1$), unemployment ($v = 2$), or non-participation ($v = 3$).

HOUSING STATE

- y_t = a dummy indicator, which equals 1 if an employee is a homeowner at time t, for $t = 1 \ldots T$.

We assume that the censoring times are stochastically independent of the corresponding job durations; i.e. we assume that censoring is independent. Since the job durations are distributed exponentially, conditional likelihood of $\{T, b\}$ of a particular individual can be described as:

$$f_T(T, b | \mathbf{y}, \mathbf{X}, \mathbf{v}) = \exp\left[- \Sigma_t^T \left\{ \theta_1(t) + \theta_2(t) + \theta_3(t) \right\} \right]$$
$$\times \left[\theta_1(T)^{I(b=1)} \times \theta_2(T)^{I(b=2)} \times \theta_3(T)^{I(b=3)} \right]^{(1-d)} \quad (8.6)$$

where I ($b = 1, 2, 3$) is an indicator function of the event in parentheses. In particular, this concerns the destination following the jobs spell. The first part of (8.6) represents the survival probability. Within the context of our model, this is the probability of not having found another job, having become unemployed, or having become non-participant, up to time T. If T is censored ($= 1$), the likelihood of $\{T, b\}$ equals the survival probability. If T is uncensored ($= 0$), Eqn. (8.6) consists of two parts: the probability of survival until T and the likelihood of a transition, into either another job ($b = 1$), or unemployment ($b = 2$), or non-participation ($b = 3$).

The individual conditional likelihood of $\mathbf{y}$—consisting of a sequence of housing states over the job spell of an individual—that follows from the (panel) logit model (8.5) is:

$$\Pr(y|X, h, u) = \Pi_t^T \Pr(y_t = 1|X_t, h_t, u)^{I(y(t)=1)} \times \Pr(y_t = 0|Z_t, h_t, u)^{I(y(t)=0)} \tag{8.7}$$

The joint, individual likelihood of the observed variables—given the unobserved variables v and u—is obtained by multiplying (8.6) and (8.7). For the unobserved variables, we have K combinations of mass points for $\{v_1, v_2, v_3, u\}$, with probability weights, $P_1, P_2 \dots 1 - P_1 - \dots - P_{k-1}$, respectively. Thus, the joint, integrated likelihood can be written as:

$$L = \Sigma_i^K \left[P_i \times f_T(T, b|y, X, v_i) \times \Pr(y|X, h, u_i) \right] \tag{8.8}$$

where i indicates the mass-point combination. This expression is maximized with respect to $\{\alpha, \beta, \gamma\}$, as well as K mass points of $\{v_1, v_2, v_3, u\}$. Obviously, more combinations of mass points may help in increasing the fit of the model. As stated before, we use a likelihood ratio test to determine the optimal number of combinations.

8.4. Data

The IPR database consists of a sample of about 75,000 individuals who are followed yearly by tax authorities, over the period 1989–98. In the IPR, a number of possible housing and labour market states are distinguished. The states for the labour market are based on individual income states, like social assistance (SA) benefits, unemployment insurance (UI) benefits, income, and no income. From these income states, one can derive the data as to when a person becomes unemployed (SA or UI benefit), or non-participant (no income or disability benefits). Further, since we know the identity of the employer, it is possible to keep track of job-to-job changes. Behaviour regarding moving can be derived from address changes. Housing market states consist of rental housing, homeownership, or other types (e.g. housing for the elderly). These are observed on a yearly basis. For each individual, we observe a complete or incomplete job spell, together with various individual characteristics.

Our data consist of a flow sample of employees. This means that we select individuals entering a job, avoiding the problem of left censoring. This leaves us with 9,426 observations of individual spells. The construction of a flow sample has one major advantage: for each employee we observe the exact job tenure. Obviously, this variable is crucial to identify the impact of job commitment, in particular the impact of (negative) duration dependence.

We also select employees who are either homeowners and/or tenants during the time span covered by the interviews. Thus, employees living in 'other house types' are left out of the sample. As the vast majority of individuals in this category are students or pensioned, this does not reduce the size of our sample (consisting of employees) substantially.

Given the IPR, the following variables are used in the empirical analysis:

1. Age at time of entry into the sample.
2. Gender.
3. Higher or university education. This (proxy) dummy variable indicates whether a person has received recently a scholarship for higher or university education at the moment of inflow into the sample. Thus, this level of education is not observed for older employees.
4. Having children that receive child support, or not.
5. Having a partner who earns income, or not.
6. Marital state: being married, or not.
7. Wage in logs.

In Table 8.1 we present the characteristics of employees at the end of 1998. The majority of the employees are male (59 per cent), 40 per cent have a working partner, 31 per cent have children, 7 per cent have studied recently. As we have a flow sample, a large fraction of the sample consists of employees who are more likely to switch jobs, and/or start their labour market career. Consequently, on average, employees are rather young (34 years), and job durations relatively short (almost twenty months). The mean percentage of homeowners is 53 per cent. In the first year of a job spell, we observe a mean percentage of homeowners of about 25 per cent. Thus, a large fraction of employees are observed to buy a home during their job spell.

As we have yearly observations of housing state (measured at the end of calendar years) and monthly observations of labour market state, this may cause

Table 8.1. Description of variables (mean and standard deviation)

	Employees	
	Mean (*fractions*)*	Standard deviation of mean
Job duration (including censored, in days)	596.25	7.44
Percentage of right-censored	0.232	0.004
Female	0.475	0.005
Working partner	0.345	0.005
Children	0.31	0.005
High education	0.176	0.004
Age (years)	30.6	0.106
Married	0.41	0.005
Wage	4.47	0.05
Percentage of homeowners	0.53	
Number of observations	9,426	

*Unless defined otherwise.

measurement problems. For example, an employee becoming unemployed may be faced with a drop in income and therefore have to sell his home and move to a rental home. Suppose this employee is registered as being a tenant for the whole year, the new housing state may be misperceived as having caused an increase in job mobility. Similar problems arise if, for example, an employee decides to move to another region, and only temporarily moves into the rental sector. If then, after a while, the tenant becomes a homeowner again, the new housing state may seem to have caused an increase in job mobility. Thus, measurement errors may occur in some cases. However, there are no strong a priori beliefs that this will lead to a strong bias in our estimation results.

8.5. Estimation results

8.5.1. *Two separate models*

Initially—as we have stated before—the job duration model and the housing model are estimated separately, and without the inclusion of time-invariant random effects. This is the model for $K = 1$. Obviously, no possible interaction exists between the job duration and the housing model when unobserved heterogeneity is not included in the model. Thus, the comparison between the two models helps us to identify the possible impact of endogeneity effects. Endogeneity can be tested by examining the difference in the coefficient estimates of homeownership in the two models—the null hypothesis being that this difference equals zero and there is no endogeneity (see e.g. Wooldridge 2002). At the end of this section, we will employ this endogeneity test.

We first assume that the hazard of leaving a job is not affected by duration in a job. Then, as we have a flow sample of employees, we allow for the presence of (negative) duration dependence in both models. The results of these two model versions are presented in the first two columns of Table 8.2.

From the first column, we may conclude that homeowners indeed experience fewer job-to-job transitions, but they also have a smaller risk of becoming either non-participant or unemployed. Obviously, as will be shown in the sequel, these findings may be biased for various reasons.[1] Further, most coefficients are in line with economic intuition. That is, the probability of job-to-job transitions decreases with age and wage level. Also, we find women, as well as married employees, showing less job-to-job mobility than other employees do. The risk of non-participation first decreases, and then increases with age. Students often have temporary jobs, which explains the relatively high inflow into non-participation of younger employees. On the other hand, older employees often enter into disability insurance or pre-retirement schemes. Remarkably, we find the 'higher education' dummy to have a positive impact on the risk of becoming non-participant. This reflects the fact that this dummy is measured

Table 8.2. The (simultaneous) job duration and housing model with unobserved heterogeneity (N = 9,426)

	Without unobserved effects; no job tenure included		Without unobserved effects; job tenure included		With unobserved effects; job tenure included	
	Estimates	Std. error	Estimates	Std. error	Estimates	Std. error
Parameters, job duration model:						
Risk of job changes						
Constant	−0.8905	0.0302	−0.1830	0.0406	−0.1747	0.0550
Homeowner	−0.3460	0.0374	0.0397	0.0459	−0.0084	0.0555
1–2 years tenure			−1.7229	0.0583	−1.7199	0.0585
3–5 years tenure			−2.2921	0.0660	−2.2853	0.0661
More than 5 years			−2.7514	0.1365	−2.7302	0.1356
Age 25–35 years	−0.0575	0.0395	−0.2032	0.0512	−0.1903	0.0521
Age 35–45 years	−0.3181	0.0522	−0.4333	0.0667	−0.4333	0.0678
Age > 45 years	−0.5873	0.0691	−0.8013	0.0838	−0.8046	0.0849
Women	−0.1929	0.0310	−0.0988	0.0393	−0.0974	0.0395
Children	−0.2055	0.0380	−0.1682	0.0476	−0.1741	0.0478
Working partner	−0.0061	0.0389	−0.0482	0.0483	−0.0369	0.0484
High education	0.2504	0.0412	0.1184	0.0546	0.1139	0.0549
Log wage	−0.3727	0.0152	−0.1769	0.0182	−0.1757	0.0183
Married	−0.0356	0.0454	−0.0748	0.0562	−0.0727	0.0563
Random effects: 2nd point of support: v_{21}					0.0893	0.0624
3rd point of support: v_{31}					−0.0820	0.0733
Risk of non-participation						
Constant	−1.6860	0.0455	−0.9838	0.0543	−0.9509	0.0758
Homeowner	−0.3392	0.0553	0.0119	0.0630	0.0529	0.0800
1–2 years tenure			−1.8735	0.0841	−1.8745	0.0841
3–5 years tenure			−2.2942	0.0941	−2.2983	0.0943
More than 5 years			−2.5341	0.1765	−2.5410	0.1774
Age 25–35 years	−0.1669	0.6430	−0.2977	0.0737	−0.3073	0.0749

	Coef.	S.E.	Coef.	S.E.	Coef.	S.E.
Age 35–45 years	-0.4199	0.0800	-0.5153	0.0919	-0.5267	0.0932
Age > 45 years	-0.1159	0.0878	-0.2640	0.1042	-0.2774	0.1062
Women	-0.0449	0.0443	0.0455	0.0515	0.0454	0.0515
Children	-0.0271	0.0514	0.0230	0.0607	0.0222	0.0608
Working partner	-0.1483	0.0584	-0.1505	0.0664	-0.1536	0.0664
High education	0.3523	0.0553	0.2045	0.0653	0.2075	0.0656
Log wage	-0.5847	0.0172	-0.4100	0.0201	-0.4103	0.0201
Married	0.1658	0.0708	0.1185	0.0807	0.1134	0.0809
Random effects:						
2nd point of support: v_{22}					-0.0813	0.0838
3rd point of support: v_{32}					-0.0580	0.1018
Risk of unemployment						
Constant	-2.2779	0.0655	-1.5910	0.0722	-1.3931	0.0926
Homeowner	-0.8687	0.0785	-0.5837	0.0844	-0.3745	0.1173
1–2 years tenure			-1.6169	0.1051	-1.6199	0.1051
3–5 years tenure			-2.1531	0.1211	-2.1690	0.1214
More than 5 years			-3.3230	0.3584	-3.3640	0.3585
Age 25–35 years	0.2200	0.0802	0.0958	0.0868	0.0365	0.0885
Age 35–45 years	0.1971	0.0960	0.1342	0.1042	0.0431	0.1078
Age > 45 years	0.2077	0.1137	0.0447	0.1232	-0.0628	0.1275
Women	-0.0387	0.0646	0.0480	0.0692	0.0495	0.0694
Children	-0.0600	0.0746	-0.0247	0.0807	-0.0344	0.0810
Working partner	-0.2873	0.0786	-0.2796	0.0835	-0.2838	0.0836
High education	-0.0782	0.0960	-0.2122	0.1038	-0.1984	0.1045
Log wage	-0.2840	0.0383	-0.0941	0.0401	-0.0926	0.0402
Married	0.0366	0.0855	0.0180	0.0925	-0.0073	0.0926
Random effects:						
2nd point of support: v_{23}					-0.3365	0.1119
3rd point of support: v_{33}					-0.4086	0.1224

(Cont.)

Table 8.2. (Continued)

	Without unobserved effects; no job tenure included		Without unobserved effects; job tenure included		With unobserved effects; job tenure included	
	Estimates	Std. error	Estimates	Std. error	Estimates	Std. error
Unobserved heterogeneity; probability masses						
P_1: 1st point of support					0.2863	0.0055
P_2: 2nd point of support					0.3184	0.0099
P_3: 3rd point of support					0.3953	0.0100
Parameters of housing model:						
Constant	−3.2909	0.0175	−3.3851	0.0179	−9.1951	0.0904
1–2 years tenure			0.3334	0.0513	0.4922	0.0616
3–5 years tenure			0.7746	0.0297	1.4827	0.0475
More than 5 years			1.5174	0.0367	3.3260	0.0768
Age 25–35 years	0.3752	0.0103	0.4036	0.0104	1.1249	0.0327
Age 35–45 years	0.9179	0.0112	0.9332	0.0113	2.1337	0.0458
Age > 45 years	0.9872	0.0123	1.0296	0.0124	2.5575	0.0558
Women	0.3133	0.0075	0.2991	0.0076	0.3186	0.0252
Children	0.1062	0.0079	0.1008	0.0079	0.0219	0.0329
Working partner	0.6068	0.0073	0.6115	0.0074	0.6808	0.0297
High education	−0.2631	0.0155	−0.2315	0.0157	−0.4934	0.0352
Log wage	0.2885	0.0038	0.2446	0.0039	0.1837	0.0132
Married	0.9347	0.0087	0.9405	0.0088	1.4555	0.0395
Per cent homeowners	2.7560	0.0264	2.7399	0.0267	1.7655	0.0935
Random effects:						
2nd point of support: u_2					7.6423	0.0685
3rd point of support: u_3					4.8388	0.0585
Mean log likelihood	−7.1992		−6.8322		−5.0056	

only for employees who are students, or have studied in the recent past. Again, this group often works in temporary jobs.

Less pronounced effects are found for the risk of unemployment. Here, the (negative) impact of homeownership appears to be substantial, compared to the other variables. The higher the wage that is earned, the lower the probability of becoming unemployed. Employees with children have a significantly higher risk of becoming unemployed. It may be that these employees often work in part-time jobs to combine formal and informal labour activities, and are more vulnerable to unemployment.

Generally, the estimation results of the housing model are in line with economic intuition: the probability of being a homeowner increases with job duration, age, and wage level. In addition to this, individuals having children, being married, or having a working partner are more likely to own a home. Students often live in rental homes. Remarkably, women are more likely to live in owned homes than men are. It may well be that the female coefficient captures a difference in the education level—which we observe only to some extent—between men and women. In the Netherlands, labour participation of women is still relatively low compared to other countries, and women that do participate are, on average, better educated than men. As a result, the coefficient for women may be overestimated.

8.5.2. Duration dependence and job commitment

Until now, we have abstracted from the role of job tenure. Obviously, job commitment is crucial in understanding the decision to buy a home, as well as labour mobility. As job commitment and job security grow, individual employees will have a lower risk of becoming unemployed. Also, more and more they will be faced with the risk of losing the returns to job-specific investments. Thus less time will be spent searching for other jobs. The attachment to a job also reduces the probability of moving, which makes buying a home more attractive.

The results in the first and second columns of Table 8.2 illustrate the importance of job tenure as a proxy of job commitment, which is included as a (non-parametric) step function. The fit of the model increases dramatically, and all risks show that the job hazard strongly declines with tenure. A similar pattern is found in the housing model: the larger the job commitment, the more likely it is that one owns a home. This indicates that the decision to buy a home is strongly influenced by job commitment. Using job tenure as a control variable helps in reducing the estimation bias: we no longer find a significant impact of homeownership on job-to-job mobility. Also, the risk of non-participation is no longer affected by the homeownership dummy. For the risk of unemployment, we still find a (smaller) significant negative impact.

These findings suggest that the housing market is affected by the labour market, in particular the tenure of workers, rather than the reverse.

The result that there is no impact of homeownership on the risk of job changes may be quite particular for densely populated areas, where people can change jobs without changing residence. Also, moving costs may have been relatively low for homeowners. In the Netherlands, housing transactions are taxed at about 6 per cent; but it may well be that—in the time span covered by the data—these costs were compensated by strong increases in housing prices. From the perspective of tenants, in particular those in the social renting sector, the costs of moving are often high: rental prices are kept artificially low, leading to long waiting lists. Once a new job in another region is accepted, and one has to move to another region, one may be faced with much higher rental prices in the private sector.

Thus, it seems that individual employees decide to change jobs without changing residence. In contrast to this, we do find a negative coefficient describing the effect of homeownership on the risk of becoming unemployed. In a way, this is not surprising: the consequences of this event may lead to a far more substantial, and unanticipated, decrease in income. Homeowners are not entitled to social assistance if they have their own capital, and therefore have to break into their housing equity. Also, tenants are (partially) insured against loss of income, as they may receive higher rent subsidies to compensate for this. Thus homeowners have higher incentives to prevent unemployment by investing more in job-specific capital.

8.5.3. The simultaneous model

Clearly, the inclusion of duration dependence helps in obtaining a better understanding of labour market dynamics, as well as the role of the housing market. Also, it helps us in disentangling duration dependence and the mixing distribution. If unobserved effects are important in the duration model, this means that the impact of genuine duration dependence is overestimated.

As becomes apparent from the third column of Table 8.2, unobserved time-invariant effects are indeed important. The simultaneous model, which is estimated with three points of support (up to $K = 3$, the likelihood of the model increases significantly), again shows a dramatic increase in the fit of the model. However, notice that this increase is almost fully confined to the housing model; random effects are important in explaining housing state. This becomes apparent from the size and the significance of the coefficients of the parameters u_1 and u_2, the random effects in the housing model. Following the estimation results, three types of employees can be distinguished (at the three points of support), having unobservable characteristics that make them more or less likely to own a home. As a result of these characteristics, 32 per cent are very likely to own a home (P_2), and 29 per cent are very unlikely to own a home (P_1).

In contrast to this, in the job duration model the impact of unobserved time-invariant characteristics is mostly found to be small. All coefficients, except for those of the risk of unemployment (which are denoted by v_{23} and v_{33}), are found to be insignificant. Moreover, for all risks the pattern of duration dependence seems to be unaffected. Not surprisingly, the estimated coefficients of the homeownership dummy remain almost unchanged. Thus, following a Hausman Test on the difference between the coefficients for the two model versions, the null hypothesis that there is no endogeneity cannot be rejected (with P-values of 0.252 and 0.343 for the homeownership coefficient of the risks of job changes and entry into non-participation, respectively). These findings suggest that the potential biasing impact of unobserved time-invariant characteristics is not important.

Random effects, however, do matter with respect to the risk of unemployment. Employees with hidden characteristics that make them less (more) vulnerable to unemployment or non-participation, have a higher (lower) probability of owning a home. This seems to result in endogeneity effects: comparing the homeownership coefficients for the unemployment risk in the two models, we find (weak) evidence that the difference is significant ($P = 0.074$)—suggesting the presence of endogeneity effects. The intuition behind this result is that the lower the risk of a decrease in income, the higher the possibilities of buying a home. This effect may be reinforced by banks' selection criteria to grant mortgages. However, we still do find a significant (negative) impact of homeownership on the risk of becoming unemployed. This means that the unemployment risk is affected negatively by homeownership. As explained earlier, this can be driven by the stronger incentives that homeowners have to invest in their jobs.

8.5.4. The regional homeownership rate as an instrumental variable

In our model, the instrumental variable, regional homeownership, serves as an important variable for identification, in particular for the simultaneous model. This rate is observed for 538 regions in the Netherlands. We find the regional homeownership rate to have a strong impact on the individual housing status: the higher the regional proportion of homeowners, the higher the individual probability of being a homeowner. However, there are still some conditions to be met for this variable to be used as a proper instrument. Clearly, the regional proportion of homeowners is a variable pertaining to average group behaviour. As shown by Manski (1993), the identification of causality effects with these variables may be problematic for various reasons. Three types of effects that may lead to estimation biases: endogenous effects, exogenous effects, and correlated effects.

Endogenous effects occur when the propensity of an individual to behave in some way is influenced by the behaviour of the group. Within the context of our model, individual homeowners may compare their social status with that of other homeowners in their neighbourhood, and thus tend to invest in their careers. As a result, labour mobility of the individual homeowner may be small, as well as the unemployment risk. In that case, the regional proportion of homeowners would not be a valid instrument that is fully exogenous. However, in our model, such endogeneity effects are not likely to be important, as the proportion of homeowners is measured at the level of regions, and not at the level of (relevant) neighbourhoods.

Exogenous (or contextual) effects occur if the propensity of an individual to behave in some way varies with exogenous characteristics of the reference group. Within the context of our model, these effects may result from individuals having a strong labour market position and earning a high income moving to regions with high homeownership rates. To a large extent, these exogenous effects are controlled for in our model, in particular by the income variable. Still, in so far as some exogenous effects are not fully captured in our model, it is likely that most variation is between individuals within regions, and not individuals between regions. Thus, exogenous effects will be considerably smaller for the instrumental variable.

Correlated effects arise if individuals in the same group tend to behave similarly because they face similar institutional settings. In the context of our model, this would mean that unobserved neighbourhood characteristics affecting job mobility are correlated with the homeownership rate. In particular, good employment prospects may be concentrated in rich regions with a high proportion of homeowners. These effects are—by using income as a control variable—largely taken into account by the heterogeneity in our model. Further variation in job mobility between regions may be associated with differences in regional institutional settings, like property taxes set by local authorities; but these are not very likely to be related to the proportion of homeowners.

All in all, it seems that all three types of effects will not be substantial, as homeownership is measured at the level of communities, and not (smaller) neighbourhoods. Also, to a large extent the homeownership rate is regulated by local authorities, and we control for various variables, so as to avoid exogenous or correlated effects. Thus we conclude that this variable can be used as a valid instrument for identification.

8.6. Conclusions

To sum up, our estimation results suggest that the housing decision is strongly affected by job commitment; the estimated impact of homeownership strongly decreases if we control for this effect. Thus, the housing market is affected by the labour market, rather than the reverse. In particular, we do not find evidence of homeownership affecting the risk of job changes, or the risk of non-participation. Also, and not surprisingly, endogeneity effects are not likely to be important for these risks. Individual employees decide to change jobs, irrespective of their housing status, and there are various explanations for this. First, given the population density in the Netherlands, people often change jobs without changing residence. Second, strong increases in housing prices may compensate for the moving costs of homeowners. And third, the regulation of the social renting sector may result in high moving costs for tenants.

As with the risk of job mobility, we find no impact of homeownership on the outflow of the labour force. To a large extent, this concerns employees getting pensioned, or becoming disabled. It seems that these transitions are not driven by housing state, and do not (directly) affect moving behaviour.

In contrast to job-to-job changes and the probability of becoming non-participant, we do find a negative effect of homeownership on the probability of becoming unemployed. The explanation for this is that the decrease in income that comes with unemployment is far more substantial for homeowners than for tenants. In principle, homeowners are not eligible for social assistance and have to break into their housing equity. Moreover, tenants are (partly) insured against loss of income, due to the rent subsidy system. Thus, homeowners have a higher incentive to reduce the risk of becoming unemployed, in particular by investing more in job-specific capital.

To conclude, homeownership seems to stimulate job commitment in one way (lower risk of unemployment), but not at the cost of less job-to-job mobility. However, from these findings alone we cannot conclude that homeownership does not affect labour market mobility at all. Institutional settings in the rental sector—in particular rental subsidies and low prices in the social rental sector—may discourage labour mobility. From that perspective, labour mobility may be too low, both for homeowners and for tenants.

Note

1. For all model versions we also tested for possible biases stemming from the fact that job tenure is measured in months, and housing statuses on a yearly basis. In particular, we delayed the observed housing status by one year. This did not change our results substantially.

References

Abbring, J. H. (1997), *Essays in Labor Economics* (Amsterdam: Thesis Publishers).

Böheim, R., and Taylor, M. (2000), 'Residential mobility, housing tenure and the labour market in Britain', Working Paper, Institute for Social and Economic Research and Institute for Labour Research, University of Essex.

Green, R., and Hendershott, P. (2001), 'Homeownership and unemployment in the US', *Urban Studies*, 38/9, 1509–20.

Harris., J. R., and Todaro, M. P. (1970), 'Migration, unemployment and development: a two sector analysis', *American Economic Review*, 60, 126–42.

Hassink, W., and Kurvers, C. (1999), 'De invloed van woningbezit op werkloosheid: Oswald's these voor Nederland bezien' (The influence of homeownership on unemployment: Oswald's thesis analysed for the Netherlands), mimeo, University of Utrecht.

Heckman, J. J., and Singer, B. (1984), 'A method for minimizing the impact of distributional assumptions in econometric models for duration data', *Econometrica*, 52, 271–320.

Henley, A. (1998), 'Residential mobility, housing equity and the labour market', *Economic Journal*, 108, 414–27.

Holm, A. (2002), 'The effect of training on search durations: a random effects approach', *Labor Economics*, 9, 433–50.

Lancaster, T. (1990), *The Econometric Analysis of Transition data*, Econometric Society Monographs, 17 (Cambridge: Cambridge University Press).

Manski, C. F. (1993), 'Identification of endogenous social effects: the reflection problem', *Review of Economic Studies*, 60/3, 531–42.

Nickell, S. J. (1998), 'Unemployment: questions and some answers', *Economic Journal*, 108/448, 802–16.

Van den Berg, G. J. (1992), 'A structural dynamic analysis of job turnover and the costs associated with moving to another job', *Economic Journal*, 102, 1116–33.

Van Ommeren, J. N. (1996), 'Commuting and relocation of jobs and residences', Ph.D. thesis, Tinbergen Institute Research Series.

——Rietveld, P., and Nijkamp, P. (2000), 'Job mobility, residential mobility and commuting: a theoretical analysis using search theory', *Annals of Regional Science*, 34, 213–32.

Van der Vlist, A. J. (2001), 'Residential mobility and commuting', Ph.D. thesis, Tinbergen Institute Research Series.

Wooldridge, J. M. (2002), *Econometric Analysis of Cross Section and Panel Data* (Cambridge, MA: MIT Press).

9

Homeownership, Job Duration, and Wages[*]

Jakob Roland Munch, Michael Rosholm, and Michael Svarer

9.1. Introduction

In a recent survey of the micro-level consequences of homeownership, Dietz and Haurin (2003) found overwhelming evidence of positive externalities of homeownership. These positive effects range from homeowners being more environmentally conscious over housing markets for owners appearing to suffer less discrimination than renting markets to homeownership being linked with better physical and mental health. Such externalities seem to support the favourable tax treatment of the capital invested in homes received by homeowners (see Hendershott and White 2000). On the other hand, Oswald (1996) presents evidence that the unemployment rate and the share of homeowners are positively correlated for a number of countries and regions. The proposed mechanism is that homeowners are much less mobile than renters due to costs associated with buying and selling their homes, and so they are relatively inflexible in the labour market. Thus, if the homeowner share is high, the work force is immobile, which tends to give higher structural unemployment due to insufficient supply of labour. In his original work, Oswald (1996) presented evidence showing that countries or regions with a 10 percentage points higher share of homeowners have a 2 percentage points higher unemployment rate. This relationship has been confirmed by Nickell and Layard (1999) and Green and Hendershott (2001), also using macro data. These findings have inspired a number of papers investigating the impact of homeownership on labour market outcomes like unemployment duration, job duration, and wages. In the present paper, we focus on the latter two outcomes.

---

[*] This article was published in the *Journal of Urban Economics*, 63, 130–45; copyright Elsevier, 2008.

In relation to Oswald's hypothesis, a central question is whether homeowners are more likely to be unemployed? Munch *et al.* (Chapter 4 above) show that homeowners overall have shorter unemployment spells than renters, even after correcting for the possible endogeneity of homeowner status. However, they also find that homeowners are less mobile in the sense that unemployed owners have a lower transition rate into jobs outside the local labour market, thus offering some support for the proposed mechanism behind Oswald's hypothesis. This effect is, however, dominated by a stronger positive effect on the transition rate into jobs in the local labour market.

Having established that the duration of unemployment spells is shorter for homeowners than for renters, it is still possible that employed homeowners more often experience unemployment. That is, the duration of *employment* spells could be lower for homeowners than for renters? A study on Dutch data by Van Leuvensteijn and Koning (Chapter 8 above) suggests that this is not the case—in fact homeowners have a lower unemployment risk. They also show that there is no impact of homeownership on the transition rate into a new job.[1]

Another important and related issue is whether homeownership affects wages. According to the survey by Dietz and Haurin (2003), not much research exists on this relationship, but Coulson and Fisher (2002) is an exception. Based on data from US Current Population Survey and PSID, they find that homeowners have higher wages, shorter unemployment spells, and a lower probability of experiencing unemployment.

The purpose of the present paper is twofold. First, we offer some theoretical considerations concerning the impact of homeownership on job duration and wages. From a search-theoretic perspective we argue that homeowners stay longer in their jobs than renters because of reduced geographical mobility (due to mobility costs), and this in turn makes them more attractive to employers, implying that owners are offered higher wages. Second, we empirically examine *all* these predictions using a rich Danish micro dataset based on administrative registers. We estimate a competing risks duration model for job spells with a distinction between transitions into new jobs in the local labour market, new jobs outside the local labour market (where the distinction is made by realized housing mobility out of the local commuting area), and unemployment. In addition, we simultaneously estimate a standard human capital wage equation, thus allowing for an impact of homeownership on wages.

In empirical investigations of the effects of homeownership it is important to take into account the endogeneity of homeownership; if the selection process is not explicitly accounted for, the estimated parameters to the homeownership variable in the different equations cannot be interpreted causally. For example, in Coulson and Fisher (2002) it is not clear whether the positive labour market outcomes found for homeowners are causal or spurious, since the authors do not attempt to address the potential endogeneity of the homeowner variable. According to Dietz and Haurin (2003), this is a criticism that can be aimed at the majority of existing research on the micro-level consequences of homeownership, and they make a call for researchers in future work to put much more effort into identifying the causal linkage between homeownership and the outcomes of interest. In our empirical analysis we explicitly model the selection process of homeownership, and we use two different identification strategies to check the robustness of our results. First, we follow the identification strategy of Munch *et al.* (Chapter 4 above), where multiple observations for some individuals in the sample can be exploited; that is, we exploit the panel structure of our data to identify the causal linkage between homeownership and the outcomes of interest. Second, we also follow a more standard instrumental variables approach along the lines of Van Leuvensteijn and Koning (Chapter 8 above). Our empirical results are completely consistent with the theoretical predictions, and they are very robust to the different identification strategies employed.

The paper is organized as follows. The next section outlines some simple theoretical considerations about the link between homeownership and labour market outcomes. Section 9.3 describes the dataset. Section 9.4 presents the empirical model and discusses identification issues. Section 9.5 presents the estimation results, and finally Section 9.6 offers a brief conclusion.

9.2. Homeownership and labour market outcomes

To set the stage for the empirical analysis, this section presents a few theoretical considerations based on a search theoretical foundation. Munch *et al.* (Chapter 4 above) construct a search model for unemployed workers. Because homeowners have higher costs of geographical mobility than renters, they set higher reservation wages for accepting job offers outside commuting distance (requiring a residential move) than for renters. The resulting exit rates to employment outside the local labour market are therefore lower for homeowners. On the other hand, the risk of eventually having to move lowers the reservation wages for homeowners in the local labour market, thus giving them higher hazard rates for local jobs. Empirically, Munch *et al.* (Chapter 4 above) found evidence for both effects, but the latter effect strongly dominates the first one. That is, in general owners have shorter unemployment spells, but they are also less likely to leave unemployment for a job outside the local labour market.

In the present context, the focus is on employed workers rather than unemployed workers. They may also look for jobs locally or outside the local labour market (requiring a residential move), and they may quit or lose the job and search as unemployed. In the following we consider in turn the predicted impact of homeownership on the transition from employment into unemployment, into new jobs (local or non-local), and the impact on wages.

A straightforward implication of the theoretical and empirical analysis of unemployed workers in Munch *et al.* (Chapter 4 above) is that homeowners are less likely to quit the job and become unemployed, because as unemployed they are worse off relative to renters due to their inclination not to move for jobs. As a consequence, owners may accept lower-paying jobs as reflected in their lower local labour market reservation wages. Thus, *ceteris paribus*, homeowners are less likely to become unemployed than renters.

When it comes to on-the-job search behaviour (i.e. job-to-job transitions), the issues are slightly more complicated. Assume, without loss of generality, that renters have no costs of mobility. Hence, for renters the reservation wage for any job is the current wage. Homeowners must be compensated for the costs of moving, so their reservation wages for non-local jobs will exceed the current wage by the annuitized value of the mobility cost. However, the worker can always keep her old job, so the reservation wage for another local job must be equal to the current wage. Hence, in a partial equilibrium analysis, we would straightforwardly conclude that employed homeowners would be less likely to switch to jobs outside the local labour market than renters.

However, when investigating employment spells, equilibrium considerations become more important; suppose employers take these facts into account in the wage-setting process. Homeowners are likely to stay longer in a given job than renters, because they are less likely to accept a non-local job. Therefore, the expected present discounted value to the employer of a job which is occupied by a homeowner is higher than if it were occupied by a renter. Thus, employers may prefer to hire homeowners, *ceteris paribus*, and they may even set their wages somewhat higher than for renters, in order to attract them. Another argument for paying higher wages to homeowners is that the incentives to invest in these workers in terms of enhancing their human capital by providing firm-specific training are higher than for renters, since homeowners have a longer expected duration in the firm. Consequently, the firm can (expect to) recoup more of its initial investment (see e.g. Rosholm and Svarer, 2004) when training homeowners than they can when training renters. This implies that employed homeowners have higher productivity than employed renters, thus justifying higher wages for homeowners. Moreover, higher wages leads them to accept other local jobs less often than renters.

In sum, based on these simple considerations we would expect employed homeowners to

- become unemployed less often than renters (they have lower reservation wages in unemployment; cf. Munch *et al.*, Chapter 4 above)
- accept job offers outside the local labour market less often than renters (due to mobility costs)

- accept local job offers less often than renters (they have more firm-specific productivity)
- earn higher wages than renters (same reason as above).

9.3. Data and the Danish labour and housing markets

The Danish labour market shares some characteristics with Anglo-Saxon labour markets which are important in the context of this paper. The Danish labour market is very flexible due to weak employment protection, and as a consequence, turnover rates are higher than in other continental European countries. At the same time, the labour market is highly unionized, and the wage structure is very compressed. The geographical mobility of both employed and unemployed workers is modest, and regional migration rates are at the low end compared to other continental European countries; cf. OECD (2000) and Danish Economic Council (2002).

The Danish housing market is comprised of four different main segments, but in the analysis we will distinguish only between owners and non-owners. The largest part is owner-occupied housing, including more than 50 per cent of all housing units. Private rental housing and social housing each constitute almost 20 per cent, and cooperative housing accounts for 6 per cent of the housing market.

It should be noted that the markets for private rental housing, social housing, and cooperative housing are regulated by rent controls. Rents in most private rented dwellings in larger urban areas are cost-based rents, implying that landlords may pass on all costs in the operation of the property. Included in these costs is a capital charge, which is calculated on the basis of the value of the property in 1973, and allowance for inflation on this part of the rent is not possible. As a consequence, the capital payoff on the property is eroded by inflation. This means in particular that rents in older dwellings, which typically are located in city centres, are lower than market rents. In minor rural districts, local authorities use a different set of rules to regulate rents. Rents are set at the 'value of the rental unit', which is determined by comparing with similar housing units in the area, and so it is a rather vague concept. In effect the 'value of the rental unit' is typically closer to the market rent than rents in units with cost-based rents. Also housing units in urban areas can be rented at the 'value of the rental unit' if they are thoroughly improved when they become vacant. In this way substantial rent increases are allowed for, and so a large part of the private rented housing units are not seriously regulated by rent control. Thus there is considerable variation in the degree to which each unit is regulated, and not surprisingly this has an impact on tenancy duration. Munch and Svarer (2002) show that rent control distorts mobility, as tenancy duration is longer the more regulated the rent of the dwelling is.

Cooperative housing is a relatively new segment of the housing market which previously belonged to the privately rented segment. Whenever a private rented property is for sale, legislation gives current residents the right to take over the property at the offered price and convert it to a cooperative. The offered price typically reflects controlled rents, so most properties are taken over by residents under favourable conditions. Whenever residents move out of their homes, they sell their share in the cooperative at a fixed price such that the variation in the degree of initial rent control to a large extent is kept.

Social housing consists of housing associations that are run as non-profit societies with rents basically being determined from their costs, of which interest payments and amortization of the initial capital outlay are the major components. The housing associations are directly supported by the government through reduced expenditure related to interest payments and amortization of the loans, and because they are exempted from paying property tax. Again, the degree to which each unit is regulated varies, and it is correlated with the age of the dwelling.

To sum up, the alternative to being a homeowner is being a renter under rent control, where the degree of control varies substantially. Large parts of these alternative rental markets are almost unregulated, while some housing units have rents that are much lower than market rents. Thus there are costs in terms of lost rent control benefits associated with moving out of such regulated units, but overall average tenancy durations in these three non-owner segments of the housing market are still much lower than in owner-occupied housing units. According to Danish Economic Council (2001), in 1999 the mobility rate among occupants in private rental housing were on average five times the mobility rate in owner-occupied housing, while in cooperative housing and social housing it was two and two and a half times higher respectively.[2] These pronounced differences justify our focus on owners vs. non-owners.

To investigate the causes behind mobility of employed workers in Denmark, a very rich dataset, which is drawn from administrative registers, is employed. The dataset covers 1 per cent of the Danish population for the years 1993–2001. In each year, detailed information about the labour market states of all individuals, along with information on socio-economic characteristics, is available. These socio-economic variables are extracted from the integrated database for labour market research (IDA) and the income registers in Statistics Denmark. Of particular importance is the fact that a workplace identity is associated with each worker at the end of each year. A firm can have more than one workplace, so if a worker changes between two workplaces within the same firm, then this is counted as a job change in the present analysis. Job spells are then straightforwardly constructed from successive years at the same workplace.

Here we are interested in the duration of job spells and transitions into new jobs and unemployment, and for the present purposes job spells are flow-sampled such that only spells starting in 1993 and later are included in the analysis. The destination state for all spells that end before 2001 is known, and if job spells end with transitions into states other than a new job or unemployment (e.g. out of the labour force), or if spells are not completed by the end of 2001, they are treated as independently right-censored observations. In addition, if job spells end because of a firm closure, they are also treated as independently right-censored observations.[3] All students with (student) jobs have been excluded from the sample. We operate with three different destination states from a job: unemployment, a new job in the local labour market, and a new job outside the local labour market.

The local labour markets are so-called commuting areas, which are defined such that the internal migration rate is 50 per cent higher than the external migration rate; cf. Andersen (1999). The commuting areas are based on geographically connected municipalities, and the 275 municipalities in Denmark are merged into 51 such commuting areas. An employed worker is defined to find a new job outside the local labour market if he or she changes job and moves to another commuting area in the same year as the beginning of the new job spell.[4]

In the resulting dataset there are 29,878 job spells for 17,297 individuals. Table 9.1 displays summary statistics for all explanatory variables. Self-explanatory dummies for age, gender, the presence of children, the presence of two adults in the household, and education are included. Also, three geographic dummies are included to distinguish between the capital Copenhagen, five large cities, and all other localities (small city). Information on the hourly wage rate and years of working experience are also included. In the model for the hourly wage rate, we also include the elapsed duration of the job, denoted job tenure. In addition, Table 9.1 describes three variables that will act as exclusion restrictions; that is, they will enter the equation for the selection into homeownership but not the other equations in the analyses performed below. These are the proportion of homeowners in the municipality of residence,[5] the proportion of homeowners in the municipality of birth, and finally a dummy variable for the homeowner status of the individual's parents in 1980.

There are 58 per cent homeowners in the sample, which is slightly above the proportion of homeowners in the country. Presumably the over-representation is due to the selection of employed workers only, who are more likely to be homeowners than those who are unemployed or outside the labour market. A comparison of homeowners with renters reveals that homeowners tend to be older, are more likely to have children, are less likely to live in Copenhagen, and likely to have more education, more working experience, and more tenure, and to earn higher wages. This pattern is consistent with Coulson and Fisher (2002), who find that homeowners have more favourable labour market outcomes than renters.

Table 9.1. Summary statistics

Variables	All		Owners		Renters	
	Mean	Stdv.	Mean	Stdv.	Mean	Stdv.
Homeowner	0.58	0.49				
Age 18–24	0.14	0.35	0.04	0.19	0.3	0.45
Age 25–29	0.15	0.36	0.11	0.31	0.21	0.41
Age 30–39	0.31	0.46	0.34	0.47	0.27	0.44
Age 40–49	0.22	0.41	0.29	0.45	0.13	0.33
Age 50–59	0.15	0.35	0.2	0.4	0.07	0.26
Female	0.42	0.49	0.44	0.49	0.4	0.49
Children 0–17 years	0.23	0.42	0.29	0.45	0.15	0.35
Two adults	0.67	0.46	0.86	0.34	0.4	0.49
Copenhagen	0.23	0.42	0.17	0.37	0.31	0.46
Large city	0.14	0.35	0.13	0.33	0.16	0.36
Small city	0.62	0.48	0.69	0.46	0.52	0.49
Basic education	0.33	0.47	0.26	0.43	0.43	0.49
Vocational education	0.4	0.49	0.44	0.49	0.35	0.47
Further education	0.26	0.43	0.29	0.45	0.21	0.41
Experience (years)	13.3	9.1	16.2	8.3	9.5	7.6
Tenure (years)	1.3	1.6	1.8	1.7	1.1	1.4
Log wage (/10)	5.08	0.41	5.18	0.36	4.94	0.43
Owner share, region of residence	0.58	0.13	0.6	0.13	0.54	0.12
Owner share, region of birth	0.49	0.22	0.51	0.21	0.46	0.23
Parents' homeowner status, 1980	0.57	0.49	0.58	0.49	0.57	0.49
Number of individuals						17,297
Number of spells						29,878
Mean duration of spell (years)						2.78
Proportion of spells:						
right-censored spells						0.33
end with job change locally						0.4
end with job change non-locally						0.14
end with unemployment						0.08
Persons with change of homeowner status (%)						0.188
Persons with change of homeowner status and more than 1 spell (%)						0.068

9.4. Econometric model

To investigate the impact of homeownership on job duration and wages, we formulate an empirical model for job duration, wages, and selection into homeowner status simultaneously. The first step is to specify a competing risks duration model. We are specifically interested in addressing exits from employment to unemployment, to new jobs in the local labour market, and to new jobs outside the local labour market, where the distinction between local and non-local labour markets is made as described in the previous section.

We specify a duration model with a flexible non-parametric specification of the baseline hazard. To distinguish between different destinations, we use a competing risks duration model. Even if there is access to a comprehensive dataset there might still be some unobserved heterogeneity left, as no measures for e.g. ability or motivation are available. Therefore we attempt to capture unobserved worker characteristics by specifying a mixed proportional hazard model for the labour market transitions:

$$\theta_i(t|x_t, v_i) = \lambda_i(t) \exp(\beta_i' x_t + \gamma_i z_t + v_i), \tag{9.1}$$

where $i = el, en, u$ indicates the different destination states for the transition (i.e. employment locally, employment outside the local labour market, and unemployment), $\lambda_i(t)$ is the baseline hazard capturing the time dependence for transitions into destination i, and $\exp(x_t \beta_i + v_i)$ gives the proportional effects of the time-varying homeownership dummy, z_t, other observed and time-varying characteristics, x_t, and unobserved characteristics, v_i. All job spells that end with a transition to a state other than one of the three described above (e.g. out of the labour force) are treated as independently right-censored observations.

The annual observations in the data imply that the duration variable T is grouped into $K + 1$ intervals $\{[0, t_1), [t_1, t_2), \ldots, [t_k, \infty)\}$, which must be accounted for in the econometric specification. The interval-specific survival rate is defined as

$$\alpha_k = P(T \geq t_k | T \geq t_{k-1}, x_t, z_t, v)$$

$$= \exp\left[-\sum_{i=el,en,u} \int_{t_{k-1}}^{t_k} \theta_i(t|x_k, z_k, v_i) dt \right]$$

$$= \exp\left[-\sum_{i=el,en,u} \exp(\beta_i' x_k + \gamma_i z_k + v_i) \Lambda_{i,k} \right] \tag{9.2}$$

$$= \prod_{i=el,en,u} \alpha_{i,k},$$

where $\Lambda_{i,k} = \int_{t_{k-1}}^{t_k} \lambda_i(t) dt$, and $\alpha_{i,k} = \exp[-\exp(\beta_i' x_k + \gamma_i z_k + v_i) \Lambda_{i,k}]$.

To find the contribution to the likelihood function from a job spell, it is noted that the probability that a spell ends in interval k is given by the conditional probability of failure in that interval times the probability that the spell survives until interval k, or $(1 - \alpha_k) \Pi_{j=1}^{k-1} \alpha_j$. Right-censored spells contribute to the likelihood with the survivor function, $\Pi_{j=1}^{k} \alpha_j$, and so the contribution to the likelihood function from a job spell can be written

$$\mathcal{L}_e(t|x_t, z_t, v_{el}, v_{en}, v_u) = (1 - \alpha_{el,k})^{d_{el}} (1 - \alpha_{el,k})^{d_{en}} (1 - \alpha_{u,k})^{d_u} \alpha_k^{1 - d_{el} - d_{en} - d_u} \prod_{j=1}^{k-1} \alpha_j, \tag{9.3}$$

213

where d_{el}, d_{en}, and d_u are destination state indicators. If the job spell is right-censored then $d_{el} = d_{en} = d_u = 0$. Instead of imposing a functional form on the baseline hazard, we allow for a flexible specification by simply estimating the interval-specific baseline parameters $\Lambda_{i,k}$.

The wage of an individual at tenure t is specified as

$$\ln w_t = \zeta_0 + \zeta_1 t + \zeta_2 x_t + \varepsilon_t$$

where, for a given individual, the error term is composed of two components, an independently normally distributed idiosyncratic component and a random individual-specific effect,

$$\varepsilon_t = u_t + v_w.$$

The likelihood contribution from a sequence of wage observations over a job spell is thus, with σ_u being the standard deviation of the idiosyncratic component, and $\varphi(.)$ the standard normal probability density function. Note that in this model, we would have had a simultaneity problem if we had allowed the wage to affect job durations as well. In the equation above, tenure affects the wage, but one might just as well have argued that the dependence should go the other way, or rather, both ways. However, the latter is not possible to identify in the present setup, and hence a decision had to be made.[6]

To account for possible endogeneity of the homeownership variable, z_t, we simultaneously model the probability of being a homeowner, the transition rates out of the job spell, and the wage. The probability of being homeowner in year t depends on explanatory variables, x_t and y_t, and an unobserved component, v_h, and is specified as a logit model

$$P(x_t, y_t, v_h) = P(z_t = 1 | x_t, y_t, v_h) = \frac{\exp(\beta'_h x_t + \alpha'_h y_t + v_h)}{1 + \exp(\beta'_h x_t + \alpha'_h y_t + v_h)} \tag{9.4}$$

where x_t are the same explanatory variables that are included in the duration model, and y_t are variables that are included in the logit model, but not in the duration model. The corresponding contribution to the likelihood function from a job spell is

$$L_h(t | x_t, y_t, v_h) = \prod_{j=1}^{k} P(x_j, y_t, v_h)^{z_j} (1 - P(x_j, y_t, v_h))^{1-z_j}. \tag{9.5}$$

We assume that all sources of correlation between the three processes can be represented by the individual-specific heterogeneity terms. These terms are assumed to be time-invariant and hence constant across repeated spells for the same individual.

The unobserved heterogeneity is specified by the stochastic variables v_{en}, v_{el}, v_u, v_w, v_h, so the complete contribution to the likelihood function for each individual is

$$\mathcal{L} = \int_{v_{el}} \int_{v_{en}} \int_{v_u} \int_{v_w} \int_{v_h} \mathcal{L}_e(t|x_t, z_t, v_e, v_u) \cdot \mathcal{L}_w(w_1, \ldots, w_t | x_1, \ldots, x_t, v_w)$$
$$\cdot \mathcal{L}_h(t|x_t, y_t, v_h) dF(v_{el}, v_{en}, v_u, v_w, v_h), \tag{9.6}$$

where F is the joint CDF for the unobserved heterogeneity, which remains to be specified. We use a flexible and widely applied specification of the distribution of the unobservables; it is assumed that v_{el}, v_{en}, v_u, v_w, and v_h each can take two values, where one of the support points in each destination-specific hazard is normalized to zero (i.e. $v_{el} = 0$, $v_u = 0$, and $v_{en} = 0$), because the baseline hazard acts as a constant term in the hazard rates. Thus, there are thirty-two possible combinations of this unobserved heterogeneity distribution, each with an associated probability. For more details on this class of mixture distributions in duration models, see e.g. Van den Berg (2001).

9.4.1. Identification

In order to identify the causal relation between homeownership and the outcomes of interest, two identification strategies may be pursued. The first identification strategy relies on multiple occurrences of job spells and owner-ship status for the individuals. This implies that we observe some individuals in several job spells, and in some they are homeowners while in others they are not. Moreover, during a given job spell, some persons may change owner-ship status, in which case the argumentation from the 'timing-of-events' literature (Abbring and Van den Berg 2003) further adds to the identification of the model parameters. This identification approach has been used in a series of papers by Panis and coauthors (see e.g. Panis and Lillard 1994; Upchurch *et al.* 2002; and Panis 2004) and Munch *et al.* (Chapter 4 above).

Identification here requires that we—for at least a subset of individuals—observe job spells both when the individual is a homeowner and when the individual is a renter. The intuition for identification is spelled out in Panis (2004). In terms of our application, his argument goes as follows: suppose one observes only one respondent over a long period of time during which he switches homeowner status. With a sample of one, there is no heterogeneity and no correlation across equations, so that equations are independent. The effect of homeowner status on exit rates from employment is identified because of repeated observations on job spells and variations in homeowner status. More generally, conditional on heterogeneity, the equations are independent, and identification rests on repeated outcomes with interpersonal variation in homeowner status. In terms of interpersonal variation in homeowner status, 6.8 per cent (see Table 9.1) of the individuals we observe are observed both as renters and as homeowners in different job spells. In addition, 18.8 per cent change ownership status during a job spell, thus allowing separate identification of time-invariant unobserved heterogeneity and time-varying ownership effects; see Abbring and Van den Berg (2003).

The second identification strategy uses exclusion restrictions; that is, the existence of a set of variables that affect homeownership but have no direct impact on labour market outcomes is postulated. While we use the first identification strategy as our baseline scenario, we check robustness of the results by estimating the model using both identification strategies. In the literature on homeownership and labour markets, this strategy has been exploited by Van Leuvensteijn and Koning (Chapter 8 above). Like Van Leuvensteijn and Koning, we use regional homeownership rate as an instrumental variable, which only affects homeownership status. In addition, we also include homeowner status of the parents (in 1980) and the regional homeowner rate in the municipality in which the individual was born. The regional homeownership rate will naturally affect the probability of being a homeowner through a supply effect, but there is no reason to presume that this will have an impact on the individual's labour market outcomes, *ceteris paribus*. The same should hold for the regional homeownership rate in the region of birth. Finally, after conditioning on education and labour market experience, we find no reason why the parents' homeownership status should assert a current influence on labour market outcomes, given the past educational and labour market outcomes of the individual.

9.5. Results

In this section, we present the main results.[7] We first show the results from a model where we endogenize homeownership status and identify the homeowner equation by exploiting the multiple spell features of our data and time variation in ownership status—that is, the first identification strategy outlined above. These results are reported in Table 9.2. Focusing first on explanatory variables other than homeownership, the effects are roughly in line with our expectations and the established wisdom. First, by comparing the two job-to-job transition rates, it is clear that younger workers are relatively more mobile, and that this age effect is more pronounced for the job change hazard for non-local jobs. Workers living outside Copenhagen (large city or small city) have a lower job change hazard rate for local jobs, but a higher job change hazard rate for non-local jobs. With respect to the unemployment risk, older workers have a higher hazard rate. Note, however, that this impact is conditional on years of working experience, and more working experience exerts a strong negative influence on the unemployment risk. Workers with further education have a markedly lower unemployment risk than workers with basic or vocational education. We do not present the estimated baseline hazards here. For all three transitions, we find negative duration dependence.[8] This is in accordance with e.g. Farber (1999), who finds a similar pattern for job mobility in the US.

The wage equation has the traditional concave shape in working experience, and wages increase even more with job tenure in the sense that tenure is also a component in working experience. The results of the selection equation are

Table 9.2. Estimation results

Variables	Job change hazard, no mobility		Job change hazard, with mobility		Unemployment hazard	
	Coeff.	Std. err.	Coeff.	Std. err.	Coeff.	Std. err.
Homeownership	−0.0587	0.0245	−0.1597	0.0401	−0.3468	0.0597
Age 19–24	0.3472	0.0395	0.6666	0.0630	−0.6235	0.0831
Age 25–29	0.0488	0.0317	0.3315	0.0510	−0.3454	0.0718
Age 30–39	−0.1978	0.0317	−0.1885	0.0531	0.2059	0.0746
Age 50+	−0.2838	0.0430	−0.5172	0.0850	0.7257	0.0887
Female	−0.0045	0.0200	−0.4632	0.0345	0.1474	0.0493
Children 0–17 years	0.0388	0.0267	−0.0953	0.0447	−0.0140	0.0670
Two adults	−0.0709	0.0243	−0.0483	0.0406	−0.3207	0.0556
Large city	−0.3928	0.0321	1.3110	0.0683	0.2656	0.0765
Small city	−0.4417	0.0226	1.4523	0.0597	0.0531	0.0607
Basic education	−0.0594	0.0230	−0.1019	0.0373	0.0843	0.0582
Further education	−0.1978	0.0267	0.0721	0.0440	−1.0689	0.0752
Experience/10	0.0553	0.0526	0.1044	0.0893	−0.9309	0.1150
Experienced squared/100	−0.0286	0.0152	−0.0642	0.0269	0.0935	0.0352
$U_{h,1}$	−7.3118	0.0746				
$U_{h,2}$	−2.1912	0.0591				
$Ul_{w,1}$	4.8949	0.0036				
$U_{w,2}$	5.3353	0.0037				
$U_{en,2}$	2.3898	0.0585				
$Ul_{el,2}$	3.1652	0.0751				
$U_{u,2}$	1.8440	0.0431				
$P(U_{h,1}, U_{w,1}, U_{e,1})$	0.2294	0.0043				
$P(U_{h,1}, U_{w,1}, U_{e,2})$	0.0296	0.0022				
$P(U_{h,2}, U_{w,1}, U_{e,1})$	0.4146	0.0050				
$P(U_{h,2}, U_{w,1}, U_{e,2})$	0.0386	0.0026				
$P(U_{h,1}, U_{w,2}, Ue_{w,1})$	0.0884	0.0031				
$P(U_{h,1}, U_{w,2}, U_{e,2})$	0.0086	0.0014				
$P(U_{h,2}, U_{w,2}, U_{e,1})$	0.1718	0.0039				
$P(U_{h,2}, U_{w,2}, U_{e,2})$	0.0190	0.0019				
$Corr(U_h, U_w)$	0.0261	0.0115				
$Corr(U_h, U_e)$	−0.0309	0.0149				
$Corr(U_e, U_w)$	−0.0001	0.0135				

Note: Bold numbers indicate a significant parameter estimate (5% level). Since the hazard models are perfectly correlated, they are represented by v_e in the probabilities and correlations. The standard errors for the correlation coefficient and mass-point probabilities have been calculated based on 1,000 drawings from the multivariate distribution with mean and covariance matrix set equal to the estimated parameter vector and covariance matrix.
(Cont.)

Table 9.2. (*Continued*)

Variables	Wage equation		Selection equation	
	Coeff.	Std. err.	Coeff.	Std. err.
Homeownership	**0.0537**	0.0020		
Age 19–24	**−0.2317**	0.0031	**−1.3097**	0.0462
Age 25–29	**−0.0427**	0.0028	**−0.6156**	0.0369
Age 40–49	−0.0053	0.0023	**0.0920**	0.0413
Age 50+	**−0.0133**	0.0030	**0.3203**	0.0556
Female	**−0.1682**	0.0015	**0.3152**	0.0249
Children 0–17 years	**0.0088**	0.0022	**0.5183**	0.0344
Two adults	**0.0326**	0.0020	**2.1304**	0.0283
Large city	**−0.0728**	0.0022	**0.3821**	0.0365
Small city	**−0.0912**	0.0016	**1.0794**	0.0274
Basic education	**−0.1736**	0.0017	**−0.5306**	0.0288
Further education	**0.1787**	0.0018	**0.2262**	0.0322
Experience/10	**0.2198**	0.0037	**3.0468**	0.0660
Experience squared/100	**−0.0411**	0.0010	**−0.6075**	0.0199
Tenure/10	**0.0932**	0.0053		
Var(u)	**−2.7024**	0.0018		

Note: Bold numbers indicate a significant parameter estimate (5% level).

also in line with what one would expect; the probability of being a homeowner increases with e.g. age and family size.

Turning to the effect of homeownership, we find that owners are less likely to leave their jobs for unemployment—their unemployment risk is 29 per cent lower than that of renters $(1 - \exp[-0.3468] \approx 0.29)$. This result confirms the findings of Van Leuvensteijn and Koning (Chapter 8 above) on Dutch data. However, Van Leuvensteijn and Koning also found that homeownership does not affect the job change hazard rate. Since they do not distinguish between transitions into local jobs and into non-local jobs, this result could hide a negative effect on job changes to non-local jobs. Our results for the Danish labour market show that both job change hazard rates are lower for homeowners, with the effect being strongest for transitions into non-local jobs, as expected—the parameter estimates imply that homeowners have a 14 per cent (5 per cent) lower transition rate into a new job outside (inside) the local labour market. Recall that these results are completely consistent with the theoretical predictions outlined in Section 9.2. Thus, our results suggest that owners set higher reservation wages for jobs outside the local labour market relative to renters, because they have to be compensated for transaction costs. The same result is found for local jobs, and this may be explained by the fact that employers invest more in firm-specific skills for owners.

In addition, homeowners have a wage premium of 5.37 per cent compared to renters even after correcting for endogeneity. Again, this result is in accordance with our theoretical considerations; owners stay longer in their jobs, and therefore they are more attractive to employers. As a consequence, employers may be willing to offer a wage premium in order to attract owners, and they may be more willing to invest in firm-specific human capital for homeowners.

Table 9.3. Estimation results—instruments

Variables	Job change hazard, local jobs		Job change hazard, non-local jobs		Unemployment hazard	
	Coeff.	Std. err.	Coeff.	Std. err.	Coeff.	Std. err.
Homeownership	**−0.0640**	0.0244	**−0.1776**	0.0399	**−0.3847**	0.0595
Age 19–24	**0.3628**	0.0395	**0.6403**	0.0628	**−0.6259**	0.0829
Age 25–29	**0.0624**	0.0316	**0.3227**	0.0508	**−0.3399**	0.0719
Age 40–49	**−0.1985**	0.0317	**−0.2041**	0.0530	**0.1898**	0.0747
Age 50+	**−0.2927**	0.0430	**−0.5250**	0.0849	**0.6970**	0.0889
Female	−0.0060	0.0199	**−0.4623**	0.0342	**0.1507**	0.0492
Children 0–17 years	0.0410	0.0267	**−0.0883**	0.0446	−0.0019	0.0670
Two adults	**−0.0733**	0.0243	−0.0540	0.0405	**−0.3141**	0.0557
Large city	**−0.3933**	0.0321	**1.2826**	0.0681	**0.2437**	0.0764
Small city	**−0.4372**	0.0225	**1.4310**	0.0596	0.0524	0.0608
Basic education	**−0.0601**	0.0229	**−0.1202**	0.0371	0.0819	0.0527
Further education	**−0.1883**	0.0266	0.0543	0.0436	**−1.0608**	0.0754
Experience/10	0.0845	0.0525	0.0887	0.0891	**−0.8910**	0.1147
Experience squared/100	**−0.0338**	0.0152	**−0.0577**	0.0269	**0.0897**	0.0351
v_h^1	**−10.1338**	0.1004				
v_h^2	**−5.0737**	0.0846				
v_w^1	**4.8953**	0.0036				
v_w^2	**5.3361**	0.0037				
v_{en}^2	**2.4424**	0.0605				
v_{el}^2	**3.2331**	0.0766				
v_u^2	**1.9074**	0.0452				
$p_1\left(v_h^1, v_w^1, v_e^1\right)$	**0.2339**	0.0044				
$p_2\left(v_h^1, v_w^1, v_e^2\right)$	**0.0297**	0.0022				
$p_3\left(v_h^2, v_w^1, v_e^1\right)$	**0.4111**	0.0051				
$p_4\left(v_h^2, v_w^1, v_e^2\right)$	**0.0393**	0.0026				
$p_5\left(v_h^1, v_w^2, v_e^1\right)$	**0.0881**	0.0029				
$p_6\left(v_h^1, v_w^2, v_e^2\right)$	**0.0086**	0.0014				
$p_7\left(v_h^2, v_w^2, v_e^1\right)$	**0.1707**	0.0038				
$p_8\left(v_h^2, v_w^2, v_e^2\right)$	**0.0188**	0.0019				
Corr (v_h, v_w)	**0.0313**	0.0118				
Corr (v_h, v_e)	−0.0267	0.0142				
Corr (v_w, v_e)	−0.0016	0.0132				

Note: Bold numbers indicate a significant parameter estimate (5% level). Since the hazard models are perfectly correlated, they are represented by v_e in the probabilities and correlations. The standard errors for the correlation coefficient and mass-point probabilities have been calculated based on 1,000 drawings from the multivariate normal distribution with mean and covariance matrix set equal to the estimated parameter vector and covariance matrix.

(Cont.)

Table 9.3. (*Continued*)

Variables	Wage equation		Selection equation	
	Coeff.	Std. err.	Coeff.	Std. err.
Homeownership	**0.0531**	0.0020		
Age 19–24	**−0.2372**	0.0031	**−1.4841**	0.0476
Age 25–29	**−0.0426**	0.0028	**−0.6296**	0.0372
Age 40–49	**−0.0054**	0.0023	**0.3261**	0.0460
Age 50+	**−0.0134**	0.0030	**0.5949**	0.0686
Female	**−0.1681**	0.0015	**0.2654**	0.0248
Children 0–17 years	**0.0087**	0.0022	**0.4552**	0.0344
Two adults	**0.0327**	0.0020	**2.2705**	0.0290
Large city	**−0.0728**	0.0022	**0.5811**	0.0372
Small city	**−0.0912**	0.0016	**0.1395**	0.0330
Basic education	**−0.1736**	0.0017	**−0.6207**	0.0288
Further education	**0.1788**	0.0018	**0.1336**	0.0319
Experience/10	**0.2199**	0.0037	**2.9132**	0.0666
Experience squared/100	**−0.0412**	0.0010	**−0.5740**	0.0199
Tenure/10	**0.0936**	0.0053		
Var(u)	**−2.7023**	0.0018		
Owner share, reg. of residence			**0.0571**	0.0012
Owner share, reg. of birth			**0.0028**	0.0005
Owner share, reg. of birth missing			0.0577	0.7162
Parents' owner status 1980			**0.3826**	0.0279
Parents' owner status missing			**−0.1823**	0.0479

Note: Bold numbers indicate a significant parameter estimate (5% level).

When we tried to estimate the full model, we experienced problems in terms of obtaining reliable estimates for the mass points and probabilities of the thirty-two different combinations of the five unobserved heterogeneity distributions. This is not unusual in these models. In order to make the model more tractable, we therefore restrict the correlation structure between the three hazard models to be perfect. This may appear to be overly restrictive. However, it still enables us to allow for completely flexible correlation between the wage equation, the homeownership status equation, and the transition rates out of a given job. In Table 9.2, we present the implied correlations between the three unobserved components. Although some of the correlations are significant, none of them is very large, implying that the selection bias that would have arisen if the selection process had been ignored is actually quite small.

In Table 9.3, we present a version of the model where we identify the homeowner equation with instrumental variables as well as multiple spells. The results do not differ much from those presented in Table 9.2, and we can therefore conclude that the results are robust to the choice of identification strategy. This could of course also be due to the instruments included. We did try different combinations of the instruments included in Table 9.3 (results are available on request), but they all produced results similar to those reported in Tables 9.2 and 9.3.

9.6. Conclusion

We have examined the causal impact of homeownership on job duration and wages. From a search-theoretic perspective, we have argued that because of transaction costs employed homeowners should have a lower transition rate into new non-local jobs, and therefore owners overall stay longer in their jobs. This makes owners more attractive to employers; i.e. employers are more likely to invest in firm-specific human capital, and so owners are offered higher wages, and consequently they should also be less likely to leave the current job for other local jobs.

We have empirically examined these predictions using a detailed Danish micro dataset. We have estimated a competing risks duration model for job spells, with a distinction between transitions into new local jobs, new non-local jobs, and unemployment, and in addition we simultaneously estimate a standard human capital wage equation. Special attention has been devoted to identifying the causal linkage between homeownership and the labour market outcomes of interest.

Our empirical results are completely consistent with the theoretical predictions. Owners have lower transition rates into all three destinations than renters, and they also earn higher wages. The results contribute to the empirical literature on the labour market effects of homeownership in two ways. First, the reduced transition rates into new jobs are at odds with the results of Van Leuvensteijn and Koning (Chapter 8 above) for the Dutch labour market, but consistent with search theory. Second, the impact of homeownership on wages has not been the subject of intense scrutiny, and to the best of our knowledge it has never been studied in empirical models where the selection into homeownership has been carefully taken into account.

In terms of the arguments mentioned in the introduction, where positive externalities associated with homeownership have been used to argue for favourable tax treatments of homeowners, our results suggest that there are also significant labour market gains associated with homeownership. Since these gains are private, and since they might even impose negative externalities on others (because with a given budget constraint, training homeowners implies that renters do not receive training), we do not see the results as strengthening the case for favourable tax treatment of homeownership.

Notes

1. They do not distinguish between local jobs and jobs outside the local labour market.
2. The mobility rate is here defined as the number of households moving out divided by the total number of housing units.

3. The reason for this treatment of individuals losing their jobs from plant closures is that we want to investigate only job-worker separations that are, at least partly, determined by either the worker or the firm, not by exogenous forces.
4. Exact moving dates are known for all individuals.
5. This variable is also used by Van Leuvensteijn and Koning (Chapter 8 above) as an exclusion restriction.
6. We have also estimated a model with reverse causality between job duration and wages, but the results regarding homeownership still hold in that model, the results of which are available on request.
7. We do not present results for a model where we do not attempt to correct for the endogeneity of homeowner status. These results show that homeowners have 7 per cent higher wages than renters, and that homeowners are less likely to leave a current job spell for all three destinations. The results are of course available upon request.
8. Results are available from the authors upon request.

References

Abbring, J., and Van den Berg, G. (2003), 'The non-parametric identification of treatment effects in duration models', *Econometrica*, 71, 1491–517.

Andersen, A. K. (1999), 'Commuting areas in Denmark', AKF, Forlaget (Copenhagen).

Coulson, N. E., and Fisher, L. M. (2002), 'Tenure choice and labour market outcomes', *Housing Studies*, 17, 35–49.

Danish Economic Council (2001), *Danish Economy Spring* (Copenhagen: Danish Economic Council).

——(2002), *Danish Economy Autumn* (Copenhagen: Danish Economic Council).

Dietz, R. D., and Haurin, D. R. (2003), 'The social and private micro-level consequences of homeownership', *Journal of Urban Economics*, 54, 401–50.

Farber, H. S. (1999), 'Mobility and stability: the dynamics of job change in labour markets', in O. Ashenfelter and D. Card (eds.), *Handbook of Labour Economics*, iii (Amsterdam: North-Holland), 2439–83.

Green, R., and Hendershott, P. (2001), 'Homeownership and unemployment in the US', *Urban Studies*, 38/9, 1501–20.

Hendershott, P., and White, M. (2000), 'The rise and fall of housing's favored investment status', *Journal of Housing Research*, 11, 257–75.

Munch, J. R., and Svarer, M. (2002), 'Rent control and tenancy duration', *Journal of Urban Economics*, 52, 542–60.

Nickell, S., and Layard, R. (1999), 'Labour market institutions and economic performance', in O. Ashenfelter and D. Card (eds.), *Handbook of Labor Economics*, iii (Amsterdam: North-Holland), 3029–84.

OECD (2000), *Employment Outlook* (Paris: OECD).

Oswald, A. (1996), 'A conjecture of the explanation for high unemployment in the industrialized nations: part I', Warwick University Economic Research Paper 475.

Panis, C. (2004), 'Microsimulations in the presence of unobserved heterogeneity', Draft, RAND Corporation.

—— and Lillard, L. (1994), 'Health inputs and child mortality: Malaysia', *Journal of Health Economics*, 13, 455–89.

Rosholm, M., and Svarer, M. (2004), 'Endogenous wage dispersion and job turnover in a search-matching model', *Labour Economics*, 11, 623–45.

Upchurch, D. M., Lillard, L., and Panis, C. (2002), 'Nonmarital childbearing: influences of education, marriage, and fertility', *Demography*, 39, 311–29.

Van den Berg, G. (2001), 'Duration models: specification, identification, and multiple durations', in J. J. Heckman and E. Leamer (eds.), *Handbook of Econometrics* (Amsterdam: North-Holland), 3381–460.

10

Family Migration and Labour Market Outcomes: A Panel Investigation

Harminder Battu, Ada Ma, and Euan Phimister

10.1. Introduction

Though there exists a massive literature on gender inequality in the labour market, few studies acknowledge the role played by differential gender mobility patterns. As far back as the 1970s Madden (1977) noted that spatial considerations have been largely absent from the gender inequality and discrimination literature. In a much more recent review of gender differentials in the labour market there is no mention of spatial as opposed to job mobility (Altonji and Blank 1999).[1] The lack of attention paid to gender spatial mobility is somewhat surprising given the fact that females are less mobile than males both in terms of longer-distance residential moves and in terms of commuting time and distance (White 1986; Gordon *et al.* 1989).

Female immobility in terms of longer-distance moves is reflected in what is termed the 'tied mover hypothesis'. Here females in dual-career households are more likely to be the trailing spouse owing to their role as secondary earner whereby their careers weigh less heavily in the family migration decision.[2] They move at the behest of their partner, and in doing so experience a labour market loss. Household migration (alongside child rearing) may then have an important dampening influence on the life-cycle wages of married women and represent a rather hitherto unexplored source of gender inequality in the labour market. Mincer (1978) in his seminal contribution argued that families maximize total family income. Where the husband's gain outweighs the loss to the wife, the family will move. Since husbands are typically the primary earners, married women are characterized as tied movers, in the sense that they move for the benefit of the family and in doing so bear a loss. Migration whilst optimal for the family is sub-optimal for the married female. A sizeable body of research broadly confirms this hypothesis, and the deleterious impact on labour market outcomes is evident in terms of labour market participation, hours and weeks worked, income, employment, and over-education (Cooke and Bailey 1996; LeClere and McLaughlin 1997; Smits 2001; McGoldrick and Robst 1996; Büchel and Battu 2003; Nivalainen 2004).

Despite the evidence, there still exist a number of unresolved issues. First, are the disruptive effects of female migration just as prevalent in the 1990s onwards, given the rise in female participation levels, the dominance in most European countries of the two-earner household with children (see Table 10.1), and the possibility that family moves are increasingly initiated by wives for their careers, perhaps turning husbands and partners into tied movers? Second, to what extent are any negative effects transitory, and is there evidence that married females do over time recoup any losses? A number of studies find a temporary loss (Spitze 1984; Clark and Withers 2002; LeClere and McLaughlin 1997; Smits 2001). Clark and Withers (2002), using the Panel Study of Income Dynamics, find that though there is a temporary loss in terms of labour force participation, there is evidence of a gain if the focus is only on those who were out of the labour force prior to the move. Third, to what extent do existing studies account for unobserved heterogeneity and sample selection, and does correcting for these make a difference in terms of the empirical findings? A small number of studies make advances in this direction. Smits (2001) controls for sample selection bias for the Netherlands and finds that there is a disruption to earnings, but only in the short run. Similarly, LeClere and McLaughlin (1997), using the PSID from 1987, find that there is a large earnings penalty one year after migration, but that this loss tapers off. In contrast, Cooke and Bailey (1996), using the PUMS US Census data from 1980, correct for sample selection bias and find that family migration raises the probability of employment

Table 10.1. Frequency of dual-earner, single-earner, and no-earner households for couples with children in per cent, 1996

Country	Dual earners	Single earners (men)	Single earners (women)	No earners
Austria	60.6	32.0	4.8	2.7
Belgium	61.6	30.3	2.5	5.6
France	57.3	33.3	4.1	5.4
Germany, East	64.0	26.8	5.5	3.8
Germany, West	50.8	40.5	3.5	5.1
Ireland	39.0	45.4	4.1	11.6
The Netherlands	52.4	39.8	2.6	5.2
Portugal	67.1	27.3	3.8	2.0
Spain	32.7	53.5	4.1	9.6
UK	61.0	26.3	3.3	9.3
EU 13	51.4	38.6	3.4	6.5

Source: Eurostat, Labour Force Survey, 1996 (Bosch 1999).

among married females (by 9 per cent) but has no effect on the probability of working for married males.[3]

This study extends the literature in two ways. First of all we examine the effects of being a tied mover on a broader range of variables than is traditionally examined, including employment, wages, and commuting time. The focus on commute time is novel and thus requires some explanation. According to Madden and Chiu (1990), 'it is a universal and widespread empirical finding that women commute less than men' both in terms of time and distance. A number of explanations have been posited, including the lower wages of women, greater household responsibilities, and a relatively even spatial distribution of jobs. In addition, commuting may represent a form of quasi-mobility, and commuting and migration may be seen as substitutes (Clark *et al.* 2003). For a household, migration may be a mechanism for reducing commute times, so that recent movers should then have the lowest commute times. Indeed, Green *et al.* (1999) find a negative relationship between longer commutes and migration for dual-earners households.[4]

Second, we use panel data methods. Our use of quasi-panel data allows us to control for unobserved heterogeneity and state dependence. The interrupted nature of female labour market participation necessitates controlling for sample selection effects. To account for sample selection and unobserved heterogeneity, the panel sample selection model suggested by Vella and Verbeek (1999) and Nijman and Verbeek (1992) is estimated. In particular, we estimate a series of employment, wage, and commuting equations for married males and females. Here the correlation between unobserved components in the wage as well as commuting and employment equations controls for traditional sample selection effects and unobserved heterogeneity across all individuals.

The data sources employed in this paper are waves 1–13 of the British Household Panel Survey (BHPS). There is some limited evidence that married females on moving do lose out, but this is a temporary loss. There is no evidence in our analysis to support the tied mover hypothesis, since moving for spouse's job generates no discernible loss for married females. The rest of the paper has the following structure. Section 10.2 describes the data and the definitions used, and provides some basic descriptive analysis. Section 10.3 discusses the econometric specification and provides a discussion of hypotheses and model estimation. Section 10.4 presents the results. Section 10.5 concludes.

10.2. Data

The data was drawn from the first thirteen waves (1991–2003) of the British Household Panel Survey, a longitudinal survey following around 10,000 individuals representative of the British population. The labour market component of the survey has detailed information on individual earnings, hours worked, and a whole host of other individual characteristics.

In addition, the BHPS contains extensive information on residential status and mobility and why respondents moved. At each date of interview, respondents were asked, 'Can I just check, have you yourself lived in this (house/flat) for more than a year?' Using this information, a mover was defined as an individual who changed address over the previous twelve months *and* whose local authority district (LAD) of residence had also changed since their last interview. Moves are identified then in the previous twelve months but also between twelve and twenty-four months ago. There are 267 LADs in our sample, and they typically have a population of between 100,000 and 200,000. In essence, the focus here is on long moves, where long-distance moves are primarily associated with the attraction of employment opportunities in distant labour markets. On the other hand, short-distance moves (within LADs) are driven largely by attempts to improve housing and may be associated with changes in the composition of the household (birth of a child, divorce, etc.) (Buck 2000).

The BHPS also allows us to identify the main reason for moving through a set of retrospective questions. In particular, the BHPS asks whether the reason for a move was job-related, and if so, the respondent is asked to elaborate: '*Did you move for reasons that were wholly or partly to do with your own job or employment opportunities?*'

This question can be used to get a greater handle on the tied mover hypothesis. In particular, we constructed two variables to capture whether an individual moved across LADs for their spouse's job both in the previous twelve months and between twelve and twenty-four months ago. An individual is defined as having moved for their spouse's job if they themselves moved, their move was not because of their own job, and their spouse reported that they themselves moved for their own job. Previous research using this question finds that females in relationships are less mobile than men for own job reasons and more mobile for partner's job reasons. Males living with a non-employed partner exhibit higher mobility (Gardner *et al.* 2001).

To maximize the use of the available data, an unbalanced panel was constructed from individuals interviewed in three or more consecutive waves. For each individual, only information from one set of consecutive interviews was used. Hence, if data was missing in a given wave, only the information from the longest set of consecutive interviews was included for that individual.

From this basic sample, we took individuals aged between 18 and 60 who were married or cohabiting, if their marital status was unchanged (no divorces or separations), and they had full information available for the variables used in regression analysis. The retired, self-employed, and those in full-time education were dropped from the sample. The samples used for the wage and commuting time equations are a subset of those defined to be employed, being only those individuals for whom an hourly wage could be derived.

Table 10.2. Means and standard deviations of variables (employment status sample)

Variable	Females				Males			
	Full sample Mean	St. dev.	Mover Mean	Non-mover Mean	Full sample Mean	St. dev.	Mover Mean	Non-mover Mean
Employed	0.76	0.42	0.73	0.77	0.94	0.24	0.93	0.94
No qualifications	0.17	0.38	0.08	0.18	0.14	0.34	0.07	0.14
O-levels or equivalent	0.35	0.48	0.26	0.36	0.25	0.43	0.22	0.25
A-levels or equivalent	0.11	0.31	0.15	0.11	0.13	0.33	0.13	0.13
Nursing and other higher qualifications	0.22	0.41	0.26	0.21	0.31	0.46	0.28	0.31
First degree, teaching and higher degree	0.15	0.35	0.25	0.14	0.18	0.38	0.30	0.17
Age (in years)	39.52	9.88	33.19	39.73	40.10	9.47	34.65	40.30
Age squared/100	16.59	7.93	11.83	16.74	16.97	7.74	12.73	17.12
Number of children < 3 years of age	0.11	0.33	0.17	0.11	0.14	0.36	0.22	0.13
Number of children 3–4 years of age	0.12	0.34	0.15	0.12	0.13	0.36	0.16	0.13
Number of children 5–16 years of age	0.96	1.11	0.85	0.96	1.00	1.09	0.84	1.00
Mover in the last 12 months	0.03	0.17	1.00	0.00	0.03	0.18	1.00	0.00
Moved for spouse's job in the last 12 months	0.01	0.09	0.28	0.00	0.00	0.07	0.14	0.00
Non-labour income £000	3.22	5.43	2.69	3.23	2.62	4.57	2.35	2.63
No. of observations	20,654		653	20,000	17,867		622	17,245

Note: Only those who have moved homes across LAD boundaries are counted as movers; those who have moved within a LAD are counted as non-movers.

Table 10.3. Means and standard deviations of variables (wage and commuting time sample)

Variable	Females				Males			
	Full sample Mean	St. dev.	Mover Mean	Non-mover Mean	Full sample Mean	St. dev.	Mover Mean	Non-mover Mean
Log (hourly wage)*	2.01	0.51	2.12	2.01	2.35	0.51	2.45	2.35
Log (commuting time)	3.26	0.50	3.42	3.26	3.67	0.17	3.69	3.67
Log (hours)	2.62	0.90	2.95	2.61	2.80	1.02	2.97	2.79
Public transport	0.11	0.31	0.13	0.11	0.08	0.26	0.11	0.07
Private transport	0.59	0.49	0.65	0.59	0.76	0.43	0.75	0.76
Passenger	0.11	0.32	0.12	0.11	0.04	0.21	0.03	0.05
Other (walking, cycling, etc.)	0.17	0.38	0.09	0.17	0.11	0.31	0.09	0.11
Works during normal hours	0.51	0.50	0.61	0.51	0.56	0.50	0.65	0.56
Industries								
Primary, energy, and extraction[a]	0.52	0.50	0.49	0.52	0.33	0.47	0.36	0.33
Metal goods, engineering, and vehicles	0.04	0.20	0.05	0.04	0.16	0.37	0.13	0.16
Other manufacturing	0.06	0.24	0.07	0.06	0.11	0.32	0.09	0.12
Construction	0.01	0.09	0.01	0.01	0.05	0.22	0.03	0.05
Dist., hotels and catering, repairs	0.21	0.41	0.17	0.21	0.13	0.33	0.12	0.13
Transport and communication	0.03	0.18	0.03	0.03	0.09	0.29	0.09	0.09
Banking, other services	0.13	0.34	0.18	0.13	0.13	0.33	0.19	0.12

Occupations						
Managers and administrators	0.10	0.30	0.16	0.21	0.41	0.27
Professional occupations	0.10	0.30	0.12	0.11	0.32	0.17
Associate professional and technical	0.12	0.33	0.18	0.10	0.31	0.14
Clerical and secretarial	0.30	0.46	0.30	0.08	0.27	0.09
Craft and related	0.02	0.14	0.01	0.18	0.39	0.13
Personal and protective service	0.14	0.35	0.09	0.06	0.24	0.06
Sales	0.10	0.30	0.08	0.04	0.19	0.03
Plant and machine operatives	0.04	0.19	0.02	0.15	0.36	0.07
Other occupations	0.08	0.27	0.04	0.06	0.23	0.03
Workplace size: 1–9 employees	0.19	0.39	0.18	0.14	0.34	0.16
Workplace size: 10–24 employees	0.18	0.39	0.15	0.13	0.33	0.12
Workplace size: 25–99 employees	0.26	0.44	0.22	0.26	0.44	0.23
Workplace size: 100 + employees	0.36	0.48	0.46	0.47	0.50	0.49
No of observations	15,215	460	14,755	16,032	553	15,479

*Hourly wage is usual monthly labour earnings divided by usual hours worked with an adjustment factor of 1.5 for overtime hours, and commuting time is the time in minutes for the individual to get to work from home (one-way).

□This category contains SIC 1980 major groups 0 (Agriculture, forestry, and fishing), 1 (Energy and water supplies), 2 (Extraction of minerals and ores other than fuels), and 9 (Other services).

This procedure resulted in repeated observations on 3,516 married women, of whom 416 were observed in all available thirteen waves, and 2,999 repeated married male observations, with 376 observed in all waves. The corresponding figures for the wages and commuting time subset are respectively 3,489 and 384 for women, and 2,945 and 322 for men. Tables 10.2 and 10.3 report key summary statistics for the samples by gender and mover status. Between 3 and 4 per cent of the sample experienced a move, and this is not surprising since those who are married tend to have a lower propensity to migrate relative to those who are single. There were 653 (622) residential moves involving a change in local authority district for married women (men). Buck (2000) finds that around 10 per cent of the total population of Great Britain moved residence each year. Gregg *et al.* (2004) find that the residential mobility rate for those of working age is between 10 and 13 per cent from 1977 to 1999. Longer-distance moves are significantly lower, with Gregg *et al.* (2004) finding that interregional moves stand at between 1.5 and 2.5 per cent for those of working age. As one would expect, movers tend to be younger and more highly educated. Movers also tend to have higher hourly wages and longer commute times and weekly hours of work. In addition, 28 per cent of married female movers moved for their spouse's (husband's) job, compared to only 14 per cent of male movers.

10.3. Empirical model

10.3.1. *Employment status*

We assume, as is standard, that an individual's decision to work is determined by whether the offered wage is above their reservation wage, where both are influenced by observed and unobserved individual characteristics. This implies a standard reduced form model for employment as a function of all the variables affecting both the reservation and offer wage plus any individual unobserved effect (ability, preferences, etc.). However, there is considerable evidence to indicate that even after accounting for individual heterogeneity, individuals do exhibit a significant degree of persistence in their labour market state (Heckman 1981a; Hyslop 1999). The reduced form model should then allow for state dependence as follows:

$$y_{it}^* = \delta_0 y_{it-1} + \delta_1 \mathbf{z}_{it} + \mu_i + \eta_{it} \qquad (10.1)$$

$$y_{it} = I\left(y_{it}^* > 0\right) \qquad (10.2)$$

Hence, y_{it} is equal to 1 when an individual decides to work in period t, y_{it}^* is the latent variable which when positive implies the individual will work, and $\mathbf{z}_{it}$ is the vector containing the variables assumed to influence employment. In the specification below, $\mathbf{z}_{it}$ contains a standard set of explanatory variables including, education, age, number of children in various age bands, non-labour income, time and regional dummies. To capture the impact of movers, we include a dummy for whether the individual moved in the last twelve months and whether they moved between twelve and twenty-four months ago. In addition, we include two dummy variables for when the move was related to the spouse's job (moved for spouse's job in the last twelve months and moved for spouse's job between twelve and twenty-four months ago). The extent of state dependence or persistence in employment is captured by the presence of the lagged employment variables y_{it-1} (equal to 1 if the individual was working in the previous period). Employment here refers to employment post-move (up to one year after move), and lagged employment is measured before the move. Unobserved heterogeneity (time-invariant individual effects) is captured by μ_i, while η_{it} is the pure random component. Separate equations are estimated by gender.

10.3.2. *Wages and commuting time*

The equations specified to explain these three variables have a similar structure and are as follows.

$$w_{it} = \mathbf{x_{it}}\beta + \alpha_i + e_{it}, i = 1, \ldots, N, t = 1, \ldots, T_i \qquad (10.3)$$

where w_{it} represents the offered (log) wage or the log of commuting time of individual i in time t, $\mathbf{x_{it}}$ is a vector of observed characteristics, β are the returns to these characteristics.[5] In the models estimated below the exact form of $\mathbf{x_{it}}$ varies across the three equations but always includes education level, a quadratic in age, moved in the last twelve months, moved between twelve and twenty-four months ago, moved for spouse's job in last twelve months and between twelve and twenty-four months ago, plus time and regional dummies. Wages and commute time are all measured post-move (up to one year after the move). Unobserved heterogeneity across individuals in terms of productivity, preferences, and other job characteristics, is controlled for by the random effect term α_i, while e_{it} accounts for other time-varying random shocks.

The models are completed by assuming that the error terms across Eqns. (10.1) and (10.3) are jointly normally distributed with zero means and constant variances. The sample selection problem induced by the potential correlation between unobserved components in the employment and wage or commuting equations can then be incorporated by allowing for non-zero covariances between the random effects in the α_i and μ_i, and between the two shocks e_{it} and η_{it}. All other covariances between elements of the error terms are assumed zero.[6]

10.3.3. *Economic implementation*

The joint estimation of Eqns. (10.1)–(10.3) is undertaken using the two-step procedure suggested by Nijman and Verbeek (1992), and Vella and Verbeek (1999). In the first step, estimates of the parameters in the employment Eqn. (10.2) are obtained from a dynamic random effects probit. One problem is that the presence of unobserved heterogeneity μ_i in conjunction with lagged employment y_{it-1} induces an initial conditions problem, where the initial observation y_{it0} will be correlated with the unobserved random effect, and hence maximum likelihood will produce inconsistent estimates. This is addressed using the suggestion of Heckman (1981*b*), where a reduced form equation is specified for the initial period, where the error term from this equation is assumed to be correlated with the unobserved random effects.

$$y_{it0} = \mathbf{z_{it0}}\lambda + \varepsilon_{0i} \tag{10.4}$$

where $\mathbf{z_{it0}}$ is a vector of strictly exogenous variables, ε_{0i} is the error term, where this error and the random effect μ_i are correlated.

The second step of the estimation procedure is an extension of the standard Heckman approach dealing with sample selection. Consider the conditional expectation of Eqn. (10.3), conditional on y_i, the indicator of employment states of individual i in each period,

$$E(w_{it}|y_i) = \mathbf{x_{it}}\beta + E(\alpha_i|y_i) + E(e_{it}|y_i) \tag{10.5}$$

As the errors are assumed to be drawn from a multivariate normal distribution, the conditional expectations $E(\alpha_i|y_i)$ and $E(e_{it}|y_i)$ are linear functions of the covariances $\sigma_{\alpha\mu}$ and $\sigma_{e\eta}$. Specifically, Verbeek and Nijman (1992) show that

$$E[\alpha_i|y_i] = \sigma_{\alpha\mu} \left[\frac{1}{\sigma_\eta^2 + T_i\sigma_\mu^2} \sum_{s=1}^{T} a_{is}E\left[\mu_i + \eta_{is}|y_i\right] \right] \tag{10.6}$$

$$E[e_{it}|y_i] = \sigma_{e\eta} \left[\frac{1}{\sigma_\eta^2} \left(E\left[\mu_i + \eta_{it}|y_i\right] - \frac{1}{\sigma_\eta^2 + T_i\sigma_\mu^2} \sum_{s=1}^{T} a_{is}E\left[\mu_i + \eta_{is}|y_i\right] \right) \right] \tag{10.7}$$

where $T_i = \sum_{s=1}^{T} a_{is}$ is the number of periods an individual is observed ($T = \max_i(T_i)$), and $\sigma_{\alpha\mu}$, $\sigma_{e\eta}$ are the covariances between the random effects and error terms respectively. It can be shown that the bracketed terms on the right-hand side of (10.6) and (10.7) are functions of the parameters in the employment equation only. Hence, as in the standard Heckman case, once estimates of the employment parameters have been obtained, estimates of these correction terms can be obtained via numerical integration. Then Eqn. (10.5) can be estimated including the two correction terms using OLS, where standard errors are adjusted to allow for the estimated nature of the correction terms. The coefficients provide estimates of $\sigma_{\alpha\mu}$ and $\sigma_{e\eta}$, and therefore the significance of these two coefficients provides a test of the importance of sample selection effects.

In principle, the error assumptions identify all the parameters in the offered wage and commuting equations, as the selection terms are non-linear functions of the exogenous variables. However as Vella (1998) notes, the degree of the non-linearity in the selection terms may be limited, given the actual range of values of the regressors. In many static situations the choice of exclusion restrictions can be problematic. Here, however, the exclusion of the lagged employment variable in Eqn. (10.1) provides a simple and effective method of identifying the regression coefficients in the main Eqn. (10.3).

10.4. Results

10.4.1. *Employment*

The results for our employment status equation for females and males are given in Table 10.4. Two sets of estimates are provided in the table. The first set are our benchmark standard probit estimates that exclude employment in the last period, and these allow us to evaluate the effects of controlling for unobserved heterogeneity and dynamic employment. The second set are our random effects probits. The value of t-statistic is reported alongside each coefficient.

The correlation coefficient $\hat{\rho}$ is usually interpreted as the proportion of the variance unexplained by the regressors in the random effects probit and accounted for by variation between individuals (Arulampalam *et al.* 2000). Here unobserved individual heterogeneity accounts for 54 per cent (47 per cent) of the unexplained variation in the probability of employment for females (males). The associated standard error indicates whether taking account of unobserved heterogeneity in the employment equation is important. Consistent with previous studies, this correlation is significant for all specifications in Table 10.4; controlling for unobserved heterogeneity matters supports the use of the random effects estimation.

The key result here is that whilst there is a clear penalty for moving for married females in terms of employment, this penalty is transient. Controlling for unobserved heterogeneity and employment in the last period does not reduce the size of this penalty (in fact, the penalty rises). On the other hand, for married males there is only a negative effect in our simplest estimation (no controls for unobserved heterogeneity and employment persistence). There is no discernible impact on the probability of working for those married males that migrate (they experience no gain) in our more sophisticated estimations.

Table 10.4. Employment model

	Females				Males			
	Probit		Random effects probit		Probit		Random Effects probit	
	estimate	t-stat	estimate	t-stat	estimate	t-stat	estimate	t-stat
Constant	-0.820	-4.359	-1.061	-2.457	-1.236	-4.200	-1.385	-2.195
Employed in the last 12 months			1.679	35.128			1.583	16.764
O-levels or equivalent	0.399	13.525	0.478	6.237	0.544	11.710	0.552	4.983
A-levels or equivalent	0.573	13.845	0.634	6.246	0.703	11.610	0.752	5.295
Nursing and other higher qualifications	0.830	23.285	0.898	9.966	0.801	16.420	0.804	7.030
First degree, teaching, and higher degree	0.862	21.697	1.056	9.674	1.030	15.970	1.234	7.457
Age	0.094	9.927	0.064	2.891	0.128	8.580	0.110	3.377
Age sq/100	-0.130	-10.868	-0.090	-3.000	-0.150	-8.170	-0.140	-3.500
Number of children < 3 years of age	-0.668	-20.645	-0.783	-13.804	-0.044	-0.930	-0.149	-1.590
Number of children 3–4 years of age	-0.419	-13.648	-0.336	-5.993	-0.010	-0.220	-0.100	-1.185
Number of children 5–16 years of age	-0.312	-25.514	-0.261	-8.505	-0.149	-8.530	-0.146	-3.746
Mover in the last 12 months	-0.202	-2.835	-0.312	-2.773	-0.201	-2.170	-0.224	-1.289
Mover 12–24 months ago	-0.029	-0.373	0.052	0.440	-0.302	-3.190	-0.383	-2.325
Moved for spouse's job in the last 12 months	-0.099	-0.763	0.028	0.169	-0.156	-0.640	-0.180	-0.401
Moved for spouse's job 12–24 months ago	-0.282	-2.057	-0.253	-1.219	0.243	0.740	0.536	1.293
Non-labour income	-0.045	-25.208	-0.031	-20.533	-0.068	-29.040	-0.041	-17.870
ρ̂			0.541	19.450			0.454	8.346
Log-likelihood	-9164.7		-5621.4		-3192.6		-2398.6	
N	20,653		20,653		17,867		17,867	

All regressions included regional and wave dummies. For the dynamic RE probit equations a separate equation adjusts for initial conditions. This equation included, own and spouse education level, own and spouse age, number and age of children, plus regional and wave dummies as regressors.

Curiously, there is a penalty for married males when one examines the moved-12–24-months-ago dummy variable. Our measure of tied migration (moved for spouse's job) indicates little either for males or for females.[7]

The other variables behave very much as expected. The probability of working rises with education level, and is negatively associated with the presence of children (the penalty is more acute for females) and non-labour income. Employment rises with age (a proxy for work experience), but at a decreasing rate. State dependence is an important influence on employment. An individual employed last year, controlling for observable and unobservable influences, is more likely to be employed compared to someone who was not in employment last year. This is evident across both sets of specifications and for both sexes.

10.4.2. Wages

Tables 10.5 and 10.6 provide our wage equation estimates for females and males respectively. The dependent variable of the earnings equation is the log of hourly wages. Wages are usual monthly labour earnings divided by usual hours worked in a month, with an adjustment factor of 1.5 for overtime hours. Four separate specifications are run, with the first being a standard least squares regression. The other three specifications are our sample selection models, albeit with different specifications.

In the sample selection models, the coefficients on the two selection terms provide estimates of the covariance between the random effects, $\sigma_{\alpha\mu}$, and the covariance between the random shocks, $\sigma_{e\eta}$.[8] The results indicate that sample selection is important for men and women. For both samples the estimate of $\sigma_{\alpha\mu}$ is positive and significant (the correlation between individual effects in employment and wage equations is positive), while the estimates of $\sigma_{e\eta}$ are negative and significant for both sexes.[9]

There is a mobility wage premium for married males of around 6–8 per cent, with the largest premium being evident in the second sample selection model (7.7 per cent). The premium disappears in our broadest sample selection specification where we control for sample selection and include various industrial and occupational dummies (the third sample selection model). The earnings of movers are much more closely aligned to occupation, industry, and size of employer, with most of the coefficients for these dummy variables being highly significant (not shown in the tables). There are similar findings for females. However, in the first two sets of results, the premium is slightly higher for males compared to females, and this is consistent with the view that there is a relative loss for females in moving. There is also some general indication that the size of the premium rises over time; the return is higher for those who moved twelve to twenty-four months ago, though again this disappears in our

Table 10.5. Wages model (females)

	OLS		Sample selection (1)		Sample selection (2)		Sample selection (3)	
	estimate	t-stat	estimate	t-stat	estimate	t-stat	estimate	t-stat
Constant	1.049	17.680	1.112	10.398	1.111	10.391	1.629	18.880
O-levels or equivalent	0.212	18.660	0.206	9.335	0.206	9.334	0.066	3.698
A-levels or equivalent	0.307	21.300	0.308	10.126	0.308	10.145	0.117	5.049
Nursing and other higher qualifications	0.424	34.620	0.418	16.057	0.418	16.060	0.172	8.239
First degree, teaching, and higher degree	0.876	66.440	0.882	30.281	0.883	30.306	0.401	14.072
Age	0.032	10.850	0.030	5.501	0.030	5.506	0.023	5.411
Age sq/100	-0.037	-9.890	-0.035	-5.000	-0.035	-5.000	-0.027	-5.400
Mover in the last 12 months	0.032	1.560	0.058	2.410	0.078	2.639	0.031	1.228
Mover 12–24 months ago	0.047	2.250	0.057	2.569	0.090	3.374	0.036	1.527
Moved for spouse's job in the last 12 months					-0.071	-1.562	-0.054	-1.238
Moved for spouse's job 12–24 months ago					-0.121	-2.728	-0.092	-2.515
Industries dummies	No		No		No		Yes	
Occupational dummies	No		No		No		Yes	
Firm-size dummies	No		No		No		Yes	
$\sigma_{\alpha\mu}$			0.070	4.600	0.070	4.606	0.054	4.958
$\sigma_{\epsilon\eta}$			-0.129	-7.848	-0.129	-7.826	-0.045	-3.378
N	15,215		15,215		15,215		15,215	

t-statistics are robust to autocorrelation and heteroskedasticity. In the sample selection model they are also adjusted for the two-step estimation process. All regressions include a common set of regional and wave dummies. Industry dummies are: metal goods, engineering and vehicle industries; other manufacturing industries; construction; distribution, hotels and catering, repairs; transport and communication; banking; and other services (reference category). Occupational categories are professional; associate professional and technical; clerical and secretarial; craft and related; personal and protective service; sales; plant and machine operatives; other occupations and managerial (reference category). Firm-size variables are whether workplace employs 10–24 employees, 25–99 employees, or more than 100 employees; reference category is employing fewer than 10 employees.

Table 10.6. Wages model (males)

	OLS		Sample selection (1)		Sample selection (2)		Sample selection (3)	
	estimate	t-stat	estimate	t-stat	estimate	t-stat	estimate	t-stat
Constant	0.323	5.140	0.381	3.148	0.381	3.144	1.056	10.440
O-levels or equivalent	0.228	18.750	0.222	8.494	0.222	8.501	0.159	7.409
A-levels or equivalent	0.384	27.850	0.376	11.693	0.376	11.696	0.232	8.778
Nursing and other higher qualifications	0.462	39.420	0.454	16.364	0.454	16.366	0.252	10.872
First degree, teaching, and higher degree	0.798	61.310	0.795	25.834	0.795	25.813	0.438	14.585
Age	0.082	26.380	0.079	12.902	0.079	12.907	0.062	12.629
Age sq/100	−0.09	−23.870	−0.087	−10.875	−0.087	−10.875	−0.069	−11.500
Mover in the last 12 months	0.058	3.090	0.077	3.241	0.064	2.441	0.011	0.452
Mover 12–24 months ago	0.067	3.390	0.071	3.223	0.070	2.957	0.015	0.765
Moved for spouse's job in the last 12 months					0.083	1.473	0.081	1.605
Moved for spouse's job 12–24 months ago					0.005	0.081	−0.006	−0.123
Industries dummies	No		No		No		Yes	
Occupational dummies	No		No		No		Yes	
Firm-size dummies	No		No		No		Yes	
$\sigma_{\alpha\mu}$			0.062	3.005	0.062	3.021	0.044	2.869
$\sigma_{\varepsilon\eta}$			−0.203	−4.499	−0.202	−4.462	−0.136	−3.699
N	16,032		16,032		16,032		16,032	

t-statistics are robust to autocorrelation and heteroskedasticity. In the sample selection model they are also adjusted for the two-step estimation process. All regressions include a common set of regional and wave dummies. Industry dummies are: metal goods, engineering and vehicle industries; other manufacturing industries; construction; distribution, hotels and catering, repairs; transport and communication; banking; and other services (reference category). Occupational categories are professional; associate professional and technical; clerical and secretarial; craft and related; personal and protective service; sales; plant and machine operatives; other occupations and managerial (reference category). Firm-size variables are whether workplace employs 10–24 employees, 25–99 employees, or more than 100 employees; reference category is employing fewer than 10 employees.

final estimation. This perhaps reflects an initial difficulty in adjusting to the destination labour market and obtaining a better match with higher pay.

Though moving for one's spouse's employment does reduce earnings for females and raises earnings for males, these effects are not on the whole statistically significant. However, the lagged version of this variable is negative and significant for females (moved for spouse's job 12–24 months ago). That is, whilst females who moved for their husband's employment do not receive an instant penalty in terms of earnings, there is some evidence that they do experience a delayed penalty when moving at the behest of their husband's job. For the other variables the results are in line with expectations. For both married males and females earnings rise with education level. Age has a positive impact on earnings for both sexes. The square of age has a significant negative coefficient, indicating that rising experience has a non-linear effect. The effects for both age terms are larger for married males.

10.4.3. Commuting time

The results for our commute time regressions are given in Tables 10.7 and 10.8. We might expect mobility and commuting time be negatively related on the grounds that moving may be used as an opportunity to reduce commuting burdens. On the other hand, it might be the case that after a residential move longer commutes are accepted on a temporary basis, since they may be reduced by a more local residential move in the near future. This conforms to the view that most households will change jobs first (longer moves) and then change residence. The analysis here is complicated by the fact that we are focusing on those who are married. For couples it may be more difficult to find satisfactory job and residence arrangements, and we may then find that dual earners have longer commutes.

There is no evidence from our results that there is a trade-off between migration and commuting times. Our descriptive statistics in Table 10.3 reveal that movers have higher commute times relative to non-movers, and this holds more strongly for females. Our empirical estimations indicate that those married females who have moved experience longer commutes; they are less likely to minimize commuting time after a move, compared to men. This perhaps indicates that females have to adjust to migration by searching for employment over larger distances (and larger labour markets). The moved-for-spouse variable has no discernible impact on the commute times for males or females.

The effects of the other variables are in accordance with the existing literature (Van den Berg and Gorter 1996; White 1986; Dasgupta *et al.* 1985; Crane 1996). There is a positive relationship between education level and commute times for both sexes. In line with Van den Berg and Gorter (1996) we find that a rise in the number of children in the household reduces commute times for both sexes though the effect is much larger for females. The greater the number of

Table 10.7. Commuting time model (females)

	OLS		Sample selection (1)		Sample selection (2)		Sample selection (3)	
	estimate	t-stat	estimate	t-stat	estimate	t-stat	estimate	t-stat
Constant	2.114	16.550	2.164	9.009	2.163	9.005	1.964	9.131
O-levels or equivalent	0.170	7.350	0.178	3.637	0.178	3.639	0.055	1.352
A-levels or equivalent	0.201	6.830	0.206	3.216	0.206	3.222	0.044	0.817
Nursing and other higher qualifications	0.261	10.470	0.273	5.114	0.273	5.121	0.121	2.616
First degree, teaching, and higher degree	0.472	17.570	0.484	8.158	0.486	8.197	0.250	4.199
Age	0.036	5.480	0.034	2.744	0.034	2.742	0.014	1.330
Age sq	−0.057	−6.910	−0.055	−3.438	−0.055	−3.438	−0.023	−1.769
Number of children < 3 years of age	0.137	4.720	0.158	3.761	0.157	3.741	0.130	3.499
Number of children 3–4 years of age	0.060	2.240	0.077	2.255	0.077	2.260	0.079	2.697
Number of children 5–16 years of age	−0.160	−18.24	−0.147	−8.756	−0.147	−8.735	−0.083	−5.727
Mover in the last 12 months	0.185	4.410	0.163	3.269	0.209	3.884	0.161	3.282
Mover 12–24 months ago	0.084	1.980	0.108	2.228	0.143	2.450	0.097	1.865
Moved for spouse's job in the last 12 months					−0.169	−1.394	−0.104	−0.986
Moved for spouse's job 12–24 months ago					−0.130	−1.298	−0.074	−0.798
Public transport							1.267	27.266
Private transport							0.478	12.254
Passenger							0.396	8.754
Works during normal hours							0.175	7.294
Industries dummies	No		No		No		Yes	
Occupational dummies	No		No		No		Yes	
Firm-size dummies	No		No		No		Yes	
$\sigma_{\alpha\mu}$			0.044	1.408	0.043	1.396	0.007	0.266
$\sigma_{\varepsilon\eta}$			−0.149	−4.701	−0.148	−4.644	−0.083	−3.068
N	15,215		15,215		15,215		15,215	

t-statistics are robust to autocorrelation and heteroskedasticity. In the sample selection model they are also adjusted for the two-step estimation process. All regressions include a common set of regional and wave dummies. Industry dummies are: metal goods, engineering and vehicle industries; other manufacturing industries; construction; distribution, hotels and catering, repairs; transport and communication; banking; and other services (reference category). Occupational categories are professional; associate professional and technical; clerical and secretarial; craft and related; personal and protective service; sales; plant and machine operatives; other occupations and managerial (reference category). Firm-size variables are whether workplace employs 10–24 employees, 25–99 employees, or more than 100 employees; reference category is employing fewer than 10 employees.

Table 10.8. Commuting time model (males)

	OLS		Sample selection (1)		Sample selection (2)		Sample selection (3)	
	estimate	t-stat	estimate	t-stat	estimate	t-stat	estimate	t-stat
Constant	2.410	15.790	2.331	8.980	2.333	8.991	1.755	7.011
O-levels or equivalent	0.048	1.710	0.045	0.799	0.044	0.788	−0.032	−0.641
A-levels or equivalent	0.255	8.040	0.266	4.092	0.266	4.084	0.101	1.712
Nursing and other higher qualifications	0.264	9.770	0.268	4.923	0.267	4.907	0.090	1.816
First degree, teaching, and higher degree	0.482	16.080	0.479	7.483	0.477	7.446	0.196	3.101
Age	0.022	2.850	0.025	1.933	0.025	1.929	0.017	1.400
Age sq	−0.00024	−2.520	−0.00027	−1.688	−0.00027	−1.688	−0.00018	−1.200
Number of children < 3 years of age	0.047	1.950	0.061	1.851	0.062	1.885	0.042	1.410
Number of children 3–4 years of age	0.003	0.120	0.018	0.610	0.018	0.618	0.007	0.244
Number of children 5–16 years of age	−0.061	−6.770	−0.064	−3.759	−0.063	−3.744	−0.037	−2.354
Mover in the last 12 months	0.096	2.210	0.052	0.951	0.029	0.485	−0.014	−0.255
Mover 12–24 months ago	0.108	2.370	0.106	2.085	0.095	1.817	0.045	0.905
Moved for spouse's job in the last 12 months					0.161	0.988	0.232	1.736
Moved for spouse's job 12–24 months ago					0.080	0.587	0.080	0.693
Public transport							1.428	22.201
Private transport							0.690	13.312
Passenger							0.596	8.454
Works during normal hours							0.170	5.435
Industries dummies	No		No		No		Yes	
Occupational dummies	No		No		No		Yes	
Firm-size dummies	No		No		No		Yes	
$\sigma_{\varepsilon\mu}$	0.003	0.095	0.003	0.095	0.003	0.092	−0.021	−0.772
$\sigma_{\varepsilon\eta}$	0.090	1.332	0.090	1.332	0.086	1.258	0.095	1.495
N	16,032		16,032		16,032		16,032	

t-statistics are robust to autocorrelation and heteroskedasticity. In the sample selection model they are also adjusted for the two-step estimation process. All regressions include a common set of regional and wave dummies. Industry dummies are: metal goods, engineering and vehicle industries; other manufacturing industries; construction; distribution, hotels and catering, repairs; transport and communication; banking; and other services (reference category). Occupational categories are professional; associate professional and technical; clerical and secretarial; craft and related; personal and protective service; sales; plant and machine operatives; other occupations and managerial (reference category). Firm-size variables are whether workplace employs 10–24 employees, 25–99 employees, or more than 100 employees; reference category is employing fewer than 10 employees.

children, the smaller the willingness of women to pay for commuting time. This implies either that the value of leisure is higher for women with children or that the pecuniary costs of children rise with hours of work and number of children. However, this holds only for those with older children (aged between 5 and 16). As the number of children less than 3 years old and between 3 and 4 years old rises, commute times for females actually rise.

Those who utilize public transport tend to have the longest commuting times. This is unsurprising given the inefficiency of public transport relative to other forms of transport. Passengers have higher commute times, and those who work during the daytime have longer commute times than those who have unorthodox work patterns. This accords with the view that increased congestion at these times increases commuting times. The region dummies indicate strong regional effects, with most regions having significantly shorter commute times than the omitted category, i.e. the South-East (not shown in tables). The estimates of the two covariances in the male sample (Table 10.8) are both insignificant. This suggests that sample selection is not particularly important for males.

10.4.4. *Alternative specification*

An alternative approach was also tried. This differed from the above in two ways. First, we tried an alternative test of the tied mover hypothesis, distinguishing between the following reasons for moving: moved for own job, moved for spouse's job, moved for both own and spouse's job, and moved for other reasons (non-employment reasons). Second, we added an additional control for private homeownership. These results are provided in Tables 10.9 and 10.10, and we report only our broadest sample selection estimates. The results indicate that females who move for their spouse's job have a lower probability of being in employment, although the penalty is short-lived. No such penalty is evident for tied males (Table 10.10). There is also no effect of tied migration on the wages of males or females. Female tied migrants do, however, experience a rise in their commute times, though the effects are smaller than those for male tied migrants. Where the female move is for both partners' jobs, there is a gain in employment and a fall in commute times. Where the female move is for 'other reasons' (non-employment), there is somewhat unsurprisingly a fall in the probability of employment and a rise in commute times. Homeowners in these estimations have a higher probability of being in employment, have higher wages, and a higher commute time, although care needs to be taken here owing to the endogeneity of housing tenure. We also interacted our mover dummy variables with homeownership to decipher whether tied migration and homeownership together had any impact. The results, which are not reported here, revealed little.

Table 10.9. Alternative mover variables (females only)

	Employment: Participation model		Wages: Sample selection (3)		Commuting time: Sample selection (3)	
	estimate	t-stat	estimate	t-stat	estimate	t-stat
Constant	−0.988	−2.273	1.598	18.542	1.948	9.050
Employed in the last 12 months	1.673	34.634				
O-levels or equivalent	0.456	5.889	0.059	3.352	0.050	1.224
A-levels or equivalent	0.602	5.804	0.106	4.607	0.034	0.640
Nursing and other higher qualifications	0.874	9.546	0.164	7.913	0.114	2.479
First degree, teaching, and higher degree	1.021	9.223	0.390	13.736	0.244	4.134
Age	0.055	2.482	0.020	4.817	0.012	1.131
Age sq/100	−0.080	−2.667	−00.024	−4.623	−0.021	−1.574
Number of children < 3 years of age	−0.793	−13.864			0.124	3.35726
Number of children 3–4 years of age	−0.344	−6.119			0.078	2.659
Number of children < 16 years of age	−0.256	−8.325			−0.081	−5.623
Moved for own job in the last 12 months	−0.477	−1.148	0.020	0.205	0.086	0.405
Moved for own job 12–24 months ago	−0.131	−0.215	0.012	0.148	0.096	0.513
Moved for spouse's job in the last 12 months	−0.507	−3.479	−0.028	−0.728	0.278	2.917
Moved for spouse's job 12–24 months ago	−0.246	−1.292	−0.069	−2.000	0.032	0.407
Moved for both own and spouse's jobs last 12 months	0.681	1.764	0.051	0.701	−0.295	−1.620
Moved for both own and spouse's jobs 12–24 months ago	−0.043	−0.113	−0.010	−0.199	0.051	0.327
Moved for other reasons in the last 12 months	−0.298	−2.468	0.035	1.350	0.170	3.341
Moved for other reasons 12–24 months ago	0.065	0.532	0.040	1.640	0.097	1.808
Homeownership	0.183	3.015	0.107	7.034	0.084	2.292
Non-labour income	−0.030	−20.133				
Public transport					1.265	27.335
Private transport					0.470	12.134
Passenger					0.394	8.727
Works during normal hours					0.172	7.173
$\sigma_{\alpha\mu}$			0.05634	5.24295	0.00881	0.35035
$\sigma_{\varepsilon\eta}$			−0.03526	−2.65253	−0.07614	−2.79126
$\hat{\rho}$	0.538					
Log-likelihood	19.353	−5612.58				
N	20,653		15,215		15,215	

t-statistics are robust to autocorrelation and heteroskedasticity. In the sample selection model they are also adjusted for the two-step estimation process. All regressions include a common set of regional and wave dummies. Industry dummies are: metal goods, engineering and vehicle industries; other manufacturing industries; construction; distribution, hotels and catering, repairs; transport and communication; banking; and other services (reference category). Occupational categories are professional; associate professional and technical; clerical and secretarial; craft and related; personal and protective service; sales; plant and machine operatives; other occupations and managerial (reference category). Firm-size variables are whether workplace employs 10–24 employees, 25–99 employees, or more than 100 employees; reference category is employing fewer than 10 employees.

Table 10.10. Alternative mover variables (males)

	Employment: Participation model		Wages: Sample selection (3)		Commuting time: Sample selection (3)	
	estimate	t-stat	estimate	t-stat	estimate	t-stat
Constant	-0.877	-1.433	1.042	10.395	1.759	7.071
Employed in the last 12 months	1.575	16.199				
O-levels or equivalent	0.402	3.911	0.137	6.489	-0.047	-0.943
A-levels or equivalent	0.486	3.689	0.199	7.608	0.078	1.319
Nursing and other higher qualifications	0.554	5.127	0.223	9.777	0.072	1.441
First degree, teaching, and higher degree	0.893	5.893	0.404	13.712	0.178	2.810
Age	0.063	2.013	0.057	11.768	0.012	0.985
Age sq/100	-0.090	-2.250	-0.065	-10.799	-0.013	-0.870
Number of children < 3 years of age	-0.183	-1.973			0.037	1.253
Number of children 3–4 years of age	-0.106	-1.281			0.003	0.125
Number of children < 16 years of age	-0.095	-2.520			-0.031	-2.026
Moved for own job in the last 12 months	0.232	0.517	0.0623	1.5833	-0.174	-1.759
Moved for own job 12–24 months ago	-0.077	-0.210	0.057	1.587	-0.052	-0.632
Moved for spouse's job in the last 12 months	-0.442	-0.856	0.108	1.466	0.470	2.752
Moved for spouse's job 12–24 months ago	-0.363	-0.768	-0.006	-0.085	0.002	0.011
Moved for both own and spouse's jobs last 12 months	-0.124	-0.214	0.127	2.266	0.145	0.964
Moved for both own and spouse's jobs 12 to 24 months ago[a]	–	–	–	–	–	–
Moved for other reasons in the last 12 months	-0.248	-1.281	0.013	0.438	0.060	0.923
Moved for other reasons 12–24 months ago	-0.431	-2.419	0.008	0.352	0.078	1.313
Homeownership	0.673	7.568	0.173	10.377	0.158	3.628
Non-labour income	-0.036	-17.850				
Public transport					1.422	22.273
Private transport					0.672	13.198
Passenger					0.582	8.363
Works during normal hours					0.167	5.376
$\sigma_{\alpha\mu}$	0.3678		0.03298	2.35619	-0.01846	-0.72264
$\sigma_{\varepsilon\eta}$			-0.10939	-2.79821	0.16959	2.4569
$\hat{\rho}$	6.182					
Log-likelihood	-2357.44					
N	17,867		16,032		16,032	

t-statistics are robust to autocorrelation and heteroskedasticity. In the sample selection model they are also adjusted for the two-step estimation process. All regressions include a common set of regional and wave dummies. The wage and commute time regressions also include dummies for occupation and employer size. Industry dummies are: metal goods, engineering and vehicle industries; other manufacturing industries; construction; distribution, hotels and catering, repairs; transport and communication; banking; and other services (reference category). Occupational categories are professional; associate professional and technical; clerical and secretarial; craft and related; personal and protective service; sales; plant and machine operatives; other occupations and managerial (reference category). Firm-size variables are whether workplace employs 10–24 employees, 25–99 employees, or more than 100 employees; reference category is employing fewer than 10 employees.
[a] That variably perfectly predicts a large number of outcomes and has therefore been dropped.

10.5. Conclusions

This study undertakes a panel investigation of the tied mover hypothesis for the UK for the 1990s. The use of a panel dataset mitigates the traditional cross-sectional econometric problems of sample selection and unobserved individual heterogeneity. Cross-section data do not allow us to disentangle the effects of unobserved characteristics on labour market outcomes (i.e. earnings) from idiosyncratic shocks.

We find that despite the rise in female labour force participation there is still some limited support for the notion that females lose out from mobility, especially with respect to the probability of employment. However, and in accordance with the existing literature, we find that these negative effects are on the whole transitory. For example, the lower probability of being in employment from moving dissipates over time for married females. In one case, namely commute times, we do find some evidence of a longer-term effect with moves generating higher commute times for married females. In addition, there is no support for the tied mover hypothesis, since moving for spouses' employment has no bearing on labour market outcomes for both males and females. In most cases we find that controlling for sample selectivity and unobserved heterogeneity matters.

Notes

1. A notable exception is a study by Ofek and Merrill (1997).
2. Sociologists argue that gendered family roles play an important role in the family migration decision (Bielby and Bielby 1992) and downplay the importance of potential economic returns.
3. A number of recent studies have examined tied migration using the BHPS. Rabe (2006) examines the decision to migrate and the role played by expected wage gains of both husbands and wives and finds that dual-earner couples place roughly equal weight on each partner's expected wage gains. Moving wives are also found to experience a temporary fall in employment. Taylor (2006) finds that tied migrants (husbands and wives) have a lower probability of employment, although no distinction is made in the analysis between short and long moves, and there is no evaluation of whether the losses were transitory.
4. Green *et al.* (1999) discuss dual-location households, with partners living apart during the week, with one individual having long-distance weekly commutes and returning to the family residence at weekends.
5. Commuting time is the one-way commute time in minutes.
6. The sample selection model controls for labour market participation but not for the potential endogeneity of location. However, informal estimates using sub-samples of 'less mobile' individuals, e.g. those with lower education levels, indicate that the results are robust to this limitation.

7. We do not include spouse's employment or income in the employment equation, since both are likely to be endogenous.
8. The sample selection terms are generated using the coefficients from the appropriate dynamic probit estimation results in Table 10.4.
9. The significance of this second selection term provides a form of validation for the model, as formally, the covariance between the two errors must be zero for the fixed effects estimator to be consistent.

References

Altonji, J., and Blank, R. (1999), 'Race and gender in the labor market', in O. Ashenfelter and D. Card (eds.), *Handbook of Labor Economics*, iii (Amsterdam: Elsevier Science), 3143–259.

Arulampalam, W., Booth, A., and Taylor, M. (2000), 'Unemployment persistence', *Oxford Economic Papers*, 52, 24–54.

Bielby, W. T., and Bielby, D. D. (1992), 'I will follow him: family ties, gender-role beliefs, and reluctance to relocate for a better job', *American Journal of Sociology*, 97, 1241–67.

Bosch, G. (1999), 'Working time: tendencies and emerging issues', *International Labour Review*, 138/2, 131–49.

Buck, N. (2000), 'Housing, location and residential mobility', in R. Berthoud and R. J. Gershuny (eds.), *Seven Years in the Lives of British Families* (Bristol: Policy Press), 133–60.

Büchel, F., and Battu, H. (2003), 'The theory of differential overqualification: does it work?', *Scottish Journal of Political Economy*, 50/1, 1–16.

Clark, W. A. V., and Withers, S. (2002), 'Disentangling the interaction of migration, mobility, and labor-force participation', *Environment and Planning*, A34, 923–46.

—— Huang, Y., and Withers, S. (2003), 'Does commuting distance matter? Commuting tolerance and residential change', *Regional Science and Urban Economics*, 33, 199–221.

Cooke, T. J., and Bailey, A. J. (1996), 'Family migration and the employment of married women and men', *Economic Geography*, 72, 38–48.

Crane, R. (1996), 'The influence of uncertain job location on urban form and the journey to work', *Journal of Urban Economics*, 39, 342–54.

Dasgupta, M., Frost, M., and Spence, M. (1985), 'Interaction between urban form and mode choice for the work journey: Manchester/Sheffield, 1971–1981', *Regional Studies*, 19, 315–28.

Gardner, J., Pierre, G., and Oswald, A. (2001), 'Moving for job reasons', unpublished paper, University of Warwick.

Gordon, P., Kumar, A., and Richardson, H. W. (1989), 'Gender differences in metropolitan travel behaviour', *Regional Studies*, 23, 499–510.

Green, A. E., Hogarth, T., and Shackleton, R. E. (1999), 'Longer distance commuting as a substitute for migration in Britain: a review of trends, issues and implications', *International Journal of Population Geography*, 5, 49–67.

Gregg, P., Machin, S., and Manning, A. (2004), 'Mobility and joblessness', in D. Card, R. Blundell, and R. Freeman (eds.), *Seeking a Premier League Economy*, NBER (Chicago: University of Chicago Press), 371–410.

Heckman, J. (1981a), 'Heterogeneity and state dependence', in S. Rosen (ed.), *Rosen Studies in Labor Markets* (Chicago: University of Chicago Press), 91–139.

—— (1981b), 'The incidental parameters problem and the problem of initial conditions in estimating a discrete-time–discrete-data stochastic process', in C. F. Manski and D. McFadden (eds.), *Structural Analysis of Discrete Data with Econometric Applications* (Cambridge, MA: MIT Press), 179–95.

Hyslop, D. (1999), 'State dependence, serial correlation and heterogeneity in intertemporal labor force participation of married women', *Econometrica*, 67, 1255–94.

LeClere, F. B., and McLaughlin, D. K. (1997), 'Family migration and changes in women's earnings: a decomposition analysis', *Population Research and Policy Review*, 16, 315–55.

Madden, J. F. (1977), 'A spatial theory of sex discrimination', *Journal of Regional Science*, 17/3, 369–80.

Madden, F., and Chiu, L. C. (1990), 'The wage effects of residential location and commuting constraints on employed married women', *Urban Studies*, 27/3, 353–69.

McGoldrick, K. M., and Robst, J. (1996), 'Gender differences in overeducation: a test of the theory of differential overqualification', *American Economic Review*, 86, 280–4.

Mincer, J. (1978), 'Family migration decisions', *Journal of Political Economy*, 86, 749–73.

Nijman, T., and Verbeek, M. (1992), 'Nonresponse in panel data: the impact on estimates of a life cycle consumption function', *Journal of Applied Econometrics*, 7, 243–57.

Nivalainen, S. (2004), 'Determinants of family migration: short moves vs. long moves', *Journal of Population Economics*, 17/1, 157–75.

Ofek, H., and Merrill, Y. (1997), 'Labor immobility and the formation of gender wage gaps in local markets', *Economic Inquiry*, 35/1, 28–47.

Rabe, B. (2006), 'Dual-earner migration in Britain: earnings gain, employment and self-selection', ISER Working Paper 2006-1.

Smits, J. (2001), 'Career migration, self-selection and the earnings of married men and women in the Netherlands, 1981–93', *Urban Studies*, 38, 541–62.

Spitze, G. (1984), 'The effect of family migration on wives' employment: how long does it last?', *Social Science Quarterly*, 65, 21–36.

Taylor, M. (2006), 'Tied migration and subsequent employment: evidence from couples in Britain', ISER Working Paper 2006-5.

Van den Berg, G. J., and Gorter, C. (1996), 'Job search and commuting time', Tinbergen Institute Discussion Paper, T1 3-96-2.

Vella, F. (1998), 'Estimating models with sample selection bias: a survey', *Journal of Human Resources*, 33, 127–69.

—— and Verbeek, M. (1999), 'Two-step estimation of panel data models with censored endogenous variables and selection bias', *Journal of Econometrics*, 90, 239–63.

Verbeek, F., and Nijman, T. (1992), 'Testing for selectivity bias in panel data models', *International Economic Review*, 33, 681–703.

White, M. J. (1986), 'Sex differences in urban commuting patterns', *American Economic Association Papers and Proceedings*, 76/2, 368–72.

Index

Note: page numbers in *italics* refer to Figure and Tables.

Index